MISTER

The Men Who Taught the World How to Beat England at Their Own Game

RORY SMITH

**SIMON &
SCHUSTER**

London · New York · Sydney · Toronto · New Delhi

A CBS COMPANY

First published in Great Britain by Simon & Schuster UK Ltd, 2016
This paperback edition published by Simon & Schuster UK Ltd, 2017
A CBS COMPANY

1 3 5 7 9 10 8 6 4 2

Simon & Schuster UK Ltd
1st Floor
222 Gray's Inn Road
London WC1X 8HB

www.simonandschuster.co.uk

Simon & Schuster Australia, Sydney
Simon & Schuster India, New Delhi

The author and publishers have made all reasonable efforts to contact
copyright-holders for permission, and apologise for any omissions or errors in
the form of credits given. Corrections may be made to future printings.

A CIP catalogue record for this book
is available from the British Library.

Paperback ISBN: 978-1-4711-5156-9
Ebook ISBN: 978-1-4711-5157-6

Typeset and designed in the UK by M Rules
Printed and bound by CPI Group (UK) Ltd, Croydon, CR0 4YY

MIX
Paper from
responsible sources
FSC® C020471

Simon & Schuster UK Ltd are committed to sourcing paper
that is made from wood grown in sustainable forests and support the Forest
Stewardship Council, the leading international forest certification organisation.
Our books displaying the FSC logo are printed on FSC certified paper.

Rory Smith is a football reporter for *The Times*, covering everything from the daily machinations in the soap opera of the Premier League to the impact of the game as far afield as Mexico, South Africa and Argentina. His work has also appeared in the *Mirror*, the *Daily Telegraph* and the *Independent*, as well as *FourFourTwo*, *eightbyeight*, *ESPN.com* and the *Blizzard*, while he is also a regular contributor to BBC radio. He lives with his wife, Kate, near Manchester. *Mister* is his first book.

Further praise for *Mister*:

'It is in the small details of how the destinies of this band of proselytisers were forged that the book delivers such delights.' *i*

'As well-travelled and erudite a journalist as you will find ... the candour of Smith's writing is one of the book's most endearing traits.' *When Saturday Comes*

'Superbly researched story ... An ideal read in front of a warm log fire.' squawka.com

For Kate, like everything

And for Bernard, so that even those who
are forgotten might be remembered

Contents

Foreword

BY ROY HODGSON

It is 40 years since I got the call from Bob Houghton in Sweden. I had known Bob since we were at school together in Croydon. We had first worked together at Maidstone United in the early 1970s: him as manager, me as a player. By 1976, he was in Sweden, coaching Malmo FF to consecutive league titles. When one of their rivals, Halmstads BK, decided they wanted an English manager, too, they asked Bob for a recommendation. Fortunately, he chose me.

That would prove the start of a long career. I spent the best part of the next three decades abroad, my work taking me to Sweden, Switzerland, Denmark, Italy, Norway, Finland and even the United Arab Emirates. I had some success, including eight league titles, with Halmstads, Malmo and FC Copenhagen, and countless wonderful experiences. I will never forget taking charge of a Milan derby at San Siro, reaching my first European final or tasting my first World Cup with the Swiss national team in 1994. Along the way, I met some remarkable people and worked with some exceptional players.

I travelled so far that I ended up where I started: back home, working at Fulham, Liverpool, West Bromwich Albion and, the crowning glory, being offered the chance to manage my country in a European Championship finals and World Cup, the greatest honour and privilege of my career. But while that was my eventual destination, there can be no question that I was irrevocably shaped by all I learned, all I saw and all I did during the course of my journey.

Travelling broadens the mind: that is true for anyone, whatever their profession. It certainly improved me as a manager. My view of how the game should be played might have been forged in England, but being exposed to new cultures, new ideas, new languages and new worlds served to expand my horizons and polish my ideas. I witnessed at first hand the game growing, developing, advancing everywhere I went. Being able to harness so many different perspectives opened my eyes in a way that, perhaps, would not have happened had I remained in one place. All of those countries I worked in changed me in some way, hopefully for the better.

I would like to think I gave something back, too. I would hope some of the players with whom I worked can look back and feel they benefited from our time together, and that some of the clubs and countries where I found myself would have fond memories of my time there. I have always been afforded warm welcomes whenever I have had the chance to visit my erstwhile teams; I often find myself meeting former charges, reminiscing about all that we did. I have even been awarded the equivalent of a knighthood in Finland. Obviously, I did something right!

I was not the first Englishman to strike out abroad. Indeed, Bob and I may well have owed our presence in Sweden to one of our predecessors, the remarkable George Raynor. George remains an almost mythical figure in Sweden, thanks to his achievement in taking the country to the World Cup final on home soil in 1958. To many of that generation of players, he is the father of Swedish football.

Yet he is typical, in many ways, because his reputation remains considerably higher abroad than at home. Here was a man who fell short of football's ultimate triumph only because his side ran into a 17-year-old by the name of Pele in the World Cup final, and yet he struggled to find work when he returned to England. It was a fate I avoided, but which befell so many who, like George, like me, left home to offer the benefit of their experience.

We are often guilty, in football's ever-shrinking world, of looking overseas for inspiration. We look on the achievements of the Spanish, the Germans and the Dutch – among many others – with envy, wondering which elements of their success we might be able to co-opt into our own thinking, asking why we cannot do things quite like they do. We see the exotic as superior. We talk about needing to leave our own history, our own traditions behind.

As George's story shows, though, many of the ideas we eulogise now all grew from an English seed. England did not just invent and codify football as we know it, it did not just demonstrate to the rest of the world how to play it; it took a leading role in teaching the craft of the game, too. Those ideas may have been improved, finessed, developed by others, but they came first from a group of men who made the same journey I would make, decades later, leaving England for distant shores.

Men like Jimmy Hogan, credited with inspiring the Magic Magyars who bewitched Wembley in 1953; William Garbutt, the father of Italian football; and Fred Pentland and Jack Greenwell, figures who shaped the destiny of the game in Spain. They are just the most famous names: there are many others who never achieved any sort of celebrity but whose impact, whose legacy, endures to this day. Not only did they help the countries where they worked fall in love with football; they changed the way the game was played. In many ways, though it was not their intention, these visionaries and pioneers helped bring about the end of England's presumed superiority on the pitch. They made it the world's game.

When I first arrived in Sweden, it was a country with a tremendous passion for football, but in need of modernisation. Bob Houghton and I tried to encourage our players to think in a different way about how they played the game, tried to take them away from the sweeper system they had played for so long, to deploy a style that might allow them to take their place among the best teams in the world. I was fortunate enough to win five league titles, at Malmo, a feat that remains unmatched. I would like to think I contributed a little to the culture of the country, too: if the 1994 World Cup was good for me, it was better for Sweden. They reached the semi-finals of the tournament, with a side containing several players who had worked with me at Malmo. Not quite what George Raynor managed, but a source of pride nonetheless.

I can imagine, then, the joy that some of the men described in the pages to come would feel at seeing the nations where they worked – whether it be Spain, Italy, Germany, Holland, Hungary or Austria – playing such a key role in the game's history. We must not seek to monopolise credit, to claim it when it belongs to others, but some must be due to the men we sent out from these shores. These were the men who taught the world to play. I would like to think I might one day be counted among their number.

Introduction

Bulldozers and Craftsmen

Daniele Verde was born in 1996. He grew up in the shadow of Mount Vesuvius, in a suburb of Naples called Rione Traiano. It is a tough, dilapidated sort of a place, the kind of neighbourhood that is only ever mentioned in the newspapers in connection with a gangland killing. Its inhabitants refer to it as Baghdad.

Football was Verde's escape. He stood out playing in the area's youth sides. He was spotted by a scout working for Roma and taken to the Italian capital before he had even hit his teens. Early in 2015, he broke into the first team, making his full debut in a win away at Cagliari. He set up both goals. Still breathless from the game, he was interviewed by Roma's in-house television channel. '*Voglio ringraziare il Mister per la fiducia,*' he said.

It is the sort of anodyne statement footballers across the world make every day, the kind of sentiment that constitutes the overwhelming majority of column inches and air-time dedicated to the sport. There is a word in there, though, that catches the eye. 'I want to thank the Mister for his faith.' Verde was an 18-year-old kid from one of the most deprived parts of Italy, a world of drugs and guns and organised crime, using a word drawn straight from Italian football's Edwardian ancestry. Not manager. Not coach. Not *allenatore*. The plain old English 'Mister'.

There is a story, related by the author David Goldblatt, of a meeting in the 1960s between Denis Healey, then defence secretary, and Sir Richard Turnbull, the penultimate governor of the province of Aden, modern-day Yemen. 'When the British Empire finally sinks beneath the waves,' Turnbull told Healey, 'it will leave behind only two monuments: the game of association football, and the expression "fuck off".'

Nothing illustrates the truth of Turnbull's assertion – about the first of those two legacies, at least – better than that word. *Mister*. It is the word they use for manager in Italy even now, even when they were born at the tail end of the 20th century in parts of Naples that could not be further removed from the Italian game's genteel, aristocratic origins. They use it in Spain, too. It is almost unique in transcending the ethnic and geographical divides that crisscross the country: Jose Mourinho was *el Mister* at Real Madrid, just as Pep Guardiola was at Barcelona and Marcelo Bielsa at Athletic Bilbao. Andalucian, Basque, Catalan: everyone is and everyone says *Mister*.

In Portugal, the official title is *treinador*, but it is always *Mister* in conversations in bars and cafes; it is the *Mister* who bears the brunt of the fans' frustrations when Benfica or Sporting or FC Porto dare to lose. Across the Atlantic, although in Argentina they prefer *director técnico* and in Brazil *Professor*, the word lingers, too. Everyone knows what *Mister* means. It is not transliterated – as the word *time*, for team, has been in Brazil – but it stands, in its original English form, a remnant and a relic of where football came from, a memory of how these countries first encountered the sport, a tribute not to the men who first imported the game but to those who helped nurture and stimulate it.

As Turnbull acknowledged, football is one of Britain's gifts to the world. Geoffrey Green, football correspondent of *The Times* and legendary chronicler of the game, described it spreading 'with a speed that defied all opposition', becoming 'a cord of understanding amongst the nations and the true link of the universe'. If that sounds overblown, the rather more sober historian James Walvin suggested it functioned as the country's 'most durable export', not just for how it lasted but for how far it spread, way beyond the bounds of empire, infiltrating even those parts of the map that were not coloured imperial pink.

In much of western Europe, it was first introduced by expat aristocrats, encouraged by embassy staff or imported by upper-class students who had been educated at England's public schools. Genoa, initially, was a football and cricket club, populated exclusively by the English. Fiorentina was founded in an English tea shop. Bologna was established by a group of academics at the city's university. In Habsburg Austria, there was a craze for all things English at the turn of the 20th century – art and couture and culture – and football was seen as just as sophisticated, just as civilised. In the coffee houses of Vienna, they pored over theories of how to play the game. It was as much an intellectual as a physical pursuit.

As Walvin notes, though, the game only seeped deep into the public consciousness when the masses took hold of it. In Spain, engineers in the Basque region and miners in the south of the country brought it with them and inspired locals to play. In industrial Milan and Turin, factory owners saw it as a way to curry favour with their staff. It was oil workers manning the derricks at Ploiesti who brought it to Romania; two Lancastrians at the textile factory at Orekhovo-Zuyevo in Moscow established the team that would thrill the world as Dynamo; sailors and railway workers took it yet further afield, to Brazil and Argentina and Uruguay.

In this, football's global spread followed the pattern that had been laid down in Victorian England. The great teams of the Northwest, the founders of the Football League, were established by local grandees as a way of directing their workers' energies in a constructive fashion. Football as an organised sport, rather than as an informal game, was as much a by-product of the Industrial Revolution as soot and urban squalor.

And, like so many of the other innovations of that period, it was not exported complete, seeded on foreign shores and allowed to develop on its own. As with the textile mills and the factories, there was an appetite not simply for English ideas but for English expertise as well. Locals could provide manpower, workers, but it was to the homeland and the heartland that they looked to for management. Someone had to show them how best to use this new-fangled idea. That is where the *Misters* come in.

English football has long been charged with standing apart. A sense had endured that, as soon as the game started to catch on, England looked on in horror at what the foreigners were doing with it and promptly, in a fairly literal sense, took its ball home. It is this reactionary isolationism, in most interpretations, that led to England losing its primacy at its own invention. As early as 1955, that was Brian Glanville's assessment: 'The story of British football and the foreign challenge is the story of a vast superiority, sacrificed through stupidity, short-sightedness and wanton insularity.' Green was not nearly so furious, but he was almost as scathing, describing the home nations' refusal to join the nascent Fifa before World War I as 'a monumental example of British insularity'.

And yet there is an alternative story which runs perfectly contrary to this accepted narrative. It is one not of haughty dismissal but of intense generosity, of first an individual and later a collective desire to see football grow and thrive across the planet, to make sure everyone could benefit from Britain's great invention.

It is a story that starts with those men credited with spreading football to all four corners of the globe, famous names like Charles Miller, father of football in Brazil, and James Richardson Spensley, the doctor so central to the establishment of Genoa, Italy's first club. This part of the story is relatively well known. These were the men who gave the world the game.

They were the pioneers, but the story does not end with them. Just as in Argentina, where once the English had built the railways, English engineers were dispatched to manage them and English coaches and English engines were purchased to stock them, Miller, Spensley and the rest were followed by a second wave of emigrants, charged with teaching the savages – and, in this case, that term applies to anyone from Calais and beyond – how to play, how best to use the gift they had been granted.

These were the *Misters*. Not the inventors, but the innovators, a handful of dedicated proselytisers, a gang of mavericks, pioneers and outcasts taken far from home by football, tasked with winning converts and showing them the way. They were men who wanted to bring light to the darkness. If the foreigners were going to play our game, they thought, we might as well show them how to do it properly.

Their reasons for going were far from uniform; likewise, the effects they had and the fame they found. Before and immediately after World War I, a clutch went of their own accord, men like Steve Bloomer, Fred Pentland, Jack Greenwell, William Garbutt and Jimmy Hogan.

For them, travelling abroad was to some extent a simple business decision. They had reached the end of their playing careers and they lived in a country where the overriding belief was that football could not be taught, or learned, but was innate. This was a time when, as Garbutt admitted, 'no club [in England] would hire a professional coach.' The role of the trainer was to keep players fit, to improve speed and stamina and strength; professionals, they felt, could not be improved. Most clubs did not train with the ball for much of the week, the theory being that absence would make the heart grow fonder. Deprive them of it in training and they would seek it out more hungrily on match days. Hogan, Garbutt and the rest disagreed. They felt that skills could be practised, tactics fine-tuned, techniques honed. They went abroad to teach because they were in possession of a specialist knowledge, one that made them more valuable commodities in foreign climes than in England.

After 1945, though, a different pattern emerges, not so much one of adventurers striking out into the world of their own accord but of apostles, consciously trained and dispatched by the Football Association. That may not have been the primary intention, but it was an incontestable effect, one that strikes a note of discordance in the theory of English insularity.

By 1948, the FA had established its own coaching scheme, under the auspices of Walter Winterbottom. Many of the clubs in the Football League were still not convinced of the need for anything other than physical training, so many of its graduates were sent out beyond these shores to improve standards elsewhere. One, George Raynor, took Sweden to an Olympic gold medal and a World Cup final. Alan Rogers and Harry Game never came quite so close to achieving such glory, but they are remembered, still, by those they encountered, those they educated across the world, from Antwerp in Belgium all the way to Tehran and Kampala.

Just like their predecessors, though, these men not only found a respect on foreign shores that they were not afforded at home, but in their own way they forged and formed the football traditions of each of the countries where they worked. They developed players, built teams, raised standards, and brought the backwaters into the mainstream. These were not the men who gave the world the game, but they were the men who taught it how to play.

If two teams stand for everything continental football has that English football does not, they are Barcelona and Holland. They boast intertwined visions, mutual traditions of attractive, expansive tactics, a trademark style that has made the former the club the world supports and the latter football's aesthetes, its arbiters of good taste. Barcelona and Holland stand for football done right. Johan Cruyff, Pep Guardiola, La Masia, Lionel Messi, the Ajax Academy, tiki-taka, Total Football: there is a clear line linking the Barcelona of today with the great Dutch tradition, conceived in Amsterdam and proselytised by the country's national team. They are the embodiment of sophistication, of exotic glamour. From Barcelona and Ajax, in particular, England has imported more than just players: it has brought in ideas, too, on how to nurture talent and how to instil technique; how, in short, to make the game beautiful. More than anywhere else, it is to Barcelona and Holland that England looks for inspiration.

And yet all of it stems, undeniably, incontrovertibly from Britain. 'The seeds were sown by the British, and this is the harvest that has been gathered in,' as Geoffrey Green wrote. The likes of Bobby Robson and Terry Venables – who managed Barcelona in the 1980s and 1990s – can be given some modicum of credit for that, but much of it belongs to men who came long before, men who have all but been struck from history.

Rinus Michels might have invented Total Football, passing his teachings on to Cruyff, mentor to Guardiola, patron saint of La

Masia, but the man who laid the foundations for his work was English: Vic Buckingham, who had started his career as manager of West Bromwich Albion in the 1950s. Further back, into the haze of the distant past, there are others as well, names that are never mentioned now. There was Jack Greenwell, who may well have been the longest-serving coach Barcelona have ever employed. Their link is less direct but the likes of Fred Pentland and Jimmy Hogan may also have some part in the story, their ideas observed and co-opted by Barcelona as the club sought to become Spain's pre-eminent power. Barcelona may stand for everything that we admire most when we look abroad, but all of it, every delicate pass, every inventive tactic, comes laced with a distinctly British history.

It is a story replicated wherever English coaches went: all the way from the steppes of Iran to the Californian coast, from Montevideo to Montreal. The names of many of them may not have resonated in history quite as much as they might have hoped, and few of them ever achieved the recognition in their homeland that they craved, but their impact was seismic and their legacy lasting – not just in all four corners of the globe, but in England, too.

The best measure of how successful they were, these visionaries banished overseas, is in the one place that was not willing to heed their warnings: home. All of those coaches England sent abroad, whether they went of their own volition or whether they were dispatched by the FA, reported back at regular intervals. They were all, by and large, hopeful that they would one day be invited back, their work on faraway shores enough to impress clubs in the all-powerful Football League. The call never came. George Raynor, veteran of a World Cup final, struggled to find work in England so much so that he ended up at Skegness Town.

Perhaps the reason why their accounts of the vast strides being made abroad were disregarded is that it was seen as self-promotion: who knows? All we can be sure of is that Pentland, Garbutt, Hogan and the rest repeatedly warned the game's authorities that the foreigners were coming, and that they were consistently ignored.

As early as 1928, Pentland was calling for 'new methods to be adopted' to prevent England slipping behind the continentals. Two years later, Hogan added his weight to the argument, cautioning that 'British training methods are out of date'. Raynor perhaps captured it best, writing in his autobiography in the 1960s that in England 'bulldozers are now more important than craftsmen; what we need is football at speed, but with the artists back in command'.

England was ceaselessly told the world was changing by those who had not only seen the revolution but had set it in train. Their clamour went unheard. The charge of insularity may not be fair, but the one of wilful ignorance most certainly is. The end result is where we find ourselves now, a time when England looks abroad for its players: bulldozers, sometimes, but definitely craftsmen. It looks abroad to see how they teach the game. It looks abroad for managers, too, for expertise. That is the measure of how well England's missionaries did their job, of how important they are in football's history: put simply, thanks to the lessons they gave, eventually the masters became the pupils.

English football's multiculturalism – a philosophy born as much of necessity as ambition – has helped turn the Premier League into the world's favourite division. All over the planet, fans watch it with awe and admiration, tuning into games early in the morning in the United States and in the dead of night in China, Malaysia and Japan.

But there is an irony to its popularity. It is somehow separated from its birthplace, its home. Everyone watches English football, but few seek to ape it or to learn from it. Quite the opposite. The example it sets is that any football culture can be improved by importing the best from a global marketplace, and so that is what they look to do. They watch a football competition that is held in England, but that does not mean they esteem English football.

'There's not a great amount of respect for English managers,' says Scott Cooper. There are still English coaches striking out for distant climes, heirs to the proud tradition started by Bloomer, Garbutt and the others. Cooper is one of them. He was appointed at Muangthong United, in Thailand, after a stint at Leicester City's academy. His nationality, he believes, was held against him; others in the same position recount the same story.

'The perception of how we play the game means it is hard for us to win people over. They think an English manager means long balls, diagonals, everything in the air. There is a huge demand for Spanish, German and Dutch coaches, but not the English. When I first got the job at Buriram United, my first side in Thailand, there were a lot of people at the start asking what English coaches have ever done. There were a lot of doubters.'

This book is an attempt to find out how we got from there to here; how the world changed beneath our feet; how a country that the planet once looked to for guidance has now become so thirsty for knowledge. It is, in part, a story of how England paid the price for its blindness to change and its deafness to suggestion. It is the story of how football's motherland lost its place at the top table through – to borrow from Glanville – 'extraordinary complacency and infinite self-deception'.

But it is also a story about how England, without realising it, fired the very revolution that would remove its crown. And at the heart of that story are a group of other stories, each of them a branch of the vine, that take as their stars a handful of men who sowed the seeds, across the planet, of the inversion of football's natural order. They were the men who wrote football's history and shaped its destiny, who changed the way it looks, the way it is played, the way it is discussed to this day. If the first wave – Spensley, Miller and the rest – gave the world the game they knew, these were the men who gave us the game we have. They were the men who taught the world to play. This is the story of these men. This is the story of the *Misters*.

I

All Our Yesterdays

Alan Rogers' flat is a riot of photos. They litter every available surface, stuff every drawer, lurk under tables and in cupboards. There are folders full of them, some sepia-tinted, some black and white, some with the occasional flash of colour. There are newspaper cuttings and pages ripped from magazines, all a little frayed at the edges.

Here, he shakes hands with the Empress of Iran. Here, rather unsteady on a malnourished horse, he treks down a path with spear-clutching tribesmen in Lesotho. Here he is in Chicago, here in Bloemfontein, another in Tehran. He even has a photo, from a summer long past, when he formed part of the same football team as Des O'Connor.

He was nearly 90 when I went to visit him at the start of 2014. He is still in good shape. He was running four or five miles a day until a few years ago, round the lake in Southport. He is a little slow going down stairs, but he goes up them at quite a lick. His mind is clear and his tongue is sharp, and he has a good head of hair. Looking at his photos, you suspect that is quite important to him. He was a good-looking man, Alan, a bright smile, glinting blond locks, a tale to tell.

Alan lives in a grand old Victorian house, long since converted to flats, on a quiet road just around the corner from Lord Street, the town's main drag. Most of the apartments were abandoned when the absentee landlord put up the rent. It is just Alan and one neighbour now. In Alan's, the paint on the ceiling is mottled with damp. The roof above the rotting bay window looks eerily like it might cave in, but it is a pleasant enough spot. From the lone armchair, he can see the grey clouds scudding in off the Irish Sea, and the corner of the lake. The decor is sparse: a single bed, a sofa, a couple of old filing cabinets. He has a sink and an oven in a small kitchen hived off the main room; he and his neighbour share the bathroom along the hall. It is what an estate agent would call bijou.

As he sits in his armchair, though, he tells a story of grand adventure. Each time he picks up another photo, points out another image, he embarks on another anecdote, dredges up another memory, veers off down another winding road. These are the highlights of a story that spans three decades and encompasses four continents.

The list of countries he called home, however briefly, is enviable: the Philippines, South Africa, Uganda, Swaziland, Zambia, Iran, the United States, Iceland, Qatar, Cyprus. He describes winning trophies and titles and medals and honours. There is one story in which he was feted by royalty and another in which he was, he says, swindled by mobsters. Another picture reminds him of the time he spent defying South Africa's apartheid laws to sneak into Lesotho. That leads on to one about his brush with Iran's SAVAK, once the world's most feared secret police force. And then he explains how he wandered out for breakfast one morning in Libya and saw three bodies strung up from the trees.

If it was not for the photos, for that documentary evidence of each and every one of his escapades, you would be inclined to believe that there was a degree of embellishment. The stories seem a little tall. A simple check, though, a trawl through Google, removes any doubt.

It was in Iran that Alan had his greatest success. He won a clutch of championships; he was hailed as a hero. One of his stories was about being invited back, in 2006, alongside Frank O'Farrell, the former Manchester United manager who had taken charge of the country's national team for a while. He recounted being greeted at Tehran airport by a sea of people. It was, he says, crammed to the rafters: there was a military band there, standing to attention, clutching their weapons of choice, trumpets and trombones, close to their chests, and a phalanx of photographers and reporters clustered together, cameras and notepads at the ready. He remembers the huge roar that greeted them as they appeared, flanked by a security team. It is a scene so unlikely as to be unbelievable: two men, pensioners now, cheered as heroes thousands of miles from home, in a country widely seen as a pariah state.

As they made their way out of the airport, Rogers said, he caught sight of a familiar face in the crowd, beckoning him over. 'It was one of my former players,' he explains. 'He was shouting my name, above all of that noise. He was shouting, "Mr Rogers! Mr Rogers!" He had this big grin on his face. When he saw me looking, he just shouted: "Bollocks!" Then he let out this enormous laugh.'

A flicker of a smile crosses his face, his eyes glinting behind his Dennis Taylor bifocals. 'Still, at least he'd remembered the first thing I taught him.'

Sure enough, there on a Farsi blog site is a picture of Alan, a few years younger, standing awkwardly next to O'Farrell, not looking at the camera. The 'bollocks' story is not mentioned. They were indeed there for an anniversary, though, and had been invited to give a press conference. 'In person,' the correspondent wrote, 'they were incredible.' His name might not mean much in England, but the Iranians certainly remember Alan Rogers.

To some extent, Alan is a curious place to begin the story of how English coaches taught the world to play. He was not the first to go abroad: he may not have known it at the time, but when he took his first job away from England, he was becoming part of a tradition that already stretched back half a century.

Nor was he the most successful. He was not the father of a school of thought that lasted for a century. He did not reach a World Cup final or leave his stamp on one of the world's pre-eminent football nations. There may be some, in East Africa or the United States or the heart of Asia, who would concede that he played some small part in helping them develop their game, but it would be a stretch to suggest that his influence stretches much beyond that. Alan, by the extraordinary standards set by some of those whose stories are to come, was pretty ordinary.

So, then, why start here, in this Southport bedsit? In part, it is for the simple reason that it is here that the story of the book begins. At the age of 17, as World War II raged, Alan signed up for military service. He was posted to the destroyer HMS *Oribi*, as a gunner. He would take part in the Arctic convoys, the route by which the Allies transported vital supplies to the Soviet Union. Winston Churchill described the journey undertaken by the merchant ships as 'the worst in the world'. It was not an exaggeration. German planes buzzed overhead. U-boats prowled beneath the surface. Over the course of the war, 120 ships were sunk, if not by the enemy then by the monstrous storms or the drifting ice floes. *Oribi* came under heavy fire off the coast of Norway. It survived, and Alan with it.

Seventy years after the end of the war, his service and his courage were recognised. In the summer of 2013, it was announced that he was one of just a handful of survivors of those hellish journeys who would be awarded the Arctic Star. There was a piece in Southport's local newspaper about the town's newest, oldest hero. Beneath his recollections of life on board the *Oribi* was a brief description of what he did when the war ended. A friend brought it to my attention. It spoke volumes that the details of his life after the convoys sounded, if anything, even more remarkable than what he had experienced at sea. It was with that curt list of the countries where he had worked that the germ of this book started to grow.

That is not the only reason. Alan makes an apposite place to start because of the contrast between how he is viewed at home and how he is viewed in those countries where he worked. In England, it is not so much that he has been long forgotten, more that he has simply never been known.

He was never a professional footballer. He had a trial for Everton as a teenager, but his eyesight let him down, and he played for non-league Redhill after being demobbed, but that was about it. 'I'm one of these,' he says, gesturing with a ham sandwich, 'like Wenger or Mourinho. I never played for anyone, not really. I was a coach. But I won people over – all of them – because I got results.'

His lack of playing experience essentially precluded him from ever getting a job in the Football League. English football's mistrust of anyone who has not played at the highest level is not a new phenomenon – in the 1960s, nobody on these shores was prepared to be won over by anyone's results. Alan was forced to go abroad and stay abroad to build his career. The effect was a curious one: a man totally unknown in his homeland, but with some measure of fame in places more faraway than he could ever have imagined. This, too, makes his story a fitting place to start, because this was a fate suffered by the vast majority of those who followed the same path as him. No matter how famous they became elsewhere, nobody in England was prepared to give them a chance. What happened to Alan stands for what happened to countless others, too.

And so does his approach to his career abroad. There is a little of all of the stories that follow in Alan's account of his life. His first job, after the end of the war, was on a farming camp in Reigate. In 1952, he moved from there to Butlin's holiday camps, working at Pwllheli, in north Wales, at Clacton-on-Sea, at Skegness. His time as a Redcoat lasted for a decade. He married a beauty queen. Wenger and Mourinho might have had unorthodox routes into management, but they never had to run a tombola in the middle of a boxing match.

It was here that he first discovered that he had something of a gift for coaching players. He had organised the football competitions at the camps, working with professionals who were paid to be there for the summer: Ivor Allchurch at Pwllheli, Ronnie Clayton at Skegness. He enjoyed the work; he knew, as he says, that he 'could organise these people'. He suspected management might be his forte. In 1960, inspired by his success running teams, Alan decided to go on a Football Association training course in Durham. His initial aim was to hone his skills, not start a new career.

The course Alan went on was run by the man who would become Sir Walter Winterbottom. He is best known, of course, for his work as England manager, but in truth his legacy extends some way beyond that role. Winterbottom is the father of coaching in a form that we would recognise in this country. It was during that course that Rogers caught Winterbottom's eye. 'He said I did very well,' Rogers remembers. 'All sorts came down, from all sorts of different clubs. I was the best on the course.' His certificate, signed by the chairman of the Football Association, Stanley Rous, does not quite bear that assessment out: he passed his Theory of Coaching and Practical Performance evaluations, and was deemed 'satisfactory' in his Practical Coaching module. His strong suit was Laws of the Game. He was officially recognised as 'Good' at that.

Rogers returned to Skegness for a year, and then travelled to Lilleshall for a refresher course. His world had been turned upside down in the intervening period. As he recalls it, his wife had gone to Jersey 'and never come back'. That would prove the defining moment of his life.

'On that course, Winterbottom asked me what I was going to do,' he says. 'He was the top man, and he was asking me if I was thinking about coaching full time. I sat down all night and thought about it. It would be a big job to get anywhere in England, I knew that. The people taking training at clubs in those days did not have badges, nothing like that. They were not coaches. I thought I would like to coach, but I knew I would have to start right at the bottom, and that it'd be difficult getting a good wage. The results counted then like they do now: it was a risk.

'The next morning, he asked again. "What do you want to do?" He said there were jobs abroad that he could offer me. There was one in Tripoli, in Libya, and one in the Philippines. I thought: "I've just got divorced. I'll make some money, I'll get stuck in out there."'

The story of the first 70 years of England's direct involvement in world football can be divided neatly into two parts. The first half is populated by mavericks, men who set out for far-flung corners of the globe because they possessed the nerve and the courage to take a chance but also because they found themselves in a position of economic necessity, where they were almost forced to do so. The second is a tale of missionaries, men dispatched by the Football Association to help spread the word of the game to every part of the planet. Alan makes a fitting first case study because he has a little of both traits. He was a maverick, from an unorthodox background, who saw going abroad as a way to earn a better living than he might at home, but he was also a missionary, part of a greater plan to help foreign countries improve their standard of play.

He was certainly not a natural traveller. Offered the choice of Libya or the Philippines, he plumped for the latter. He remembers Manila as being 'like walking into sauna, it was so hot and humid'. He was there to work with Brian Birch, once a player of no little repute with Manchester United, who was dispatched to coach the country's senior team. Rogers would be in charge of the under-19s. He remembers their first meeting. 'Brian came in, sopping wet. It wasn't raining. His first words to me were: "It's not what you think."'

He was told that he could not select any players of Chinese origin. 'They were the best, technically,' he says. He battled the insects, and did his best to cope with the violence that stalked the city's streets. 'Every day someone would get stabbed. Everyone had a knife. That did not happen in England.' He hated the insects, and the heat, and the country's predilection for baseball, and the fact that he was not coaching every day. He would arrange games only for them to be cancelled at the last minute. He gives the impression that he did not relish being abroad. That, too, is true of many of those English coaches who went out both before and after him. They did not necessarily go because of some form of wanderlust. They wanted, more than anything else, to be given a chance at home. Like Alan, they left England harbouring the desire to come back, hoping and believing that if they showcased their talents abroad, they might one day get what they craved: a position at a Football League club.

Like Alan, most never got that chance. Like Alan, they kept travelling, desperately hoping that at one point they would be able to stop. That is why this book starts with Alan. Not because he was the first, or the best, or the most influential, but because in his story there is a touch of all of the others.

To celebrate his 90th birthday, Alan's army of nephews and nieces arranged a party for him at the Royal Clifton hotel in Southport. They dug out old photos of their uncle from all his various postings; they tried to piece together the jigsaw of his peripatetic career. Alan is a little fuzzy on dates and details now, understandably, but seeing it as one coherent narrative brought a realisation. 'I gave a speech,' he says. 'I told them I have had a marvellous life. I had a good life. Don't worry about that. I've seen Niagara Falls and stood on Hollywood and Vine. I've been to the Alamo and to Rorke's Drift. I said I might be a 90-year-old now, but back then, I was buzzing.' He glances out of the window. 'I was fucking buzzing.'

Alan, though, was not in any of the countries he visited to sightsee. He was no mere tourist. There is no question he saw his coaching career as an unparalleled opportunity to expand his horizons, to see things he might otherwise never have been able to see, but he was working, and working hard. In the course of his time abroad, he coached many thousands of players. He can take credit for stimulating the development of the game in half a dozen countries, perhaps more.

In Africa, he defied South Africa's brutal apartheid regime to coach in what is now Lesotho. He was sent by the Football Association to report on the state of the game and run coaching courses in Zambia and Swaziland. He concentrated much of his work on helping introduce more sophisticated tactics. 'Where most African clubs fall down is in tactics and in defence,' he told the *Lusaka Times* after landing in Zambia. 'Their individual ball control is good, although there are still some skills they can develop. But their game is usually based on attack and often they come apart defensively under pressure. Tactically, I think I can do a lot here.' As a measure of how demanding his schedule was, the newspaper confirms that his first session, working with players at Nchanga Rangers, was due to start that very evening. Alan's life was no sinecure.

His first trip to the United States, in the early part of 1966, was no easier. In a three-month tour of duty, he crisscrossed the country, hosting 52 coaching sessions in 26 cities, travelling from Chicago to California, Miami to New York and all points in between. He spoke to packed auditoriums of wannabe coaches, discussing tactics and techniques and the importance of raising players in the right way. He visited Mexican and Italian and Polish clubs, trying to craft something lasting from scratch sides playing in amateur leagues. He taught, he says, a modern style of play, influenced by the Hungarians and Brazilians of the 1950s, with a touch of the wonderful Dutch teams of the 1970s thrown in later on.

It would be dishonest to suggest Alan was a visionary. There is not an English equivalent to Rinus Michels sitting in a flat in Southport. But it would be equally unfair to deny him the place in history that he warrants. Because of Alan's work, many thousands of players were just a little bit better than they might otherwise have been. Nearly a dozen countries across four continents became slightly better at football slightly quicker than they might. That is his legacy, and it is one that he should be both proud of and celebrated for. Alan played his part. It might only be the briefest of cameos, but he has a role nonetheless in football's history, and that is more than most of us can manage.

Of course, his influence was most deeply felt in those countries where he stayed for some period of time. After his sojourn in the Philippines, he returned home. He wrote to Allen Wade, director of coaching at the FA, asking if he had any positions available.

Wade offered him the chance to coach in South Africa. Rogers, exhausted by his experiences in Asia, must have been tempted to turn it down, but he had little prospect of earning money elsewhere. In 1963, he got on the boat.

His job would be in Bloemfontein, what he describes as 'the worst place' for the strictures of apartheid. There is, as with everyone who agreed to work in South Africa at the time, a moral ambiguity to his criticism of the regime, but he does not seem to have enjoyed his encounter with institutionalised racism. 'Blacks were not allowed to watch the games,' he says. 'They had to stand outside the stadium. It was terrible. They had to leave the town when the siren went at 7pm. They had to walk back to the townships on the edge of the city. They came in every morning, the nannies and the cleaners, but in the evening it was only white people. It was a very strange way to live.'

Frustrated by his experiences coaching 'a white team in an all-white league', Alan spread his wings a little. 'I went down to Maseru in Basutoland – what's now Lesotho – on my days off,' he says. He is pointing now at the photo in which he sits, not entirely comfortably, on that rather hungry-looking horse, being guided down a steep, rocky path by tribesmen. 'A white fella contacted me while I was down there. He had married a black woman, so could not operate in Bloemfontein. He asked me to come and do some coaching. It was only just over the border, about 90 miles away. They were not organised, and because of apartheid they obviously could not come and play in the Orange Free State, which was the closest place to them. I felt sorry for the players.'

A year in Bloemfontein was enough for him. He thought he had a job lined up at Wanderers, in the less hard-line surrounds of Johannesburg, but was pipped at the post by Alex Forbes, the Arsenal player. 'He pulled rank on me.' Instead, he would spend much of 1964 and 1965 on that FA tour of Lesotho, Swaziland and Zambia, assessing the facilities each nation could boast and the abilities of the local players.

'Zambia was the best organised,' he says. 'That was the heart of the copper belt, so there was a real mix of people. Every town I went to, they had the best stadia, everything was well maintained. The crowds were quite good, and they were good players. Far better than in Swaziland and Lesotho. Jackie Sewell was there. He had played for Notts County and England but he had ended up playing for Zambia. I'm not sure how: I fancy he had a pal there who had got him a job in Lusaka, paying well, and he was playing for them as well. For an international-standard footballer to be playing for Zambia was remarkable.'

Rogers' reports on what he found in each of the nations he visited clearly impressed his paymasters, even if the messages he sent back had a tendency to make life a little awkward. He had written to Wade from Lesotho to express his belief that apartheid was stymying the game's development in Lesotho. Wade responded, in April 1965, by admitting that 'many of the clubs in South Africa are unhappy with this situation', but insisting that he 'did not feel qualified to express an opinion on this matter'.

They were sufficiently satisfied with his work, though, to send him on a similar jaunt to the United States at the start of 1966. There, too, he found life frustrating, although this time the issue was the reluctance of the television companies to try to finance football and the desire of many of the authorities he encountered to promote what was seen as 'the European game'. By May, he was back home. His career had already taken him to six countries, each of them now just a little affected by what he had taught them. That would have been legacy enough. Rogers was only just getting started.

*

Rogers is not a shy man, nor a bashful one. He was, as he says, 'a good coach', 'always pushing, learning, presenting my ideas'. That this is no idle boast can be proved by one, very brief, stop in his career. He spent the 1966 World Cup on Merseyside, where Hungary were billeted for the tournament. He watched all of their games, attended their training sessions, picked the brains of their coaching staff. He did not stay still for long: no sooner had the country stopped celebrating a triumph that disguised quite how far it was losing touch with football's zeitgeist than he was off again, called to take charge of Uganda for the Gossage Cup, a sort of East African regional championships.

It was not, on the face of it, a promising assignment. After casting an eye over a few club games, he named a squad for the tournament. Newspapers in Kampala confirmed he had asked 30 players to attend his training camp. Only 12 of them turned up, and two of them were goalkeepers. Rogers embarked on a frantic series of phone calls to try to muster a team. He wrote letters, registered requests with various clubs. He describes a week or so of total chaos. Uganda made the final of the competition. He was indeed, it seems, quite a good coach.

Judging by his next move, he was not afraid of a challenge, either. His work in the United States had been enough to establish something of a reputation there, and later in 1966 he was offered the chance to take charge of the Chicago Spurs, one of the ten founding members of the National Professional Soccer League, a forerunner of the North American Soccer League. 'I had coached in Chicago on the trip in early 1966. Three sessions. They thought I was the man for the job. There was the social life and all that stuff, so I went.'

Again, he would find his preparations disrupted by difficulty in getting a team together. The NPSL was not recognised by the US football authorities, the USSF, or by Fifa. 'They had jumped the gun, I think,' he said. 'That made it hard to get players: we had a couple of local lads, a couple of Mexicans, and I brought Joe Haverty across from Arsenal. We could only play at Soldier Field. It held 80,000. Jack Dempsey boxed there. It's right on the waterfront. It's so big, but it was no football stadium. We had to play on top of the baseball diamond. It was terrible. The gates weren't very big. The television companies did not like football because it's harder to film than basketball, so you had to play at midday.'

Results were respectable – Rogers, not given to unnecessary modesty, says he 'did well' – but it was more the lifestyle Chicago afforded him that he enjoyed. 'I found [a partner] out there who wasn't too bad, and that was going OK,' he says. The adventure would end prematurely. The NPSL was forced to merge with the United Soccer Association to form the NASL; the Spurs were relocated to Kansas City because another franchise, the Mustangs, had already arranged a deal to play in Chicago. Rogers, in dispute with the team's owners, would not go with them.

Before he left, though, he had the chance to go out for a drink with Malcolm Allison, the legendarily bombastic Manchester City manager. His side had come out to Chicago to play a money-spinning pre-season game. 'He was a real John Wayne type, a great big cigar clamped between his lips,' smiles Rogers. 'We were talking about who the best coaches in the world were. I said Helenio Herrera, at Inter Milan. Allison said he was a coward, too defensive. So I asked him: "Who do you think the best three in the game are?" And he looked at me and replied: "Well, the other two are ..."'

He laughs as he tells the story, amused by the brazen cockiness of the remark. It is not long, though, before Rogers is remembering his own golden age, and declaring that, in a certain place and at a certain time, he stood comparison with one of the most decorated managers in history.

*

O'Farrell and Rogers landed back in Tehran in January 2006. It was the height of the War on Terror; Iran was the heart of what George W. Bush had dubbed the 'axis of evil'. Fears over Iran's nuclear programme were mounting. Mahmoud Ahmadinejad, the country's hard-line, anti-American president, had been elected just a few months previously. He would, it is fair to say, have been unimpressed at the sight of two Englishmen – ancient or not – being mobbed at the airport. He probably would not even have laughed at hearing Rogers' former player shout 'Bollocks!' at him.

The pair had been invited to return for eight days by Persepolis, the country's most famous, most successful club. The Iranian embassy had sent envoys to Rogers' home in Southport, and O'Farrell's in Torquay, to persuade them to attend a gala dinner held in honour of some of their former players. Neither was entirely sure; both were in their eighties, long cocooned from the rigours of international travel. 'We had a chat, and decided we might as well,' says Rogers.

O'Farrell might have been the more famous face, as erstwhile coach of the Iranian national team, but it was Rogers who was the star turn. He, after all, had led Persepolis to four league titles; he had helped them to victories over some of the most glamorous teams in the world. He flickers with pride as he remembers it. 'I was recognised everywhere,' he says. 'I was with the best team. I was winning all the time. It sounds stupid, but I was a bit like Fergie, really.'

Rogers had arrived in Iran, after his American adventure, in 1969. His employers were not Persepolis, but a club called Paykan. 'It was the FA who recommended me,' he says. 'Ken Aston – the referee – had done a course in Tehran for people from all over Asia. When he travelled back, [the Iranian football authorities] asked him if the FA could find a coach for one of their clubs, Paykan. I had been doing well, so they told me there was a job going. The way it worked was that the local FA would fly you out, you'd see if it was OK, and then you'd make up your mind. I didn't speak a word of the language, of course, but the facilities were good, and the club was backed by a big car firm. I agreed to take it. I flew back to London, where I had a flat, closed that down, and flew back out.

'The standard would have been the same as at the bottom of the Second Division in England. People have the wrong idea: they are not professional teams, but they train the same as they do here because they're on the payroll of the ministry or the company or whatever. They just don't go into work, you see. I could get them any time I wanted. If it was too hot, or there was a downpour, I could knock training back a couple of hours and they would still turn up. That first year, we won the league and the cup. Paykan begged me to stay.'

He rejected their overtures. An ownership tussle meant that Paykan, as a club, would cease to exist, with most of their players joining Persepolis. Amid the uncertainty, an offer arrived from the United States. There had been a change of ownership at his old team, the Spurs, now based in Kansas City, but many of his old allies in the club's administration remained. It was an appealing prospect, but his stay lasted only a year. He was tempted back east by Persepolis, a new club full of familiar faces from Paykan. It would prove a defining move in his career, such a successful time that he would be invited back 30 years later to speak to the club's most famous players. It was at Persepolis that he would become the Persian Ferguson.

In the space of his four years at the club, he would win two league titles and establish Persepolis as the pre-eminent force in Iranian football. He would be introduced to the Empress Farah; he would be carried aloft by his players in front of 30,000 screaming fans. 'I did very well,' he says. 'You can tell when you're doing well, because nobody argues with you. The crowds liked me. I never used to have to pay in restaurants, all that stuff. We would get a full house every game. These were big matches, big teams. The supporters were good, certainly in Tehran. It was a bit different in the oil fields, down south. You'd get people chucking rocks at you there.'

It is his victories over visiting touring sides – from the Soviet Union, from South America, from England – that brought him most pleasure, though. He remembers 'stuffing' CSKA Moscow to win the 'Friendship Cup' with Paykan; at Persepolis, he managed a 1-1 draw with Manchester United, the same scoreline with Stoke City and a victory over Bournemouth. They drew with Sao Paulo in a tense, fractious game described as 'more like a wrestling match'. Only Crystal Palace, he remembers, dispatched Persepolis with any ease.

'We were playing a four-three-three,' he explains. 'They had never had that in Iran. I took it there. I had two fullbacks: one went to Bayern Munich and the other ended up playing in the States. I made those two. I had a midfielder, Ali Parvin, who was captain of the national team. We were a good side.

'I remember Chelsea came out. We got a draw with them. We ran Newcastle off their feet: they had been on tour in Hong Kong and were on their way back. But my biggest win was against Nacional, the Uruguayan team who were world champions. We stuffed them 1-0. They were all surprised by how good we were. Of course, we were three or four thousand feet up, so it was easier for us.

'Teams came out with the wrong impression about some of the sides they were going to face. It was very difficult to win those games and if you were at the end of a long tour and your energy levels were down, the local players would run you into the ground. Nacional had played three games by that stage and they had won them all, but we stuffed them. My record in those matches was good. They have never done anything like that with a club side since.'

The local press agreed. One newspaper noted that the city had gone 'wild with joy' after the victory, with 'young Persepolis supporters singing and dancing' so much that 'a few people fainted among the crowd'. After the win, they took to 'marching around the streets, cheering their club'.

It was not just on the pitch that Rogers enjoyed life in Tehran. The Iranian capital was, then, a cosmopolitan, welcoming place for westerners, a place of bistros and embassy garden parties and lush hotel bars. Rogers cautions that there were 'certain things you could not do in Iran', but for an expat, beyond criticising the Shah, it is not immediately clear what those things were.

'I enjoyed it,' Rogers says. His priorities become clear. 'I found it peaceful. They had bars, you could get a drink. All of the women that had been to Europe were wearing miniskirts and everything. It went so well. There were different crowds. I used to mix with the people from the embassy. There were garden parties, and I'd be invited to their homes and everything. They had a place up the hill, in the mountains that ring the city, where it was a lot cooler in summer.'

It sounds idyllic, but even in the gilded bubble he had created for himself, Rogers knew things were not quite right. 'They used to have secret police chasing the revolutionaries,' he says. 'I remember walking home from the bar at the US embassy one night and I suddenly found myself surrounded by all these dogs. They all had rabies, all the strays. I remember thinking: "How do I get out of this?" If I ran, they'd chase me. If I stopped, they stopped. Anyway, all of a sudden, a car screeches around the corner, coming out of one of the narrow back streets. No lights on. Really gunning it. Twenty yards behind them was another car. The dogs bolted, and it saved me. But it was the SAVAK, the secret police, chasing someone. One of my players was in the SAVAK. We knew he was in the SAVAK, all of the other players knew he was in the SAVAK. That is what it was like. They had someone everywhere.'

Discontent at the Shah's brutal regime was mounting. 'If you go downtown in Tehran, right down at the bottom of the hill, they were the bad areas. They had sluices open at the side of the road running from the rich areas at the top to the poor ones at the bottom. They would open them up at the top and the water, the waste, would end up in the south part of the city. That is how the Ayatollah got involved. First it was those people, and then it was in the universities.'

Rogers had other concerns, too. He had left Persepolis in 1974 after a row with the owner about what team he should select to face Aberdeen; the club's president, A.H. Abdoh, stressed that 'there was nothing more' Rogers could do for the club, claiming that he 'needed a fresh face and fresh ideas'. The separation was sufficiently amicable for Persepolis to write the 50-year-old a warm letter of recommendation. Rogers used it to go back to Iran, in October 1975, in charge of newly promoted Shahbaz. The political situation, though, was deteriorating.

'The Ayatollah was on the radio every day,' he says. 'He was agitating from Paris, and then from over the border. Two Americans were shot dead in the south. The revolution was coming. Shahbaz were a new team, a smaller team than Persepolis, but they wanted me to go down and put it together. They gave me a contract, but the committee were not unanimous. They did not really want an overseas coach, not in that climate. We did well in the first division, and we put a good team together, but after a year we started arguing about salary. There was a row with the press: I accused a reporter of writing rubbish, the papers did not like it, and so I was sacked. It was all just prior to the revolution. You could see what was coming.'

The sky is darkening over the lake by the time we finish. Rain is spitting against the windows. Alan Rogers has been talking for five or six hours about all the people he has met, all the places he has been, all the things he has done. Throughout, one phrase has recurred. He says it as he remembers the adventures, the experiences, the girls. He uses it to describe finding himself on a boat in the Bahamas when he had been told his services were no longer required in Chicago. He uses it to recall drinking in a hotel bar in Tehran with Peter Osgood. He uses it when he thinks about Lesotho, about Zambia, about meeting his ex-wife, the beauty queen, a lifetime ago in the holiday camps. It is a phrase laced with sadness, about a life that has been lived, but a life, too, that was worth it. He says it with a smile and a sigh: 'All our yesterdays.'

Rogers' career did not finish in Iran. He went from Shahbaz to Benghazi, in Libya, when a local side made him a lucrative offer to come and coach them. Things were so basic that, after returning to England for a holiday, he travelled back to North Africa with a proper garden roller to improve the standard of the pitches. He did not, presumably, take it as hand luggage.

'The problem was that I used to go out to get breakfast from a bakery,' he says. 'Nice bread. Leavened bread. Anyway, so I walked round the main square to find three bodies strung up, hanging from the trees. Colonel Gadaffi had been to Benghazi. He'd taken over a hotel on the outskirts. He had commanded that three fellas be hung in the main square and another in the docks. I thought a year there would probably be enough.'

Next, he travelled to Iceland, the place where, he jokes, they filmed the moon landing. His team, in Akureyri, 60 miles from the Arctic Circle, had to fly everywhere to games because the roads were not good enough to be used. 'There were a couple of places where you landed right next to the pitch. I'd had a problem with my eye, so I wasn't allowed to jump, to head a ball, to swim, anything like that. It was too cold to be up there, standing around.'

He would not make that mistake again. Qatar was next – 'the money was quite good,' unsurprisingly – long before the notion that the tiny Gulf State might one day turn into world football's power broker. He stayed for two years. There would be one more stop, one more stamp for the passport, in Cyprus, before he decided to call time on his career, return home, hang up his clipboard. 'Wherever I went, the longer and better my CV was. These teams do not take a chance. I was a good coach.'

He was more than that. There is time for one final photo. He is pictured standing on the right, beaming smile, gleaming blond hair. It is from a Butlin's camp, probably the late 1950s. It is before Walter Winterbottom, before Bloemfontein, before Chicago, before Tehran, before Rogers' life, his second life, had even begun. It is a picture of a man who is about to start on an adventure that will change not just him but the lives of countless people he encountered, while also, unlikely as it seems, in some way altering the course of football's history. All of those people whose paths he followed, all of those who would travel in his footsteps, will have a photo like this one, a snapshot of who they were before it all started. It is a picture of a maverick and a missionary, a man who may not have been known here but who will never be forgotten out there. Alan looks at the photo for what seems like an age. 'All our yesterdays,' he says. 'All our yesterdays.'

2

Boys and Men

Fred Pentland spent the afternoon of 31 July 1914 watching the German war machine rumble into gear. One by one, the lamps were going out all over Europe. It was three days since the Austro-Hungarian Empire had declared war on Serbia, two since the Russian army mobilised, less than 24 hours since the bombardment of Belgrade had begun. Pentland was supposed to be making his way to Strasbourg, where he was due to take a coaching clinic, but found himself trapped in Freiburg, witnessing at first hand the Kaiser's response. 'At four in the afternoon,' he later wrote, 'the troops began to file out of the barracks in full war kit.' He had turned 31 on 29 July, just as the last hopes that conflict might be avoided were evaporating. He had been in Germany for two months.

He had travelled out in May, employed as one of three coaches engaged to try to harness the country's growing enthusiasm for football in time for the 1916 Olympics, due to be held in Berlin. South Germany was his patch. His job, explained to him at his interview with a man by the name of Walther Bensemann at the Adelphi hotel in Liverpool, was to 'teach, advise and choose the best players' from all of the club sides he encountered. He had spent those first few weeks in Karlsruhe, Pforzheim and Stuttgart, assessing what talent there was to be found.

What he saw that afternoon in Freiburg did not seem to trouble him unduly; after all, 'nobody supposed Britain would enter the war' at that stage. Still, he was clearly alert enough to get in touch with Bensemann once more, asking if he might be permitted to travel home in light of the worsening crisis. 'He was very kind to me,' Pentland recalled, 'and did his utmost to find a way for me to travel home, but it was impossible.' All of the trains were being used to transport troops. Bensemann assured him that once the 'first rush of mobilisation' was over, arrangements would be made for all foreigners to leave. The chance never came. On 4 August, Britain declared war on Germany. The police were instructed to round up all resident aliens. Pentland was thrown in jail.

According to his own account, given to *All Sports Weekly* in 1921, he remained there for 'several days'; given the subsequent timeline of events, it is likely his stay was somewhat longer. He does not complain about the treatment he and his fellow prisoners received, but it was sufficiently bad that, at one point, he claimed to be a professor in the hope of improving his lot. It worked, for a while, until the guards noticed that 'about 95 per cent of the crowd' had afforded themselves the same status. The question was asked again. He said he was a professor of sport. 'I was immediately transferred to the masses,' he wrote.

Prison was just a short-term measure. Germany was busy preparing a more permanent home for its enemies within. The army had commandeered Ruhleben racetrack, six kilometres to the west of Berlin, to serve as an internment camp. The stables, straw still on the ground and the stench of manure in the air, were converted into 11 barracks to house the detainees, as many as 400 men crammed into a space meant for 27 thoroughbreds.

By early November 1914, Ruhleben was ready to welcome its first inmates. By the time Pentland got there, hundreds, possibly thousands, of others had already arrived. His first sight of the place that would be his home for the next four years must have been a miserable one. Each barrack had a standpipe for cold water. There were no beds, just the horseboxes and haylofts and the concrete floor. There were only strips of sackcloth, crawling with lice, for protection against the bitterly cold nights. The prisoners wore wooden clogs on their feet and donated coats on their backs. A couple of hundred guards watched over them. Ruhleben was encircled by what one prisoner described as 'more barbed wire than I have ever seen in my life'.

In Pentland's recollection, he had only just arrived when he was summoned to the loft in Barrack 11. There, deep in enemy territory in the middle of a war that would claim millions of lives, hundreds of miles from home, a friendly face awaited him. 'I had only been in the camp a few minutes when I was taken to the loft where Steve Bloomer lived,' he wrote. 'He was at that moment giving the same earnestness to a game of Ludo with a crowd of racing men as the old warrior would have done to an international match with Scotland.'

Steve Bloomer was English football's first superstar. He did not, at first glance, look the part, boasting what James Catton, the great-grandfather of football journalism, described as 'an ashen countenance' and a slim, almost elfin figure. That did not stop him earning fame – first for his club, Derby County, and then for his country – as a preternatural goalscorer, a player who 'did nothing like anyone else'. To his peers, he was 'incomparable Steve, the greatest inside forward who has ever played for England'. To the nation, his prowess in the Home Internationals earned him the nickname 'the Hammer of the Scots'. He was so famous that even

P.G. Wodehouse had heard of him: in 'The Goalkeeper and the Plutocrat', the football enthusiast Daniel Rackstraw reveres a pair of 'Bloomer's boots'.

Bloomer first burst into the country's consciousness in his debut season at the County Ground in 1892. It was his ruthless finishing that stood out. It was a gift he had honed as a child, when he would go 'out on my own into the fields near my home with a football; I would drive sticks into the ground and dribble round them, or just shoot at one from all angles, learning to keep the ball low, the most difficult shot for any goalkeeper to save'. All of that practice would serve him well. As an 18-year-old, he scored 11 goals in his first season for Derby, 19 in his second, and he won international recognition in his third. By the time he retired, in 1914, he was the leading goalscorer in Football League history and had managed 28 goals in 23 games for his country. It would take the combined might of Jimmy Greaves and Dixie Dean to deprive him of those records.

Fred Pentland's playing career was not quite so glittering. Even he knew that: when he published his life story, in a series of articles in *All Sports Weekly*, it was self-deprecatingly titled 'It Ain't All Lavender – the life story of a very ordinary professional footballer'. He had been rejected, as a youngster, by Hereford and, more brutally, West Bromwich Albion, where the club's secretary told him he should consider giving up the sport altogether.

Undeterred, he managed to win a place at Small Heath – the club that would eventually become Birmingham City – in 1900. Even that was something of a fluke. Pentland was working in a factory and planning to join the army when he attended an open trial at Small Heath as a fan. Hearing that one player had not shown up, he asked if he might fill in. His application was accepted only because his father had run an amateur team for disadvantaged children in Birmingham, Pentland's Robins, for many years. His father's good name was enough to gain him entry. It was the chance he needed, performing well enough as an outside right to earn his first professional contract, for 10 shillings a week, at his hometown club.

He would spend three years at Small Heath, largely as a reserve, balancing his career as a player in the Birmingham and District League with his work in the factory, persuading his manager and chief foreman to give him time off every weekend to play. 'Every week leave was given me for the very last time,' he wrote, 'but I always obtained it.'

Small Heath released him in the summer of 1903, forcing him to write to 'nearly 30' different clubs in the hope of finding another contract. He received just one reply, from Blackpool, but remained there for just a matter of weeks before being sold to Blackburn. His stay there lasted three years and saw him once again cast in the reserves. By 1906, he had been trapped by the retain-and-transfer system: because his contract had expired, Blackburn did not have to pay him, but they would only agree to sell him if a buyer matched their £250 asking price. He could not join another Football League club without their permission, so he was forced to drop into the Southern League, which was exempt from the pernicious regulations. He joined first Brentford and then Queens Park Rangers, two more stops in an increasingly wandering career. Pentland only settled in 1908, thanks to a move that, in hindsight, arose in highly suspect circumstances.

Strictly speaking, Pentland still could not move to another Football League club without Blackburn's permission. All of a sudden, though, he was in demand: QPR had won the Southern League in the 1907-08 season and, at the age of 24, he had even been selected to play for the South against the North in a game at Manchester. When he refused to sign a new deal in west London, he was threatened with total excommunication from the game.

QPR demanded £700 for his transfer, £250 of which would go to Blackburn. 'Another club informed me that if I could get away for £500, including Blackburn's £250, they would give me £250 for myself,' he wrote.

That club was Middlesbrough, the richest team in the country, riding the heavy industry boom that gave the city the nickname Ironopolis. Three years previously, they had made Alf Common the first £1,000 player, a move that had drawn stinging criticism from the press – described by the *Athletic News* as the dishonourable practice of 'retention of place [in the First Division] by purchase' – as part of a transfer spree that had sparked a Football Association investigation into financial irregularities and, eventually, earned manager Alex Mackie a lifetime ban from football. Judging by Pentland's account, his tricks for signing players endured even after his departure.

Pentland would remain on Teesside for four years, his longest spell at a club. Moreover, he would win full international recognition while there, not bad at all for a player who had not long since been told it would be in his interests to give up the game altogether. He described himself, upon being selected to represent the English against the Scots, as 'the proudest man in all the world'.

More significant, though, it was at Middlesbrough that Bloomer first crossed his path. 'Incomparable Steve' had arrived in the Northeast in 1906 in another deal that owed much to Middlesbrough's creative approach to transfers. He had been sold by Derby as part of a £750 double deal which also included Emor Ratcliffe. In order to comply with FA rules over payments – introduced after the Common deal – the two players were officially ascribed the same value in the sale, a perfectly reasonable £375 each. In reality, that did not quite ring true. Bloomer was arguably the most famous player in the country. Ratcliffe, on the other hand, was a reserve left back.

Bloomer and Pentland were together at Ayresome Park for only two years, deployed together at inside and outside right. Their partnership did not bring the club any particular success on the pitch. As Pentland wrote, though 'no-one could deny the players were of the highest international reputation, as a whole it did not work well, or as well as might have been expected. It was the same old story of individual names being preferred to a harmoniously-working team. This sort of team never does much in championships or cup ties.'

Off the pitch, though, the two men struck up a firm friendship. Pentland struggled for form after his transfer – 'the change of air had so affected me I had no energy or desire to do anything' – but found his new team-mate willing to bail him out. 'Bloomer did not ask; he understood,' Pentland wrote. 'He always tried to do an extra bit to cover my errors, and to put chances in my way of rehabilitating myself.' Quite how close they became is evident from Bloomer's reaction to Pentland's first international call-up, in 1909, a game he had not been selected for. 'I am glad,' he told him. 'You have got the biggest honour in all the world. I only wish I was playing with you.'

From this remove, granted the chance to assess their lives, it is not hard to see why they got on so well. They had far more in common than just the dubious circumstances of their arrival at Middlesbrough and the fact they had both been born in the Black Country, Bloomer at Cradley and Pentland at Wolverhampton.

Once Pentland had got over Bloomer's rather rudimentary rhetorical style – 'he did not exactly say what he had to say as the Archbishop of Canterbury would say it' was his euphemistic way of pointing out that Bloomer swore a lot – he discovered in him a resource he was keen to tap. Pentland had always been obsessed with perfecting his craft, with making the most of what he saw as his relatively meagre abilities; in Bloomer, he had found someone whose knowledge of the game was encyclopaedic. 'I found every-thing he said was right,' Pentland wrote. 'He has always been, in my view, the greatest inside forward the game has ever known or is ever likely to know. He could see a thing going to happen minutes before any other player. He knows the playing of football from A to Z. In fact, one could truthfully say he knows absolutely everything there is to know about football.'

However, that is not to say theirs was a master and pupil relationship, based on Pentland's admiration for Bloomer. They were both forward thinkers. Bloomer's biographer, Peter Seddon, quotes one of his former team-mates at Derby, Jimmy Methven, as describing him 'sampling different pairs of boots and testifying they were all the ideal boot. I should think he averaged a different pair every fortnight. He must have spent a small fortune in ink writing testimonials for the different firms.' They were far from the only commercial endorsements he sought in order to capitalise on his substantial, but by no means lucra-tive, maximum wage: he was a regular face on cigarette adverts for more than a decade. Bloomer was in the habit of pulling his socks up over his knees, too, a century before Thierry Henry thought of it, and performing cartwheels 'in ecstatic joy' when-ever he scored.

Pentland, not nearly as famous and perhaps not quite as showy, had a similar penchant for challenging the status quo. As early as 1921, in that series of articles in *All Sports Weekly*, he was proposing that players might benefit from a winter break. 'I have suggested to league clubs many times that, in their own and in their players' interests, it might be advisable to give all their best players a rest for a couple of weeks a season.' He would not be the last to have that particular idea. Thirty years before Gabriel Hanot dreamed up the European Cup, and many more before the continent's super-clubs started discussing abandoning their domestic leagues altogether, he even 'dreamed' of a 'Europe-wide league'. 'The day will come when we shall see a league comprised of teams in all the countries in Europe,' he wrote. His vision even stretched beyond football, his field of expertise, and took in the delights of private air travel. 'Each club, of course, will have its own flying machine. Fancy seeing the placards out for Chelsea against Madrid, or Newcastle against Prague in the final of the cup.' His was a remarkable foresight. Pentland, like Bloomer, was considerably ahead of his time.

It is fortunate, then, that they found each other at Middlesbrough; not simply for them, but for the game, too. Their friendship would last until Bloomer's death in 1938, but before then it would help both men survive a war; it would provide the spark for one of the most remarkable stories in the sport's history, set against the barbed wire and misery of Ruhleben.

Most significantly of all, though, it would take them both to Spain, where the roles would be reversed, where Bloomer would enjoy success but Pentland would find fame. It was in Spain that their friendship would have its most long-lasting effect, where a bond first forged in Ironopolis would irrevocably shape the destiny of one of football's modern superpowers. It was in Spain that both men would put their knowledge to use and see their vision of how the game should be played become reality. It was in Spain that both would become *Misters*.

Like Pentland, Bloomer faced a stark choice as the end of his career drew near. It was one few had encountered before them: they were members of almost the first generation of professionals who had to find a way, when age caught up with them, to continue earning a living from football or be forced to return to the trades they had learned before they made their way in the game. Bloomer, like his father, had trained as a blacksmith; Pentland might have been able to return to factory life. Neither, it seems, found the prospect desperately enticing.

Yet football offered no obvious path, even to a player as famous as Bloomer. He had, by the standards of his day, done well from his time at Derby and Middlesbrough. His wage, for many years, was £5.10s. a week, not far off the maximum permitted of £6, with a further £1 as a win bonus. He and his wife, Sarah, lived relatively comfortably with their children in Derby, but the days when a player was set for life were nearly a century away.

Just as far-fetched was the idea that a player of Bloomer's standing might be able to pass on to a new generation the wisdom accrued during his 20-year career. The constituent clubs of the Football League all had managers, but they were either administrators or, at best, 'trainers': employed to keep the players in shape. Ball-work – let alone tactics – did not really feature. Pentland's description of an average week's training during his playing days bears this out: Sunday and Monday were days off, Tuesdays involved an hour's football in the morning and a brisk walk in the afternoon, Wednesdays and Thursdays concentrated first on sprinting and then a couple of longer-distance runs round the stadium, and then Friday was reserved for gym work, if the player in question felt up to it.

It was an ideology that would prove peculiarly persistent, leaving dozens of thinkers and pioneers with little choice but to leave their native shores and indulge their educational instincts abroad. For Bloomer, a keen student of the technical side of the game but by his own admission 'not a natural trainer', it seemed to limit his employment opportunities. Pentland was in the same position. In 1912, he had found himself in Middlesbrough's reserves, his primary role to help teach the club's young players a degree of game craft. It was a task he relished. 'They were,' he wrote, 'some of my happiest days.'

When his contract expired, he volunteered to stay on – at a reduced rate – so he could continue his work, but was told there was no position for him. He left on good terms, though, for Halifax then Stoke, with the words of the club's chairman, Philip Bach, buzzing in his mind. 'It was his advice that gave me the idea of being a continental coach.' So when he was summoned to the Adelphi hotel to meet Herr Bensemann, he had long been sold on the idea that perhaps his future would lie abroad.

Bloomer was a little different. He seems to have had no desire to spend his days barking orders at young players as they sprinted around the pitch, but equally there is little to suggest that he had any great longing to travel. He would certainly have been aware, though, that foreign clubs and countries had already started to recruit experts from the motherland to aid in their footballing development. By the time he was recommended – his reputation was such that he did not require an interview – for the managerial job at Britannia Berlin in the spring of 1914, there were already a handful of Britons abroad. John Madden, a Scottish international and former Celtic player, had joined Slavia Prague as early as 1905. William Townley, once of Blackburn, had been in Germany for some time, working in Karlsruhe, Furth and, eventually, at Bayern Munich. William Barnes, a former team-mate of Pentland's at QPR, was at Athletic Club in Bilbao. William Garbutt – of whom much more later – had joined Genoa in 1912.

Perhaps their examples served to convince him that the Berlin post was worth taking, that this was a valid way of supporting his family without returning to the smithy. Whatever the reasoning, he arrived in the German capital on 14 July 1914, a few weeks after Pentland had arrived to take up his post. His assessment of his new charges was not entirely positive: '[the Germans were] very earnest, although never anything like so skilful as the Britons at the game.' He had precious little opportunity to help them along.

Three weeks later, as Pentland wandered around Freiburg, war was declared.

Bloomer was not quite as phlegmatic as Pentland about his situation. 'Rumour followed rumour of disquieting nature until all foreign-borns knew they were in the midst of very unhealthy surroundings,' he wrote in *Navy & Army Illustrated* magazine in 1922. 'Finally a body of British men proceeded to a local recruiting depot and asked if it were possible to secure train accommodation in order to get back to England. To their enquiries, the Teuton officer replied in perfect English, saying in dramatic and grandiose manner: "Oh, it would be impossible. We want all our trains to transport our troops to the East and West."'

Soon, he described 'notices being placed in public places notifying all British subjects to report to the nearest police station'. Any chance of slipping away unnoticed had evaporated: according to Seddon, his biographer, he blamed a number of 'rotters' among his squad at Britannia for turning him in. He was given instructions to report to the authorities 'every third day'.

Despite the restrictions, he seems to have lived relatively freely in Berlin until November. By that stage, though, the Germans had worked out what they were going to do with the enemy aliens in their midst. Bloomer was instructed to report to Charlottenburg, to the west of the city. He was joined by 600 or so British and French subjects, rounded up by the police the previous evening, each of them clutching 'all the worldly possessions one felt advisable to take'. 'It was,' he wrote, 'a dishevelled and lamentable-looking procession ... subject to the worst [their guards] could do.' They began to march. As they trudged through the crowd that had gathered to watch them leave, they were 'battered about' by men wielding walking sticks, women brandishing umbrellas and children throwing missiles. They were heading to Ruhleben, their bleak new home.

For the first six months of their incarceration, Bloomer, Pentland and their fellow prisoners suffered badly. They were counted on the racetrack at 7am every day and then dispatched to their daily tasks: loading and unloading railway carriages, unwilling cogs in the wheel of the Kaiser's war machine. Rations were Spartan: 'Breakfast consisted of black bread and something undefinable which they christened coffee,' Bloomer wrote. 'Dinner saw us rushing with our mess tins for more black bread and soup, its relationship to soup being due to the fact that a few pieces of potato, carrot or cabbage had found within it a watery grave.' Inmates would forage in the bins for leftovers. Anyone found guilty of 'talking, shuffling or whistling' would be beaten with the butt of a guard's bayonet, or forced to eat from a swill bucket; the worst offenders were sent to the 'birdcage', a makeshift isolation unit surrounded by razor-sharp barbed wire. They were spat upon and sworn at during the day; at night, they were packed so tightly in their barracks that 'you could not raise your arm above your head'.

Bloomer and Pentland were not the only notables suffering at the hands of Baron von Taube, the sadistic deputy camp commandant, and his henchmen. 'When the Germans cast their net for the enemy alien resident in the country, they made a varied catch,' Bloomer told the *Sunday Chronicle* when he returned home in 1918. 'The camp opened to receive a good many people whose lot in life had been to entertain others: we had musicians and vocalists who had appeared before royalty, accomplished actors and music-hall artistes, and quite a selection of professional athletes.' Most of all, they had footballers, and good ones.

Among them were John Cameron, once of Tottenham Hotspur and Scotland, John Brearley of Everton and the former England international Sam Wolstenholme. All of them, as the days dragged on and freedom did not come, grew convinced that they had to do something to keep themselves occupied, to try to 'make the best of a bad lot'. It was a sentiment felt throughout the camp. Prisoners made concerted attempts to improve their dire situation, nominating a 'captain' to negotiate with the German authorities for better food, lodging and treatment. Given the experience among their number, it should be no surprise that football was prime among their thoughts.

Their chance arrived early in 1915. When the second most powerful man in the Fatherland, General Gustav von Kessel, was charged with reporting on how the inmates were being kept, the camp's democratically elected captain, Joseph Powell, was deputed to negotiate with him. He requested that they might be allowed to use the grass field inside the racetrack as a football pitch. Von Kessel, persuaded that such activity might stave off the threat of 'barbed wire syndrome', agreed. On 22 March 1915, five months after they had first arrived, the Ruhleben Football Association was formed. The announcement that they would be allowed to play football, according to the magazine the prisoners had started to produce within the camp, was 'greeted with a magnificent roar of approval' from the internees.

It is perhaps a measure of where their strengths lay that, while Pentland took a leading role off the pitch, Bloomer remained a draw on it. It was the former who was tasked with getting the field ready for play, armed with a tape measure and a bucket of whitewash to mark out two pitches. The latter, meanwhile, was nominated as the captain of one of the teams that would play in the opening game, on 26 March. Bloomer's XI, containing Pentland, Wolstenholme, Brearley and Cameron, would take on 'The Rest'. In an attempt to curry favour with Von Taube – who was felt to be against the move to allow football – he was invited to kick off the game. Bloomer's team won 4-2.

That match would be the start of a league that would run for the next three years and which, to both Bloomer and Pentland, served to 'save the sanity of the camp'. Teams were organised by barrack – aside from a 'Boys' Team' – and into two leagues and a cup competition. Games were played over two 35-minute halves and in great numbers. Cameron wrote to Frederick Wall, the secretary of the Football Association, to say that some 300 games had been played in a 'hurricane' of a first season, in the space of just six weeks.

By October 1915, Pentland could write in the camp magazine that, for the second campaign, the Football Association intended 'having goal nets, and shall also place ropes and posts around the ground for the convenience of all concerned'. Players could buy all of the requisite kit from the camp's athletic store, though footballs, more expensive, had to be sent out as gifts by the FA and 'some of John Cameron's friends in Chiswick'.

So in demand were the two pitches that a rigorous schedule had to be drawn up for their use. One was reserved for league games, the other for friendlies: 'to allow ample opportunity for those who are not involved in the league to have plenty of football'. 'Taking it for granted that the ground is open from 9 to 11.30am and 2 to 5pm,' Pentland wrote, 'we have five and a half playing hours per day. This gives 39 hours a week for non-league players, or three hours per barrack.' Each league team, in the week ahead of the start of that second season in October, were meanwhile given a pitch for four hours' practice to assess the players at their disposal. Such a workload, of course, came at a cost: by Christmas 1915, Sam Wolstenholme could complain that the league pitch had 'cut up pretty badly' and, because of 'the lack of proper utensils to keep it in order', was preventing teams from playing the sort of football they desired.

Not surprisingly, Bloomer became 'the central figure of Ruhleben football'. His team, Barrack 1, lifted the inaugural league title, leading his old friend Pentland to praise his 'generalship' and his 'keenness for the success of his side'. Though Barrack 9, captained by Wolstenholme, went on to win the championship the following season, Bloomer was always the main draw. 'Although he has had his 41st birthday among us, his interest in the game has been so great that he has only missed ... one match,' Pentland wrote at the end of 1915.

The camp followed the league with a remarkable intensity. Attendances numbered in the thousands – more than 3,000 watched the cup final in May 1917 – and, at one game, the spectators had to be warned not to make too much noise in case they made the German guards skittish. Some 1,600 votes were cast when, in September 1915, the camp magazine ran a competition to pick the sides for an England against the Rest of the World game; when the teams they chose did not feature, they complained bitterly and at length to the magazine.

That was not the only controversy the football sparked. In 1915, the magazine's sports correspondent, writing under the pseudonym Young Bird, had criticised the performance of two inexperienced players in a league game. Pentland took exception. 'To slate a man as Young Bird did ... is hitting below the belt,' he wrote in response. 'Neither of these players, in my humble opinion, deserved the condemnation passed upon them.'

Young Bird was affronted. 'I am exceedingly surprised that a player of Mr Pentland's standing should take up an attitude with regard to criticism which I can only define as "namby pamby",' he replied. He accused Pentland of losing his 'mental perspective in Ruhleben' and defended the duty of the critic 'to criticise, not to encourage young footballers'. He suggested that if Pentland's sensibilities were offended by that, 'it is time he gave up football and took to croquet'. A year later, there followed a fevered debate over whether it would be better for camp morale to do away with the league, which some felt served to engender 'a spirit which often oversteps the bounds of friendly rivalry'. Pentland was against such a move. 'The men who play the game will do so, whatever the contest, and whatever the prize,' he wrote.

That football assumed such importance speaks volumes about the mentality of the prisoners at Ruhleben. 'One only realises the tremendous part the Sports Ground plays in our circumstances when the Racecourse is closed,' Pentland wrote in the Christmas 1915 edition of the camp magazine. 'Hundreds of us roam aimlessly around looking for something to pass the hours.' It was not simply the chance to play and to watch, though, that they missed; it was the chance to have something to talk about, something to distract them from the situation they found themselves in. Trapped in enemy territory behind a sea of barbed wire, unfortunate to be incarcerated but blessed to be kept away from the slaughter on the fields of France and Belgium, they found that the only way of coping was to create the best facsimile of home they could. They spent their time trying to make extraordinary circumstances seem as ordinary as possible.

As Bloomer had noted, the Germans had made a varied catch when they rounded up all of the Britons resident in the country and sent them to Ruhleben, and it showed in the number of activities that sprang up: there were musical recitals, often performed by a thriving cast of female impersonators, and lectures in everything from Euripides to organic chemistry; there was a postal service and a branch of the Royal Horticultural Society and even a bijou theatre, where plays were staged. Musicals, complete with their own orchestra, proved popular; the main streets in the camp were, with a heavy dose of irony, given names like Bond Street and Piccadilly; they were packed with little shops, a cobbler's and a tobacconist's and even a library; when their occupants died or later, were released, they were sold on to new entrepreneurs for a fee. There was a printing press, churning out the camp magazine.

The obsession with football was part of the same trope. By taking it seriously, by indulging in ardent support and petty controversy, they were trying to make Ruhleben seem less like a German prison camp and more like a little patch of England. 'Let me say at once that sport was our salvation,' Bloomer later wrote in the *Sunday Chronicle*. 'How we revelled in those matches. The spectators became as enthusiastic as the players, for a healthy rivalry sprang up [between barracks].' He would suggest that the two things that kept them sane during their incarceration were the simple joys of 'food from home and sports'. Another prisoner, Henry Mahoney, wrote that the arrival of a rubber football from the Football Association 'revived our drooping spirits as speedily and completely as the sight of gold affects a prospector. The fun we extracted from football would pass all comprehension.'

At home, the reaction was less euphoric. There had been a groundswell of support for the interned Britons at the outbreak of war, a rush to send whatever people could to help them survive in the belly of the enemy. It did not last. Life slowly improved for the men in the camp. The United States ambassador petitioned the Kaiser to allow them a better diet and enough supplies to build beds and chairs. Britain granted them a relief fund of four marks a week to buy whatever they could. As reports seeped back of their apparently cosy, peaceful life – at the same time as the British public learned of the slaughter on the Somme – sympathy evaporated. Suddenly, the men at Ruhleben were the lucky ones, cocooned from the horrors of war.

Those who endured it resented that impression. Bloomer, in particular, did all he could to correct it as soon as he returned home. The account he provided *Navy & Army Illustrated* in 1922 reads like a concerted effort to contradict every single one of what his biographer, Peter Seddon, calls the 'music hall jokes and cheap newspaper gags' he and his fellow prisoners were subjected to. Ruhleben was still a place, he said, 'of more dinner times than dinners'. Many of those inside were malnourished, despite the regular packages of food from home; they were, after all, still prisoners of war. It is simply, to Bloomer's mind, that they took every step necessary to ensure they survived it. All of the life they constructed, all of the feigned normality, was partly a coping mechanism and partly a cry of patriotic defiance, proof to their guards that they would not be broken. Football, more than anything, provided the means.

'Our games,' he wrote, 'made us forget our troubles for a while. We were all brothers. We made a life for ourselves out of nothing. We were surely happier than the German guards and did our bit in upholding the spirit of the Britisher in adverse circumstances. Make no mistake that boys became men in Ruhleben, but it is far more pleasant to recall the better days when we went out to play cricket and football, and men became boys again.'

Their experiences in Germany were very nearly enough to put both men off striking out from home ever again. Bloomer was released in March 1918, a farewell football match held in the prison in his honour. The FA had managed to negotiate his exit on compassionate grounds: one of his daughters, Violet, had died in England in 1917. He was not allowed to return home immediately, being sent instead to neutral Holland to coach Blauw-Wit Amsterdam. He found a country and a continent shattered by war: in Germany, he was pestered for food by a populace hungrier than he had been; when he disembarked in Holland, he was greeted as a hero. Even then, though, football's popularity was undimmed: Blauw-Wit's stadium held 30,000 and had only been built four years previously. He had no desire to remain. As soon as the armistice was signed, he sought a way home. He docked at Hull on 22 November. Pentland, freed from Ruhleben, would arrive not long afterwards.

They both seemed intent on remaining in England. Bloomer turned down the chance to coach Poland in 1919, the same year Pentland was – rather ambitiously, it has to be said – approached to become manager of the German national side. He, at least, considered the offer: he checked with the FA to see whether they would hold working with the enemy against him. They insisted he would be 'viewed without prejudice' should any future jobs become available, but he demurred anyway when the German authorities refused to pay the balance of what he was owed from his first stint in the country, as well as compensation for four years of imprisonment. Bloomer, a father once more at the age of 45, did not even get that far. He had found a job coaching the reserves at his beloved Derby and had an extra gig on the side, as a sort of roving scout for the *Derbyshire Football Express*, to supplement his income. Pentland, in the absence of any other option, worked at a bookmaker's. He appeared occasionally for QPR's reserves, but when it became clear his playing days were over, he took a job in an office.

It would be Pentland who cracked first. In 1920, he wrote to Frederick Wall once more, asking if he knew of any posts available for coaches abroad. The reply came, tinged with bitter irony. Strasbourg were in need of a manager. Six years after he had found himself in Freiburg, watching the first embers of the blaze that would engulf the continent, unable to take the train to his next appointment in that city, he would get there at last.

His reputation, at least, remained high: he was even given the honour of preparing the French team for the 1920 Olympics, held in the Belgian city of Antwerp. It did not go especially well:

France were knocked out in the semi-finals by Czechoslovakia and the newspaper *L'Auto*, in the first available documentation of Pentland's approach to the game, reported that several of the national side's players were unimpressed with the amount of work expected of them. Pentland may have believed that a manager's role was far more than simply instructing his players to sprint, but he was obviously no soft touch. He felt players had to put in the hard yards to get anywhere, as he had. He did not tolerate shirkers.

Although the Antwerp Games were not the happiest of experiences, it was in Belgium that his future – and that of the game – turned. He was made an offer that would extend his stay abroad still further, one that would go a long way to sowing the seed for a superpower to emerge. 'While at the Olympics, a member of my present team asked me if I would find them a coach for Santander, in Spain,' he told *All Sports Weekly*. 'I decided to take the post myself. I had always had a desire to go to that country, so after the expiration of my contract in March 1921, I spent a few days in England and went to sunny Spain.'

Pentland, at that point, would most likely not have imagined that his and Bloomer's paths would cross once more on foreign shores, in a country which football was 'taking a keen grip of, as it is everywhere'. His old friend, the same year, was appointed as Derby's first-team coach – a newly minted position and concept – and although he did travel in his summers, spending three months coaching in Canada in 1922, he did not share Pentland's desire to broaden his horizons. 'Who knows,' he wrote, explaining to the *Derbyshire Express* why he wished to stay at home, 'if I did go, maybe another war would break out.'

Economic reality would force him to change his mind. Derby appointed Cecil Potter to replace Bloomer's mentor, friend and idol Jimmy Methven in 1922; he and his inherited coach did not see eye to eye. The club's most famous son left for good in the summer of 1923. He returned to his post as the local newspaper's roving scout, but it would not have been a lucrative role. In October of that year, a job offer arrived. Bloomer, too, was wanted in Spain – what he referred to as the 'land of bullfights, nuts and siestas' – by Real Irun, a team based in a small customs town about 15 miles northeast of San Sebastian.

It is unclear whether he was recommended for the position by Pentland but since, by that stage, he was also in the Basque Country, at Athletic Bilbao, it is hardly an outlandish theory. It is given further weight by what Bloomer did on the day after the train had pulled into his new home. His first was spent with Real Irun's directors, taking a trip from the town into the Pyrenees. 'Though tired, I was more than refreshed by the magnificence of this scenery. I have never seen anything like it,' he wrote to his family. The next day, he went to see his fellow Ruhlebenite.

'I made the 90-mile trip to Bilbao, where I had a long chat with Fred Pentland, who talks Spanish fluently and looks a real "Don". The lessons he gave me on the manners and customs of the country were as amusing as anything I have heard for some time. He appears to be a little tin god in Bilbao and has a courtly way with him.'

The reason for Pentland's popularity was not hard to fathom. Athletic had poached him from Santander after just a season, and were quite proud to have done so. 'Many wanted him,' wrote *La Gaceta del Norte* in August 1922. 'They included a national team: France. Maybe this detail warrants more attention than the recommendation, formidably phrased, of the secretary of the Football League. France named him as coach for the Antwerp Games, and wanted him again for the Games in Paris [in 1924]. France even offered him an order of merit. We have already seen that it was a deserved gesture.'

He had more than lived up to his billing: in his first season in Bilbao, Pentland led his side to the Copa del Rey, Spain's de facto national championship in the absence of an organised league. Given that *La Gaceta* had felt the need to remind its readers, when his appointment was announced, that 'coaches can only do human things', it seems fair to assume that achievement was not entirely expected. When Bloomer arrived, then, Pentland was flush with success. It did not take his friend long to notice the esteem in which the Basque public held him. A decade later, long after Bloomer had returned home, Pentland was no longer a little tin god. By that stage, he was positively golden.

Bloomer seemed to take to management just as naturally as he had to playing. He had been immediately impressed with the standard of player he found himself working with, recommending in one of his first letters home that scouts from England 'could do worse' than make a trip to the north of Spain to watch the talent on offer. 'I have,' he boasted, 'at least four players at my disposal who are the real goods.'

Given that the game in Spain was then still resolutely amateur, training was not always easy – 'my own boys are all "in work", some in very good positions, and it is not always that they can be freed to train' – but what he saw when he could get them together appears to have more than made up for it. 'I am down at the ground all day for there is always a chance one or two will turn up – they are as keen as mustard – and when they do come in odd ones [and twos] there is the chance for personal coaching. Their patience in perfecting tricks you show them is inspiring.'

It was this side of his work that appears to have truly appealed to Bloomer. He had greatly enjoyed his time at Derby, teaching the mechanics of the game, just as he had first fallen in love with it on the fields near his home, driving sticks into the ground and taking shots towards them. Now, given full control, he coached football as he believed it should be coached. He did not realise it – his letters, quoted by Seddon, reveal that he felt he was 'training the boys along orthodox English lines' – but that in itself made him a maverick. He concentrated on 'ball practice', with 'far less sprinting than in England'. He wanted his players to be able to control the ball as well as he could, to understand the science behind shooting that had helped him become a star. He believed the game could be taught. That was enough to make him different, the first in a long line of *Misters* who would leave England because they wanted to pass their knowledge on and could not find a willing audience at home.

At Irun, by contrast, his methods were welcomed. 'There are a number who are capable of holding their own with the best of the English league in craft and ball control,' he wrote, 'though they could never stand our climate, of course.' He seemed to revel in the enthusiasm for the game, too, describing vast crowds of 25,000 or 30,000 ardent fans, even expressing his astonishment that, in one match, armed soldiers were deployed along the touchline to maintain order.

That first season was an intensely happy one. He led Real Irun to the Basque regional title, getting one over on his old team-mate Pentland in the process, then to victory against Sevilla in the first round of the Copa del Rey, then Spain's equivalent of a national championship, before beating Barcelona, after a replay, in the semi-final. He was full of admiration for the hard-running of his players. 'The football here really is the fastest I have ever seen,' he wrote, 'the chief reason being that the grounds are harder. There are receptacles of running water where the players can every now and again plunge their heads or have a drink. They have a 20-minute interval and, believe me, they need and deserve it, for after three-quarters of an hour of hard football their faces are as red as fire.'

The final was against the might of Real Madrid. It was held at Atocha, in San Sebastian, not far off a home game for Bloomer and his team of amateurs from near the French border. They won a tense, tight game by a single goal. Real Irun were champions of Spain. In his first season as a manager, Bloomer had won the title. His vision of how football could be taught, of how players could be improved, had been right. 'Much of the glory,' a club official said at the parade to celebrate their triumph, 'goes to *Mister* Bloomer.'

It should have been the start of a career just as successful as the one he had enjoyed as a player. Bloomer might have earned himself fame not solely as one of the game's first superstars, but as one of its most influential thinkers, too. It was not to be; it would be Pentland to whom that honour fell. Bloomer, by now in his fifties, returned to Spain after a summer at home in 1924 claiming that 'another campaign in exile holds few terrors', but over the course of that difficult second season a frustration rooted in home-sickness became clear.

In his letters home, he complained of hearing little or no English spoken; the only person with whom he could regularly converse in his mother tongue was the manager of the Hotel France y Gare Norte, where he had his lodgings. His own attempts to learn Spanish do not seem to have been successful. He struggled with the 'impulsiveness' of the native character, while both the incessant rain – Spain was not quite as sunny as he had hoped – and the amount of oil on the food also attracted his disdain. 'I am like all exiles,' he wrote. 'My thoughts turn to the home country; there are many times I can see the crowds rolling up to the grounds I have played on and I can see the scenes almost as if I am among the people.'

Even the football had lost its allure. He remarked that for all their mastery of the ball, 'their chief failure is teamwork and too great a desire to shoot at inappropriate times'. He was annoyed by the tendency 'not quite to grasp the smaller points of the game and [to] overlook them as they regard them as relatively insignificant'. The crowds, which had so astonished him initially, were now described as 'unruly', while he felt the 'power of town officials and the poor refereeing' served to undermine the game's integrity.

He still managed a modicum of success on the field. No more trophies, sadly, but two famous victories over Real Madrid – 3-0 and 7-0 – in games held over Christmas. That was enough to see Irun invited to tour Switzerland as emissaries for the Spanish game, where their success saw them awarded the sash for national sporting merit on their return home. Irun remains the only Spanish club to have been given that honour. It would prove to be Bloomer's last act as a manager. His contract ran for only two years; he did not have any intention of renewing it. He wanted to return to England, to Derby, to Sarah, but that he was grateful for his experiences showed in the way he chose to leave, a model of dignity and diplomacy. 'These boys are born ball-players,' ran his final remarks to the Spanish press. 'There is nothing more to do. My work here is done.'

That was an exaggeration, of course, if an admirable one. Bloomer had, without question, left his mark on Spanish football, had helped it on its way. It would be Pentland, however, the man who had been such a significant presence in his life, who did more than almost anyone to set its course.

There is some debate as to what state Athletic, and Spanish football, were in when Pentland arrived in the Basque Country in 1921. The club's museum holds testimonies from his players, who claim he taught them to 'tie their boots', though that should probably be taken metaphorically. What is not in doubt is that by the time he, too, eventually returned home in 1935, the spectre of yet another war looming, he had changed beyond recognition the way the club he loved and the country he made his home played football.

Pentland's place in history is often boiled down to results and to records, many of them dating to his second spell in Bilbao: he had left in 1925 for Atletico Madrid and had a spell at Real Oviedo before returning to San Mames in 1929 for the first season in which Spain would have a genuine national league. The next four years would bring eye-watering success: inflicting the heaviest defeat in Barcelona's history, a 12-1 decimation in the 1930-31 campaign; masterminding a 6-0 win against Real Madrid, too, the biggest home defeat in their history. He won the Spanish title twice, unbeaten in 1930 and then again in 1931. He picked up four consecutive Copas del Rey between 1930 and 1933.

But his real impact was much broader than that. His players might have been able to tie their boots, but they were still in need of education. Unlike Bloomer, he felt that Spanish players were undermined not by a predilection for shooting from all angles but by not shooting enough; the experiences of several of those who would follow his lead and coach abroad suggest this was a fairly standard complaint. He placed this front and centre of his coaching sessions. 'The purpose of the game of football is to shoot,' he said in an interview with *Sportsman* in 1923. 'You must take a shot at goal. You must take a shot at goal constantly.'

He placed extreme importance on technique, too. He had learned from his time at Middlesbrough – a decade beforehand – that he enjoyed the experience of working with young players and Bilbao provided him with an abundance of opportunity: he would train between 70 and 80 players a season in the club's *cantera*, their youth system. 'To be a coach, you must have a lot of experience and it is essential to know how to teach,' he told *Sportsman*. He demanded respect, but believed that it 'should be earned by showing them that the coach knows more than they do, not by being excessively severe'. He preferred 'a bit of persuasion with a tinge of good humour' to 'strict discipline'.

All of those who came under his aegis were taught the need to strike the ball 'hard, rapidly, curtly', and with both feet: always with both feet. 'The first training task with the youngsters should be to show them how to kick the ball correctly with either foot,' he said. 'That is the first lesson I taught my students. It should be struck easily with either foot.' Ultimately, he saw it as his 'responsibility to train complete players'. It was a view entirely at odds with the prevailing wisdom in England at the time, where such technical training was considered irrelevant. Unlike Bloomer, though, Pentland seems to have been aware of that.

'The days are not far distant when, in addition to a secretary and a manager, the big clubs will have a coach,' he wrote in 1921. 'Some have one now. His business will be to teach the young players unity. This will do away once and forever with young players playing for themselves alone. The coach must teach them the right manner in which to use their natural ability.' This was a credo Pentland had picked up from the one manager he encountered as a player who seems to have had a lasting effect on him: James Cowan, with whom he spent just a year at QPR. Cowan, he felt, 'did not engage his men as individuals, but chose them as parts to fit in a well-running machine'. The contrast with what he had experienced at Middlesbrough, where a group of players had been thrown together with no thought at all beyond their fame, was stark.

It was this vision of football that Pentland would inculcate at Athletic, with such spectacular success that he became a hero not just in the Basque Country but something of an icon across

Spain. In 1932, fresh off the back of his two league title wins, the newspaper *AS* published a series of articles written by Pentland outlining how he put his teams together, how he coached, how he felt the game should be played. It was not just a matter of the technical, he explained, but the 'psychological and intellectual aspects of a game ... in which the morality and intelligence of a player are a prerequisite'. He seemed to care less for the reverence he attracted across the country than the esteem in which he was held in his adopted home. Bilbao, Pentland said, was 'the best city in the world'; he was determined to do it proud. 'I put my soul into my work because I am obliged to everyone. Every Athletic member is, for me, a board member.'

Asier Arrate, director of the museum at San Mames where so much of Pentland's legacy is curated, insists the Englishman 'loved' Bilbao the city as much as he adored Athletic the club. Together with his wife and daughter, he settled in the centre of town, taking rooms in the Pension Matilde. He became a regular visitor to the city's many *tascas* – its *pintxo* and tapas bars – and, by the 1930s, had even 'changed his style of dress' to fit in with the locals.

There were but two constants. Pentland was never seen without a cigar between his lips and a bowler hat – what the Spanish call a *bombín* – perched on his head. That hat became so characteristic that it not only gave Pentland his nickname, *Bombín*, but led to a curious and enduring tradition: every time his team won a game, his players would snatch the hat and celebrate by tossing it on the ground and jumping on it. Harry Homer, in a dispatch from the Basque Country sent to the *FA News* in 1953, claimed that subsequently the contrite players 'would solemnly present him with a new bowler and a box of the best Havana cigars' to apologise for their delirium. He apparently ordered as many as 20 new hats a year.

Athletic's supporters returned Pentland's affection. Homer confirms that, 17 years after his countryman left the club, that 'his name is still revered at San Mames and among fans in every Bilbao bar. They tell many stories of him and he must have been a great character. They say that every time Bilbao score three goals the crowd would turn to the stand and cry *Viva Pentland!*' In 1959, the club invited him back for a testimonial game against Chelsea, and awarded him a Distinguished Member's medal in recognition of his service. Addressing the crowd, he declared that now he had returned to Bilbao, he 'could die happy'. He would live for just three more years.

His impact, though, would last much longer: in fact, it endures to the present day. As Bloomer noted, the football both he and his old friend found in Spain was marked by its speed. To men raised on the English diet of spit and sawdust, that was not necessarily a bad thing: indeed, when Spain became the first European side to beat England, in 1929 – a feat assisted by Pentland, engaged by manager Jose Maria Mateos as a coach – it was felt that the hosts' pace, maintained despite the searing heat, had proved the crucial factor. 'The Spaniards are fast,' one member of the FA party wrote to the *Athletic News* that year. 'They are very fast, and not lacking in skill and finesse.'

However, Pentland's view of football extended some way beyond athleticism. The touchstones of his philosophy were rather different. He fervently believed that 'patience is something necessary and healthy in football. He was scornful of the 'strong kick, which is neither football nor anything'. To paraphrase Bob Paisley, he preferred neither the short nor the long, but simply the right pass. In particular, he valued what would today be called 'game intelligence' above all else. 'Intelligence is an indispensable asset in a footballer,' he said. 'That is what is of value during a match. Serenity and intelligence.'

These were the attributes he demanded of his players and his teams, the values that influenced his style. Quite how he came by such a philosophy is not immediately clear. Serenity and intelligence were not exactly hallmarks of English football in the 1920s and, although the game before the war was by all accounts rather more refined than the one that took shape afterwards, Pentland still seems something of an outlier, a purist in a pragmatist's age. Perhaps that was just because of his personal convictions, forged in his mind during his playing career. Perhaps, though, his time in Ruhleben helped spark his thoughts and focus his mind. He spent, after all, four years locked away in a little world unto itself with a self-selected cluster of adventurers and mavericks, in a place where football was a constant source of conversation. The Ruhleben Football Association's handbook, published in the camp in 1915, contained not just coaching advice but tactical discussion, too. It is, in some estimations, the very first piece of footballing literature, a written testament to the visionary thinking of the internees. It may be that Pentland's approach crystallised among the sackcloth and despair of a prison camp, that it was in the dark days of war that the theoretical groundwork of modern football was laid.

However he came by it, his style was diametrically opposed to the way football was played in Spain at the time. Just like the English, the Spanish preferred a blood-and-thunder approach to the game. This ordinary player, this quite extraordinary manager, ignored that received wisdom and spent his career preaching patience and passing. He was playing, back in the 1930s, something that sounds an awful lot like an early prototype of tiki-taka. Noting the success it brought him, others sought to ape his approach: there is even a theory that it influenced the thinking of the club that would, in time, weave his beliefs about how the game should be played into its very soul.

Pentland would be touched to think he had a part to play in crafting what Barcelona would become, but sadly the idea does not quite stand up to scrutiny. His influence on the development of Spanish football was vast. Nobody did more to set the boys of Spain on their way to becoming men, but it would be too much of a stretch to try to identify him as one of the spiritual antecedents of the modern Barcelona. The same cannot be said of his countrymen. There are, indeed, English branches on the tiki-taka family tree.

3

Render unto Caesar

There is a cross of St George on Barcelona's badge. It has been there for more than a century, right next to the yellow and red of the Catalan flag. It stands for San Jordi, as the saint is known in Catalonia, but there is another way to read it, too.

This is a club, now, that sees itself as both a resolutely local institution and a fearsome international brand. It has leveraged its identity as a gathering point for Catalan nationalism, as the only place during the dark four decades spent under Franco's dictatorship where the national language could be spoken, as the most potent symbol of the gathering campaign for independence, and turned it into something that attracts supporters across the world. Its playing squad illustrates the dichotomy: a galaxy of stars from around the globe and a core of home-grown prodigies crafted at the traditional farmhouse at La Masia – as the club's youth academy is known – where everything that Barcelona means, everything it stands for was taught to them as children. In their own way, Xavi Hernandez and Gerard Pique are as much an expression of Catalan identity as Joan Miro and Gaudi. And yet there is that one exception, that one corner of their heart and that one corner of their flag that somehow seems something else entirely: not new, not international, and not old, not local, but forever England.

The connection stretches right back to the club's founders. Three of the men who first set up the team in 1899 – Walter Wild, John and William Parsons – were English; two of its most prominent early players, the Witty brothers, likewise. But the link extends beyond distant history and into the very modern character of the club. Tiki-taka, the doctrine of rapid, short passing, is indelibly associated with Barcelona and with Catalonia. This was the philosophy that helped Pep Guardiola and then Luis Enrique turn Barcelona into the best club side on the planet over the last decade. Thanks to Xavi, Pique and the rest, Spain harnessed it to conquer the world, winning three straight major tournaments between 2008 and 2012. If any foreign influence is acknowledged in its development, it is that of Rinus Michels, Frank Rijkaard and, in particular, Johan Cruyff, who laid down the principles of La Masia and built the club's first Dream Team. Tiki-taka is Dutch in inspiration, Catalan in execution. Like the crest, though, it is somehow English.

As we will see later, many of the ideas that helped turn Michels and Cruyff into two of the most significant figures in the development of the European game came from seeds planted in their minds by Vic Buckingham. Terry Venables, too, deserves more than a passing mention: he laid the immediate groundwork in the mid-1980s for what would become known as Cruyff's Dream Team. None of it, though, would have been possible were it not for the work done by figures who appear much earlier in Barcelona's history, men whose legacies have been distorted or even eroded by time, whose significance has been all but lost even to the club they helped to create.

Alf Spouncer arrived in Spain in October 1923. He had been

recommended to Barcelona by Frederick Wall at the FA. He had
been no mean player, appearing once for his country and forging a fine career at Nottingham Forest, and he wasted no time in
presenting his new team with what might be described as his ten
commandments for how he wanted them to play. They were published, in full, by the newspaper *Libertad* a few days later.

> First: you are never individuals. Pass the ball to a player
> who is in a better position than you. Second: remember
> that one player can never beat 11 players. Togetherness
> and the effort of everyone are the keys to victory. Third: it
> does not matter who scores the goals, as long as it is our
> team that scores them. Fourth: always play the ball on the
> ground, because it is not yet possible to play in the air.
> Fifth: always keep the ball in movement from one player
> to the other, because if you hold on to it for too long you
> give the defence time to get organised. Sixth: always help
> a player when he finds himself tightly marked and in a dif-
> ficult position. Seventh: never consider another team weak
> and do not stop playing until you have heard the whistle.
> Eighth: a good attack is the best defence. Ninth: a violent,
> late or early player [in the challenge] will fall from grace.
> Tenth: remain in good physical shape and do not smoke or
> drink to excess.

These are Spouncer's principles, the cornerstones of what would
today be referred to as his managerial philosophy, and yet they
could easily have been written by Guardiola or even Cruyff. As
early as 1923, Barcelona were being told to play on the ground
and to keep the ball in constant motion. Catalan tiki-taka might
be rather older than is assumed.

Spouncer lasted just a season at Les Corts, Barcelona's first home. He returned to England in March 1924 after losing heavily in the semi-finals of the Copa del Rey, his team beaten by Steve Bloomer's Real Irun, the Derby icon getting one over on the former Nottingham Forest player. By the standards of many of Barcelona's first English coaches, that was not particularly bad going: in 1912, the year the club first appointed a specialist manager, they went through three in the space of just a few months. Billy Lambe, a former Arsenal player; a man referred to in the local press of the time as Baron, Barren and Barzon; and Jack Alderson, a goalkeeper who took on the role of coach for, at most, a handful of games in December of that year.

One of their countrymen would fare substantially better. Jack Greenwell arrived in Catalonia in 1912. He was hired initially as a player, but for the vast majority of the next decade he would also serve as the club's manager. He would shape the careers of many of the most celebrated players in Barcelona's early history – the record-setting striker Paulino Alcantara and the midfield general Josep Samitier among them – and he would lay the foundations for the club's commitment to attacking football. He would be the man who oversaw what is referred to now as Barcelona's first golden age. He is the sort of figure who should stand, if not quite alongside Joan Gamper, the club's founder, then certainly just beneath him, ranked as one of the men who turned the club into a superpower.

He is not. Too often, he is overlooked, his decade at the club boiled down to just a few sentences, a couple of curious anecdotes and a cursory list of trophies. Even among those charged with curating the club's story, his part in it is at best misunderstood and at worst disregarded. It is easy to see why his timeline has been distorted: his life survives only in fragments, in fleeting mentions in sepia-tinted newspaper clippings that span more than 20 years. As the fog of time clears, though, as the pieces start to come together, it is possible to see exactly what Jack Greenwell did. More than anyone else, he gave Barcelona its English soul.

Greenwell is a unique case. His path to management was quite different from that of Fred Pentland and Steve Bloomer, who would follow him to Spain almost a decade later. So, too, was his background. He was born in Crook, south of Sunderland, in 1884, and although he was a player of sufficient ability to be recruited by Crook Town in the amateur Northern League as a 17-year-old, he never reached the professional ranks. He spent 11 years playing for Crook: his final confirmed appearance coming in December 1911. Among the handful of British players and coaches who travelled abroad, he seems to have done so entirely under his own steam. He did not have a network of contacts who might have helped him find a lucrative teaching post. He was not sought after as a former international. He did not have any measure of fame at home, and so he did not attract the attentions of the press. All of those who left England in the first years of the 20th century to spread the word of the game were adventurers, but Greenwell was particularly ambitious. He was a miner's son who, somehow, struck out on his own.

While that lends his story an appealing edge of mystery, it comes with one significant drawback. Scraps of his life remain, traces in the rubble, making it possible to piece together where he went and what he did, who he was and why he mattered. For all that we can know, there are a number of things that we cannot: what Donald Rumsfeld might label known unknowns.

The first is quite how it all began. Thanks to the archives of *La Vanguardia*, we know the exact date he made his first appearance for Barcelona. On 1 September 1912, the club's first team met their reserves in a training game. Greenwell appeared for the first XI and clearly impressed the newspaper's correspondent.

'He guides the ball where he apparently means for it to go.' Soon enough, he was a regular feature of the side. By October, just a few weeks after he had first trained with his new team-mates, he was described as 'the well-known player, Greenwell' by *Mundo Deportivo*, the daily sporting newspaper that was as obsessed with the intricacies of life at the club then as it is now. That month he shone in a game against Numancia, 'showing he is a fine player and has great knowledge of footballing practices'.

What we do not know is what took him there in the first place. He must have arrived in Spain in the first few months of 1912; most likely, he saw out the 1911-12 season with Crook and then travelled in the summer. Why, though, remains a mystery.

The most commonly held theory is unsatisfactory. In 1909, Greenwell was invited to play for West Auckland Wanderers, another Northern League side, as a guest in the Sir Thomas Lipton Trophy, a club tournament widely regarded as a sort of unofficial forerunner of the World Cup. He travelled with the team to Turin and helped them see off German, Italian and Swiss representatives to win the competition. It has long been assumed that Barcelona spotted him in Turin and then, three years later, offered him the chance to join them. What this does not explain is either why there was a representative of a Spanish side at a tournament in which no Spanish teams were involved, or why they would wait three years to sign him.

That is not the only version, but none of the others is any more convincing. One runs that Joan Gamper, the Swiss who was the driving force behind Barcelona for many of its early years, encountered him on a trip to England and persuaded him to travel to Spain. Again, realism casts an unflattering light on the story: there is no reason why Gamper should have been in the Northeast of England, or even any record of him going there, and much less that he should have happened to take in a Crook Town game during his visit. Another suggests that he was retained after appearing for either Crook or West Auckland when they travelled to Barcelona on tour. Here, history intervenes: Greenwell was in Barcelona in September 1912. West Auckland did not arrive in Spain until December of that year; Crook only travelled out in April 1913. Greenwell predates them both.

What we can be sure of, though, is that a number of British amateur sides visited Barcelona in the early years of the 20th century. Cardiff Corinthians were there in 1910, while a host of teams from London – New Crusaders, Woolwich Polytechnic, a Plumstead FC featuring Charlie Buchan, and United Hospitals – toured in 1911 and 1912. There is no evidence that Greenwell, who had never played outside the Northeast, had any connection with any of these teams and he does not appear in any of the sides they named for their games. However, there remains the possibility that he either formed part of a travelling party or received word from a friend that there were opportunities in the city for amateur players. An even simpler explanation may be that he simply left his home for Spain for reasons unrelated to football: at least one historian has posited that perhaps he was working for an English company in Barcelona and was recommended to the club by Manuel Torres, its first true employee, without reference to his experience at Crook.

Quite why he pitched up in Spain is not the only hole in his story. His departure, too, is shrouded in doubt. Again, it is possible to date his exit relatively precisely: in May 1936, he had just finished his first campaign as manager of Sporting Gijon. After one of his final games – a 4-0 defeat to Barcelona – he afforded an interview to *Mundo Deportivo*. He seems to have had no immediate intention to leave the country. His team, he said, was packed with 'boys and some amateurs, but all of them are disciplined'. He felt confident that 'next year, we will have a team' capable of competing. Later that month, he was slated to be given a benefit game at El Molinon, Sporting's home ground. Ricardo Zamora, the legendary goalkeeper Greenwell had worked with at Barcelona, was scheduled to appear.

At some point in the next couple of months, though, his plans changed. Why they did is immediately obvious: in July 1936, Spain slid into civil war. Greenwell had been aware of the changing political climate, sending his family back to England as early as 1934 as tensions mounted. He would not be granted the chance to see what might become of that Gijon team. We can be certain that, by September of that year, he had left the country. That month, an amateur Catalan representative side travelled to Paris for a friendly game. One of the players, a Dr Amigo, informed *Mundo Deportivo* that Greenwell had been in touch. He was in the French capital for an interview with Racing Club Olympique. 'He heard a Catalan team was visiting,' Amigo said. 'He did not have time to visit us and give us advice and he could not help us during the game, as he would have wanted, because he had a meeting at Red Star at the same time. It seems he will reach an agreement with Red Star to coach them.'

In all likelihood, he left considerably sooner than that; most probably within a few days or, at most, weeks of the start of the war. The story – according to both his family and those few, brief biographies of Greenwell that have appeared in official histories of Barcelona – goes that he caught the last boat out of the city that had been his home for so long, unable to rescue any of his possessions and being forced to wave goodbye to the life he had built.

It is a compelling story, but one that remains impossible to verify entirely. We cannot even be sure that he was in Barcelona; with his family ensconced in England and his employers in Gijon, Asturias, it is not immediately apparent why he would have returned to Catalonia. All we know is that he did get out, meaning his time in Spain is bookended by two known unknowns: what was it that brought him there and how he left.

Fortunately, in the intervening period, things are clearer. In those 24 years, the fog lifts to reveal a portrait, professional and personal, of one of the most important characters in the history of Barcelona, of Spanish football and of England's influence on the world game. It is pieced together here for the first time, drawn from yellowing newspaper clippings, the long-forgotten testimonies of those who were there and, crucially, the memories of him passed down through his family. Constructing the story of Jack Greenwell was a painstaking process, one that became something approaching a labour of love, but an immensely worthwhile one. For too long, he has been denied the place in history and the status he deserves, even by the club he served so well: it will come as a surprise to Barcelona, above all, that the longest-serving manager in their history is not Johan Cruyff, the elegant superstar, but a gentle giant from County Durham.

Greenwell's greatest trait as a player seems to have been his versatility. His best position – the one in which he made the majority of his 88 appearances for the club – was in midfield, what was then known as a left half, though there were times when he played in the defensive and forward lines, too, and on one notable occasion he even slotted in as goalkeeper after the regular occupant suffered an injury. Wherever he played, he performed with 'great dynamism and magnificent control of the ball', according to *Mundo Deportivo*. When Notts County, a professional Football League team and the 'most complete side ever to visit' met Barcelona in 1914, Greenwell was, according to reports, the most impressive player on the pitch. He was seen as the side's *motor*, its engine, until he took up the post of trainer in 1917.

That, at least, is the official version, the one Barcelona hold to be true. The reality may be considerably different. As we have seen, Greenwell was not the only arrival at the club in 1912, the year Barcelona employed three English coaches: Lambe, the mysterious Baron, Barren or Barzon and, finally, in December, Alderson.

It is likely that Greenwell had a hand in this last appointment. In December 1912, West Auckland arrived in the city to play a pair of friendlies. Jack Alderson, once a team-mate of Greenwell's at Crook, was among their number. The games were a source of considerable excitement in Catalonia. *Mundo Deportivo* published a list of all of the visiting side's players, each one granted a brief description of their position and abilities. They lavished praise on the amateur team, pointing out that they had 'won a number of important trophies, including the Durham Cup and the Northumberland Cup'. The first game, on 20 December, lived up to expectations: it was 'the most marvellous exhibition of football', the visitors impressing in the first half before the stresses and strains of their 'long and accident-strewn voyage' began to tell. The two sides faced each other again a week later before the miners and shipbuilders from West Auckland began their journey home.

Alderson did not go with them. He was persuaded to remain in Spain and take up the post of trainer. It is inconceivable that, directly or indirectly, his friend did not play some part in helping him make that decision. Alderson, sadly, did not last a month. In January 1913, he received an offer to play for Newcastle United, making his debut against Arsenal in the Football League a few days later. He would go on to make one appearance for England, a decade later, after moving to Crystal Palace.

Barcelona, deprived of their goalkeeper and their manager, looked to Greenwell to step into at least one of the posts. He is referred to as *entrenador* from as early as 1913, with *Mundo*

Deportivo describing Barcelona's team as being 'set up as Greenwell intended' in March of that year. Certainly, when he was arrested on Las Ramblas in November, the satirical magazine *¡Cu-Cut!* covered the scandal as an embarrassment for the club's manager, but they stopped short of mentioning why he had been apprehended. He was sufficiently well regarded as a manager to be invited to Palma, on the island of Mallorca, to hold a coaching clinic for local players in the summer of 1916. It would seem his reign did not last six years, as some records state. Greenwell's first spell as manager of Barcelona lasted a decade. This is hugely significant. It has long been held that Johan Cruyff is the longest-serving manager the club has ever had: he managed eight years in the 1980s and 1990s. Greenwell, it would seem, was there for longer.

The reason for the confusion is what happened in 1917. As Barcelona's official history has it, the club appointed an Englishman by the name of John Barrow as their first full-time coach that year. It was not a success: he lasted just a few months before being summarily dismissed because, according to one observer, 'wine was his best and only objective'. It is at this point that Greenwell's reign as manager is thought to have begun, rather than in 1913.

Doubt swirls around the entire Barrow episode. Greenwell, as we have seen, was *entrenador* long before 1917. It is possible that this is simply a case of semantics: Greenwell was a player who took on the responsibility of coaching and naming the side; maybe Barrow was the first specialist manager to join the club. There is, though, a more serious question mark – whether Barrow existed at all.

Reading through the editions of *Mundo Deportivo* and *La Vanguardia* from that period, it is clear they would have mentioned a change of management at the club, even if it was simply Greenwell being restored to a purely playing role and a dedicated manager being brought in above him. But there is nothing. Not even a reference, among all of that forensic coverage. It is only late in the 1920s that Barrow's name and unhappy demise come up.

One possible explanation for this comes from CIHEFE, a group of independent historians of the Spanish game. They have suggested that perhaps the Barrow who supposedly took charge in 1917 is, in fact, the Barren, Baron or Barzon who coached the team before Alderson's brief stay in 1912, and that the timelines have become clouded in the intervening century. There was, they say, only one Barrow in the city in 1917: an eccentric industrialist, one who might fit the bill as an oenophile but who had no obvious involvement in football. Whatever the truth of those few months, it is agreed that by March 1917 Greenwell was the club's full-time manager, either after a brief break or midway through an unbroken ten-year spell in the position, on a salary of 12,000 pesetas a season and the cusp of the most glorious few years of his time at Barcelona.

By 1919, the club's first great team was taking shape. In goal, Greenwell had signed Ricardo Zamora, widely held to be the best goalkeeper the continent produced before World War II. The midfield was patrolled by Josep Samitier, a 17-year-old who would go on to become the highest-paid player in Spain. In attack, everything centred on Paulino Alcantara. Greenwell had, the previous season, toyed with the idea of deploying him in defence, but after both the player and the club's fans protested furiously, he relented after just a couple of games. Alcantara was restored to the forward line. He went on to become Barcelona's highest-ever goalscorer, his record unbroken for almost a century until the advent of Lionel Messi.

In an era before Spain boasted a full national league, that team can lay claim to having been by some distance the finest in the country. They won the Copa del Rey, then Spain's national

championship, twice, in 1920 and 1922, and swept all before them
in the regional Catalan competition, picking up four local league
titles in a row between 1919 and 1922. It would be easy to ascribe
that success to the quality of the players at their disposal, but that
would be to do Greenwell a disservice. He might have remained
loyal to the 2-3-5 formation he would have known in England and
that stood as an orthodoxy across Spain. His most famous tactical
experiment – playing Alcantara as a defender – was neither long-
lasting nor a success. But his influence stretched way beyond what
managers were expected to do in England. His physical training
was ahead of its time, with his players encouraged to perform
loosening exercises and jump over hurdles to improve their agil-
ity. He emphasised attack above all: as author Jimmy Burns has
noted, at one point he had some 35 forward players at his disposal,
as opposed to just 14 defenders. He worked his players hard – he
typically greeted complaints that they were exhausted with the
reply: '¡*Caramba!* Imagine how tough you'd find it if you had
to do [hard-working club secretary] Manuel Torres's job' – but
for a purpose. He wanted his side to play with greater pace and
greater intensity than any of their rivals. In the form of Alcantara,
Zamora and Samitier, Barcelona had the tools to build something
special, but it was Greenwell who made sure they were sharp
enough to do the job.

Perhaps the best gauge of how highly he was regarded at the
club is that, in 1931, eight years after his first spell in charge came
to an end, he was invited back. In the previous two seasons, Barcelona had been beaten to the title by Fred Pentland's all-conquering
Athletic Bilbao. After a presidential election, it was decided that
there should be a process of 'renovation'. The first move was to
bring Greenwell back. 'Nobody has the authority, the knowledge
and is so fully associated with the Catalan character as him,'
wrote the newspaper *ABC*. There was no doubt that he would be

able to 'obtain great fruits from his players', and he could hardly resist the club's siren call. It was not just Barcelona the team that occupied a special place in his heart, but the city, too. He had set up home there with his first wife, Florence Elizabeth Moore, after their marriage in 1922. He had endured the tragedy and trauma of her death in childbirth two years later. In 1929, he had met his second wife, Doris May Rubinson, in a British pub in the city. Once a chorus girl at the Moulin Rouge in Paris, she was performing there with her dance troupe. They lived in a well-appointed apartment on the fashionable Camino Real, together with their daughter, Carmen. Greenwell was part of the fabric of Barcelona. The city was part of him.

Football was not the only string to Jack Greenwell's bow. Just as he had been able as a player to fill any position on the pitch where he was required, so as a coach he was capable of switching his attentions to different sports. While at Barcelona, he had spent time training the city's boxers, acquiring no little respect in that discipline, too. More impressively, in 1927, at the age of 43, he travelled to Valencia alongside his partner Gil Mateus to take part in the Spanish national tennis championships. 'They play the sport very well, as individuals and together,' wrote one newspaper. The miner's son from Sunderland was something of a renaissance man.

It was as a football coach, though, that he forged his reputation and left his greatest legacy. Once his time at Barcelona came to an end, he spent two years with one of the city's lesser lights, UE Sants, before moving on to Castellon – a team based on the coast, just north of Valencia – in 1925. He was credited with turning a perennially unfashionable, provincial side into one of the most effective in Spain, and after two seasons there his work caught the eye of Espanyol, where he remained until 1930 and, perhaps, enjoyed his most remarkable triumph.

Then, as now, Espanyol were very much Barcelona's second team. They existed entirely in the shadow of their neighbours and rivals. Greenwell turned the tables. In December 1928, his Espanyol team won the Catalan championship – his sixth as a manager – and then, two months later, went one better. In February 1929, they faced Real Madrid in the final of the Copa del Rey in Valencia. They won, beating the all-powerful side from the capital 2-1. Greenwell and his team returned to Barcelona as heroes, granted a night of revelry in their honour. They were treated – if that is the right word – to a performance of *El Difunto Era Mayor*, a comedy grotesque in three acts, as well as a musical showcase from Eddy Bancroft and his Merry Makers. Greenwell was invited on to the stage to receive a gift for all that he had done for the team. The double triumph marked the most successful season in the club's history. That was the year Spain's footballing authorities, after months of contemplation, finally organised a national league. Barcelona won the first title in the history of La Liga in June, four months after Greenwell's triumph. Espanyol would be permitted to regard themselves as the country's last unofficial champions.

Spanish football, even in its earliest days, had no room for sentiment. Barely a year later, Greenwell was being accused of indulging in unnecessarily 'extravagant formations' and of making poor team selections: in the words of one particularly poetic critic, he stood charged with thinking 'the same thing worked for scrubbing as for sweeping'. Midway through the 1929-30 season, there were rumours his contract would not be renewed. That summer, he left the club and – it seems – considered leaving the game: he went to Palma, in Mallorca, to 'establish a business'. But he could not stay away, and soon found himself persuaded to help run the local team, Real Mallorca. It is a measure of Greenwell's fame that his capture was seen as a considerable coup for the club. *Mundo*

Deportivo's correspondent wrote that a coach of his stature could 'only serve to elevate football here'. His first move was to ban all spectators from his training sessions, including club members. It was a draconian policy, but anyone who might have been affronted was urged to submit to his will: 'Such an appointment requires the full enthusiasm of everyone connected to the club.'

It did not take long before he was tempted back to Barcelona. There, he added another Catalan championship, but he could not improve their performances in La Liga and, after just two years, was allowed to leave once more. There had, according to *La Vanguardia*, been a 'crisis in results' that season, though it does not seem to have affected Greenwell's standing in the game. Offers of work flooded in. 'I have a lot of options,' he told a reporter in the dressing room at Les Corts in May 1933. 'I could stay in Barcelona, I could go to Madrid or I could go to France.' In the event, he did none of the above. He signed for Valencia in 1933, where he remained for two years until, in 1935, he made the move to Sporting Gijon. Although he could not have known it then, it would prove his last appointment in the country.

What is striking is the rapturous reception he received from his new clubs: not just from Mallorca, who were aware that a club of their standing were fortunate to have contracted a man with his CV, or from Barcelona, where there was more than a tinge of nostalgia to his appointment. He was welcomed with open arms at every turn. When Valencia confirmed his appointment in 1933, he was described as 'one of the best coaches there is in Spain'. They pointed not just to his successes with Barcelona and Espanyol but to what he had done closer to home, with Castellon. 'He is indisputably one of the best there has been and with him Valencia will improve and reach great heights,' wrote one newspaper. He went down in history, too, as 'one of the most popular coaches' Sporting Gijon had ever employed.

In a way, his travels served to bolster his popularity. With a flat cap and a prominent nose, he was regularly depicted in the caricature column of the newspaper *ABC* as a draft version of Andy Capp. He spoke Spanish well, but with 'the purest English accent'. He had a reputation for being both phlegmatic – 'Will Barcelona win the title? Will it rain tomorrow?' – and plain-speaking. Asked while at Gijon to assess Barcelona, his former club, he eschewed the usual platitudes. 'You know me, I don't like to suck up,' he said. His eccentricities served to endear him even more to the Spanish public. One journalist was vastly amused, as they shared a lunch to celebrate his success with Espanyol in 1929, to see Greenwell first order a sandwich and then, satiated, nod off. 'I have not slept very much recently,' he responded, upon waking. He promptly started snoring again.

More importantly, he was respected, even by those who resented the volume of English coaches in the Spanish game. Angel Romo, coach of Atletico Madrid in the early 1930s, told the magazine *Blanco y Negro* that none of the imports had a greater knowledge than home-grown managers, but he spared Greenwell and Pentland. They had spent so much time in and given so much to the Spanish game that, he said, they were 'as good as compatriots'.

When, in 1935, a row erupted over whether foreign managers were still needed in Spain, even those who wanted to see an outright ban could not quite bring themselves to resent Greenwell. 'Maybe *Mister* Jack is one of the few coaches who have lived or do live in Spain whose work has brought important moments of lucidity,' wrote one Jose Fernandez, in a letter to *Mundo Deportivo*, even as he wondered whether much of his success was down to a calibre of player so high that 'anyone could have managed them'.

That accusation brought another side of Greenwell's character to the fore. He penned a furious response, outlining everything he had done in his time in Spain. 'When will Espanyol have similar results to those it had in 1929?' he asked, referring to his victory in the Copa del Rey. He pointed to his work with Castellon, where he could hardly have been said to have a side packed with stars, and to his most recent role, at Sporting, where he had taken his side to third place in their regional championships and steered them to top of the country's second division. He moved to defend not just Pentland, his long-standing contemporary, but Patrick O'Connell, the Irishman who took charge of Real Betis and Barcelona during his time in the country. 'With foreign coaches, as with local coaches, there are good and bad,' he wrote. 'As they say in Spain, all things exist on the vine of the Lord.' He rounded off with an English proverb. After all that he had done, all the time he had dedicated and all the energy he had expended, Greenwell was not about to be told that anyone could have matched his achievements. He was a genial man, not a boastful one, but he was a proud one, too. 'It is best,' he concluded, 'to render unto Caesar what is due to Caesar.'

The military coup came on 17 July 1936. Spain splintered, vast swathes of Castile and Leon falling to the nationalist rebels, the north and east of the country staying loyal to the Republican government. Under Franco's command, the highly trained, highly effective Army of Africa boarded Junkers transports provided by Nazi Germany and prepared to cross the Strait of Gibraltar. As the country slid into mayhem, Britain moved swiftly to rescue the thousands of her citizens trapped by the conflict. Over the next two weeks, some 40 warships were scrambled into Spanish waters, picking up as many refugees as they could find and transporting them to safety in France.

It is likely Greenwell was among their number. He may have boarded the destroyer HMS *Wishart*, which arrived in Gijon on

24 July; had he decided to spend his summer in Barcelona, he may have been among the dozens of refugees rescued by the *Gipsy*, the *Garland*, the *Grenville* or the *Douglas* and taken to Marseille. Other ships landed at San Sebastian – aiming for the resort town of St-Jean-de-Luz in the French part of the Basque Country – and at Tarragona. In the desperate chaos, no detailed passenger manifests survive. The Royal Navy were not selective in who they removed from Spain, willingly taking American, French, Italian, Swiss and even German citizens away from the theatre of war. All that is certain is that those vessels represented Greenwell's best chance of escaping alive from the country he loved, and that he made it out.

He seems, at that point, to have travelled back to England. The Durham Amateur Football Trust, who have done more than most to preserve his story, hold a newspaper clipping which they believe dates to that July and confirms as much.

> Caller yesterday was John Greenwell, who has spent the last 23 years of his life coaching soccer teams in Spain. He was under contract to Gijon when the civil war broke out but early this week he decided Spain was no place to be ... I did not ask him which battling side [in the war] he favoured, but he did mention that in his opinion level pegging represented the current state of affairs ... If any English amateur or soccer club has a vacancy he will be interested to hear of it, for, like many others, he has lost everything.

That he felt moved to contact a journalist upon his return home in the hope of finding work rather neatly encapsulates the problem he faced. Greenwell had spent the last two decades forging a reputation as one of the foremost coaches in Spain, but his fame had barely reached British shores. He had only fleetingly intruded into the country's sporting consciousness, back in 1931, when a number of newspapers had sought his view on the Spanish national team which was due to face England at Highbury. That aside, his name would have been completely unknown, even to those in the game's corridors of power; unlike Fred Pentland, say, he could not even fall back on a comparatively distinguished playing career. He had left England as an unheralded amateur. He had no favours to call in, no network in place.

It is unsurprising, therefore, that no offers of work were forthcoming at home. Greenwell, his life in ruins, had little choice but to turn his thoughts to continuing his career abroad. What happens over the next two years, though, is unclear. In the summer of 1936, there is that newspaper clipping, suggesting he has returned home, and there is the account of Dr Amigo, in Paris, which suggests he has travelled to France to look for work. There are many things he is supposed to have done, moments that form part of the accepted narrative of his life, but repetition does not make it any more true. As far as proof goes, he essentially drops off the map.

There is one compelling source, but only one: his daughter, Carmen. She was born in Barcelona in 1930 and sent back to England in 1934 because of Jack's fears over the deteriorating situation in Spain. Although the account of his life she gave her family before her death cannot be verified, it is by far the most convincing and most complete picture we have of what happened to Greenwell between 1936 and 1938.

As far as Carmen knew, no sooner had her father returned to England from Spain in the summer of 1936 than he was travelling again. She believed he worked at the Berlin Olympics in August that year as tactical adviser to the Peruvian national team. This has become an accepted part of his story, though he is not named in any of the official Olympic Games literature. Nor is it immediately clear how Peru would have come to know of his availability or even – assuming he escaped Spain in the last few days of July – if it would have been physically possible for him to return to England, speak to a journalist, and then travel to Germany in time for the start of the Games in early August. That Carmen's version is correct, though, appears to be borne out by the one piece of documentary evidence available. Greenwell appears to be in a photograph of the Peruvian delegation at those Olympics, standing behind his players, resplendent in his official blazer. It is an indistinct image, but it is the closest thing to confirmation we have, along with Carmen's memory of her father not only departing but returning, too, infuriated by the injustice he believed Peru had suffered in the tournament.

Under manager Alberto Denegri, Peru's first game on 6 August was against Finland. Few knew what to expect from the South Americans, but the first glimpse of their talents was eye-catching. Thanks to five goals from their captain, Lolo Fernandez, the Peruvians swept past their European opponents 7-3. Still, it would have been widely assumed that they would go no further: after all, the mighty Austrians lay in wait in the quarter-finals. But Peru were not easily swatted aside. Although they found themselves two goals down at half-time, they drew level late on to force extra time. They scored five times in the added period, though only two were allowed to stand by the Norwegian referee. Then, in the 119th minute, their place in the semi-final secure, the game was abandoned.

The official explanation was a pitch invasion, led by what the *Daily Sketch*, the British newspaper, described as 'a thousand Peruvian fans' brandishing weapons, including one with a revolver. Quite how 1,000 Peruvians made it to Berlin – with guns – in 1936 is not explained. Austria, complaining of the South Americans' physical approach, demanded a replay. The Peruvians were incensed, believing they were the victims of a European plot to deny them what would have been an achievement no less embarrassing to the Nazi regime than Jesse Owens' success on the track that month: five of the Peruvian team were black. Either they did not deign to attend the hearing to discuss whether the game would be replayed, scheduled for the next day, or they were held up in traffic and were unable to make it. In their absence, the authorities sided with the Austrians. Peru pulled out of the competition, despite the attempted intervention of Joseph Goebbels, who was reported by *The Times* to have called a meeting with their representatives and the country's ambassador in a bid to smooth over the situation. At home, the country erupted in fury. The German legation in Lima was attacked by a mob; President Benavides called on the other Latin American nations at the Games to withdraw in solidarity, although only Colombia complied with the request. Austria went on to win the silver medal. The Peruvian players landed at the port of Callao a month later and were greeted as heroes.

Greenwell, meanwhile, returned to England, where he informed his wife and his daughter that he was fully in agreement with the decision to pull out of the tournament, given the circumstances. By September, we know he was abroad again, in Paris – where his wife, Doris, would have had contacts, having worked at the Moulin Rouge – being granted an interview by Red Star, the Paris club. It seems, though, that he did not take that job, if he was ever offered it. Instead, Carmen recalled her father going to work in Turkey for some weeks or months later that year. There is some evidence to support it: in the raft of obituaries published in South America, where Greenwell's career and life came to an end, it was taken for fact that he had coached the Turkish national team. That country's football authorities have no record of the appointment. Turkish football, at that time, was still in its infancy; many of the clubs, especially in Istanbul, have since disbanded;

detailed histories do not survive from the period. His stay, if it happened, was brief, curtailed by a bout of ill health. He returned home early in 1937 to be treated by an English doctor.

Carmen's understanding of her father's story is compelling not simply because it is the closest thing we have to his own account, but because it has a structural logic to it. It makes sense. English coaches, for example, were the very height of fashion in Turkey in the mid-1930s, thanks to the work of the likes of Fred Pagnam and Syd Puddefoot, and a man with Greenwell's CV would no doubt have been highly prized by any team hoping to improve their station. That ill health forced his return to England also fits: as early as 1931, during his second spell at Barcelona, he had been found at the club by a reporter with his neck wrapped in a white scarf and complaining of chronic angina.

Most of all, his involvement with the Peruvian team at the Olympics fits because, when we pick up his timeline again, in 1938, he is to be found in Lima, managing both Peru's national side and Universitario de Deportes with no little success. Indeed, whatever Greenwell was doing between 1936 and 1938, wherever he was and however serious his illness, it does not appear to have blunted his abilities. He had only four years left to live, but his adventure was by no means over.

The story is tucked away on page six of the *Sunderland Daily Echo and Shipping Gazette*, just below a tale about a woman single-handedly fighting off a wolf to protect her baby, and next to an account of how a 'back-to-nature boy of nine' has 'astonished' doctors. Both are a little misleading: the wolf attack happened in Egypt, rather than on Wearside; the medical marvel turns out to be nothing more than a vegetarian, who has been taken to hospital to undergo tests because he appears to be entirely healthy despite eating 'no fish, meat, eggs or bread at home, and scarcely any milk and cheese'. Thankfully, the newspaper informs troubled readers, he is 'allowed to eat bread and butter and cake when he goes out to tea about once a week'.

With such weighty affairs to consider, it is hardly surprising that news of another child's forthcoming journey to the other side of the world was afforded a mere 294 words in the edition of 20 August 1938. 'Off to Peru,' runs the headline. 'An eight-year-old girl is leaving Crook in a few days to join her father in Peru,' explains the copy. 'She is Carmen Greenwell, daughter of Mr Jack Greenwell, former English international footballer and coach to the Barcelona Football Club. Mr Greenwell is now a football coach in Peru ... Carmen was born in Spain. She has been staying with friends of Mr Greenwell at Crook.'

It is at this point, after a lacuna of a little more than two years, that we can place Jack Greenwell once more. He was summoned to Peru – on board the steamer *Oropesa*, bound for the port of Callao – in the first half of 1938 with two tasks in mind. The first was to get a team together for the Bolivarian Games to be held in Colombia in August. The second, more important, was to build a team capable of excelling at the Copa America, which Peru would host in January 1939. That, by the end of August, he had arranged for Carmen to join him in Lima indicates how well his first challenge went. Peru, once again inspired by Lolo Fernandez, played four times in 16 days in Bogota. They won all four, putting four past the Colombians, nine past Ecuador and three past Bolivia – easing off to beat Venezuela 2-1 – to claim the gold medal. On 10 September, Greenwell and his players returned to Callao by boat to be greeted by thousands of fans. The police struggled to keep control and the crowds struggled to keep calm. 'The people broke the cordons ... and in great groups overwhelmed the sportsmen with their embraces and loud applause,' wrote *La Prensa*. In among it all stood Greenwell, the country's *Mister*, a white scarf draped over his shoulders, a look of mild bafflement on his face. He had not just left behind his home and his possessions when he departed Spain, two years previously. He had been forced to leave his reputation, everything he had worked for, too. He had lost everything. Now, on the shores of the Pacific, he was a hero once more.

That was as nothing compared to what would happen a few months later. Their victory in the Bolivarian Games ensured hopes were high ahead of the Copa America. Peru's chances were improved by the fact that neither Argentina, whose football authorities were in dispute with the continental federation, nor Brazil would be attending, both preferring to stage a special edition of the Copa Roca rather than travel to Lima. That should not diminish the scale of either Peru's or Greenwell's achievement. Uruguay, still regarded as the continent's best side, were among the five teams that did deign to enter. Over the course of a month, they would play each other once. Peru and Uruguay both won each of their first three games before, as fate would have it, meeting in the final match. In the historical novel *1939, El Primer Grito* – 'The First Cry' – there is an account of Greenwell's team talk before that game. It is, of course, dramatised, but it offers a hint of the Englishman's approach. 'How many times,' he asked his players, 'have Peru played Uruguay?' 'Five times,' his squad responded. 'And how many times have they won?' 'None – we lost every time.' 'Today, gentlemen, we change history. A few months ago, we won a final, but nobody will settle for this title. To win the Bolivarian Games is a source of pride, of course, but to win a Copa America is different. This Sunday could enter Peruvian history. It all depends on you.'

The speech worked. The hosts won 2-1. Peru, for the first time, were crowned champions of their continent. Greenwell became the first – and so far only – European manager ever to win the biggest prize in South American football.

Greenwell's golden touch spread to the club game, too. In 1939, he took up a post as coach of Universitario de Deportes, home to much of the core of the national team including, most notably, the forward Lolo Fernandez, regarded until the rise of Teofilo Cubillas in the 1970s as the greatest player Peru had produced. That year, under Greenwell's auspices, *La U* lifted the national title.

But while Greenwell was undoubtedly a success in Peru, how much he enjoyed his work there is open to question. Carmen recalled that her father regularly found himself forced to trawl the bars of Lima and Callao looking for his players, trying to urge them to go home and get some rest before games. For a manager who saw physical fitness as a crucial part of the game and who demanded an intense tempo from his teams, their apparent reluctance to keep themselves in the best possible condition was a constant source of frustration. When an offer to help prepare a Colombian national side for the Caribbean Games – due to be held in Barranquilla, on the country's Caribbean coast – arrived late in 1939, he decided to take it.

That move came at enormous cost. His wife, Doris, was not exactly enamoured of Lima, a city that did not offer the same sort of lifestyle she had enjoyed in Spain, but she had grown even more tired of the constant upheaval of moving. She decided not to travel to Colombia with her husband. The couple separated. Carmen, their daughter, remained in Peru. Greenwell had already lost everything once, to the Spanish Civil War. Now, three years later, such was his dedication to his career that he waved goodbye to his family, to his life, once more. Colombia would be his final stop.

Greenwell seems to have had two roles in his new home. He was hired not only to prepare the Colombian national team for the *Juegos del Caribe* – which would eventually be postponed because of World War II – but to act as technical adviser to the club sides of Barranquilla, too. Given his success with Peru, his arrival seems to have been regarded as something of a coup: *La Prensa*, a newspaper in the city, described his capture as 'celebrated'.

Not everyone was quite as impressed. One of Greenwell's first tasks was to name a select XI, drawn from across the city's teams, for a series of games, first against opposition from Santa Marta and then, in December 1940, the 'all-powerful' Chilean side Santiago Wanderers. As he tried to pick players and craft a side, though, he faced 'the incomprehension of some clubs and the reticence of others'. *La Prensa* remained firmly on his side, insisting the city 'owed Mr Greenwell better than this', but elsewhere he found many who were determined to 'stifle and create problems for him'.

His first training session saw just 13 players of the 19 he had selected turn up, and 'six of those were carrying injuries, and two had played just 24 hours previously'. Slowly, though, he made progress: in a column he wrote for *La Prensa* in October, in which he asked his players to 'play cleanly' in club action so as to avoid injury, he suggested they were 'in good physical condition and improving technically'.

That he took his job seriously is not in question. He used the same column to request that the games against the Santa Marta sides be held at the Estadio Municipal, where the Wanderers game would be held, so that 'the home team were not taking to the pitch in the same situation as the Chileans'. A week before that match, he joined the 16 players who had made the cut at the Hotel Buenos Aires in Barranquilla, for an intensive period of training. Whether it worked or not is unclear – the result of the game remains elusive, though Wanderers would have been formidable opposition: their tour lasted 18 months and took in 67 games across South America. They lost just 11.

Greenwell's reputation in Colombia was sufficiently enhanced, though, that he was soon in demand. Without the *Juegos del*

Caribe to detain him, in 1941 he moved to the country's capital, Bogota, where he had been invited to take charge of Independiente Santa Fe. He led the club to a state championship and won no little praise for his tactical acumen. According to *El Tiempo*, his team had 'brilliant moves' and 'played with intelligence'. They felt they were not just 'the best amateur team in the capital' but were 'ready to compete with the best professional sides'. Greenwell was no less bullish. 'After a couple of months of coaching,' he said following his first training session, 'even a game against Argentina's *Millonarios* [River Plate]' would hold no fear. Yet again, he found himself in demand: his work in Colombia had attracted the attentions of the football authorities in Ecuador, who offered him the chance to take charge of the country's national team. He turned it down.

Precious little detail of this time in Greenwell's life survives. His separation from Doris and Carmen means the family's account runs aground as soon as he departs Peru; Colombian football at the time was strictly amateur, so records are more than patchy. Indeed, the most reliable source available is his obituary. On 7 October 1942, Greenwell was driven to his apartment at the Pension Centenario in the city at around 8.15am. His driver was Rafael Urdaneta Holguin, and several of his players were in the car as he was dropped off. A few minutes later, after he had made it home, his heart, which had troubled him since at least 1931, finally gave up. His neighbours called for medical assistance, but he was dead before the doctor arrived. He was buried in Bogota's English cemetery, his funeral attended by most of Colombian football's grandees.

The differing reactions to his death in England and in Spain are instructive. It took several months for the news to cross the ocean: it is only in February 1943 that anyone in Europe would have been informed of his passing. In Britain, preoccupied with other matters, it warranted barely more than a paragraph, little more than a curiosity. In Spain, it was quite the opposite. In Gijon, he was described by *Voluntad* as not only a 'fundamentally incredibly friendly man' but a 'magnificent coach', too, 'probably the most popular' the local club had ever employed.

The sorrow would have been felt just as keenly in Barcelona, in Valencia and even in far-off Peru. That is the picture that emerges of Greenwell from all of those diverse scraps of information, all the rubble of his long-forgotten life. Time and distance mean it is an image that is torn and tattered, not quite complete, but through all of that it is possible to see a man who won the hearts of more than one nation as well as a host of trophies, who helped shape one of the world's great clubs, who warrants a place in history he has been denied for too long. He dedicated everything to football, to spreading the word, and sacrificed everything for it, too. His homeland might have taken no interest in what he achieved, but he left a legacy in all of those countries that he visited. His mark on Spanish football is indelible, and nowehere more so than at Barcelona. There is a cross of St George on Barcelona's badge. There is a corner of the club that is forever England. That, in no small part, is down to Greenwell. He was, as *Voluntad* put it, 'untouchable'.

4

Missed Opportunities

The world champions were in town, but England was unimpressed. Just a few months after lifting the World Cup on home soil, Italy arrived in London in November 1934 to be told they had achieved nothing yet. England, like the rest of the home nations, had not deemed the tournament worthy of their attention; it was widely assumed they would have sailed to victory had they bothered to turn up. Their meeting with Italy at Highbury was painted as the real World Cup final. Italy had qualified for it by winning the actual World Cup. England had qualified for it by being England. Only when the motherland was beaten, the theory ran, could the Italians consider themselves worthy of their title.

By the time Vittorio Pozzo's team arrived, England had been in fleeting contact with the European game for almost 40 years. Corinthians, that proud bastion of amateurism, went on their first foreign tour as early as 1897. Six years later, the quite brilliantly named Er Arnfield ('my father did not know what to call me, so I became Er') arranged for his club, Southampton, to become the first professional side to follow in their footsteps. The same year,

1903, the Football Association, still refusing to deign to play the continentals, rebuffed a French attempt to organise some sort of international federation to govern the game, rather haughtily suggesting that they 'could not see the advantage' of such a move. Still, it was not long before England played their first set of international matches away from the Home Championships: in the summer of 1908, they swatted aside the challenges of Austria, Hungary and Bohemia on the national team's first tour, before repeating the trick the following year.

By the 1920s, post-season jaunts were ever more common and ever more ambitious. English club sides had made it as far afield as South America – Exeter facing the first incarnation of the Brazilian national team in 1914 – and a brief sojourn on the continent, involving two or three straightforward victories against keen but limited opponents, was a regular feature of the international calendar. Indeed, so humdrum were these games that the meetings with France and Belgium in 1926 barely warranted a mention in the sporting press. The tourists won heavily, as was only expected, and everybody moved on. Assessments of their opponents varied depending on how well disposed the author was to the spread of the game. The tone of the reports from foreign fields ranged from the scathing to the patronising.

Even when the travelling Football League sides encountered rather more exacting challenges than they expected, few interpreted it as anything meaningful. Some fans assumed 'the boys had been having a good time of it' at the end of an arduous league campaign; club officials seem to have been more inclined to blame the referees, the pitches, the weather, or the fact that these foreigners did not appreciate a good, old-fashioned shoulder charge.

The response to England's first defeat to a continental team, against the Spain side coached by Fred Pentland in Madrid in 1929, followed that pattern. Although the Spanish players were praised for their speed and their technique in the 4-3 win, it was felt that England suffered largely because of the intense heat and the frenzied crowd: a correspondent wrote to the *Athletic News* from Spain to suggest that spectators had been wearing 'bandages around their heads' to keep the sweat from their eyes and that police had been required to restore order after each of the four Spanish goals. In such conditions, it was surely no surprise that England had struggled; when, two years later, Spain were beaten 7-1 at Highbury, it was generally accepted that the wrong had been righted. The defeat in Madrid was an exception, not a new rule.

By that stage, England had lost another game on foreign soil. They were beaten 5-2 by the French in Paris, but they had not – as Peter Farmer, an English coach working in France, had predicted – woken up to the fact that 'the continentals are providing opposition of a formidable nature'. As Brian Glanville pointed out in *Soccer Nemesis*, it is curious that English criticism of the foreign game often centred on a perceived determination to win at all costs – prioritising results over performance – when, if anything, that accusation could be levelled even more deservedly at England, in terms of both the national team and the clubs.

England failed to beat either Austria or Germany while on tour in 1930, prompting the Football Association's Arthur King-scott to remark that 'the men of both Germany and Austria were in every way equal' to the best team the Football League could conjure. Two years later, when the nascent Austrian *Wunderteam* arrived at Stamford Bridge and ran England mightily close, there were plenty who noted that the visitors played with more verve and panache than their hosts. Still, though, there was no ground-swell of opinion that perhaps the foreigners might be catching up. England might not have won by much, but they had still won. Results brooked no argument.

For all the hype in the build-up to the meeting with Italy, then, few perceived any genuine threat to England's unbeaten home record. Reading the match programme for that game at Highbury, it is clear that, while the Italians' victory in the World Cup a few months previously had placed them at the very summit of the football world, it was not enough to stop England looking down on them. 'Italy has attained distinction in every sphere of human endeavour,' runs the scene-setter for the game, in a somewhat patronising tone, 'and once it turned its attentions to football it is only natural it should attain distinction there, too.'

The journalist James Catton, uncharacteristically, adopted a similar tone. A long-standing advocate of the continental game, he recognised that there had been a 'great advance' in the development of Italian football in the 16 years since the end of the war, but even he was not immune to the presumption of superiority. He clearly admired Pozzo's work, but he still felt moved to describe the Italian coach's devotion to the idea of building a team – as opposed to just naming his country's 11 best players and getting on with it – as nothing but a 'fascinating hobby'. Catton found it hard, too, to treat his team as opponents worthy of respect. 'To think of Italy as a power in the world of football is rather difficult,' he wrote in the *Athletic News*. 'To play this game as a pastime is one thing, but to excel among the nations who are renowned for high skill in this manly game is another matter.'

Catton would be proved wrong pretty spectacularly at Highbury. If there was one aspect of football in which Vittorio Pozzo's team were more than a match for the English, it was in manliness. As one player told the *Guardian* after the whistle had blown on England's 3-2 win, it was 'not a game of football, it was a battle'. Italy had fallen three goals behind in a quarter of an hour and then seen Luis Monti, their captain and a veteran of two World Cup finals with two different countries, carried off the field injured.

They had not responded well. Ted Drake, the England centre forward, had his 'legs cut to ribbons'. Eddie Hapgood, his team-mate for club and country, had his nose broken. There were fractured arms and shattered ankles. Eric Brook, of Manchester City, grew so angry with his treatment that, according to the *Guardian*, he 'raised his fist' in retaliation. As Catton's match report, rather diplomatically, pointed out: 'Italy know all the tricks of the footballer's trade, and practised them.'

The outrage lasted for days; the stereotype of the Italians as masters of football's dark arts endured for far longer, burned into the English psyche even now. There were calls for England – already absent from Fifa because of a long-running dispute over compensation payments to amateurs at the Olympics – to go one step further and simply refuse to engage with the foreigners at all. There had always been occasional suggestions, whenever a club side lost a tour match, to ban such tours for fear of damaging England's 'prestige'.

Now, in the aftermath of the Battle of Highbury, the idea that the 'missionary work' to spread the game across the planet was being wasted on these savages started to gain traction. Coming only 18 months or so after the Bodyline tour, when England's cricket team stretched the bounds of acceptable behaviour to win the Ashes in Australia, here was yet another example of international sport causing more harm than good.

Lost amid all of the acrimony was one extremely pertinent fact. Italy, down to ten men and recovering from a start that most observers attributed to stage fright, had come within a whisker of snatching a draw. What had looked like a whitewash turned out to be an extremely close run thing. Catton might have been wrong about Italy's ability to match England physically, and he might have felt that Pozzo's team did not possess quite the natural grace of the Austrian team that had lost narrowly at Stamford Bridge, but he was perfectly correct to assert that there had been a great advance in Italian football since the war. Had Monti stayed on the pitch, they might even have won.

It is hard to avoid the feeling that November 1934 was a missed opportunity. Had it not descended into brute violence, perhaps Pozzo's team might have been able to shake England from its torpor. Once again, though, the result was all that mattered. England had won, in the face of considerable Italian provocation, and so it was assumed there was no lesson to learn. As Bruno Roghi, the editor of *Gazzetta dello Sport* at the time, noted: 'England displayed an enjoyable ignorance' of the rising standards on the continent. This would be a recurring trope throughout English football history: a habit, just as the country started to wake up, of taking two points and subsequently missing a much more important one; of winning individual battles and ignoring the full picture of the war. It would apply beyond even the triumph in the 1966 World Cup, when the ultimate victory set back the case for change by a decade and dissuaded anyone from addressing the reasons why it was necessary.

Italy's defeat at Highbury was not only a missed opportunity for England, though. The stain the match left on England's conception of the Italian game doomed one man to obscurity in his homeland just at the moment when his remarkable career was starting to come into the light.

William Garbutt, as a player, was not well known in England. Born in Hazel Grove, Stockport, in 1883, he had started his career at Reading, spotted playing as an outside right for the army. He played just a handful of games in Berkshire when he was snapped up, in 1905, by Woolwich Arsenal. The *Athletic News* was confident of a bright future for this 'dashing' winger. He was, readers were assured, 'destined to make a great name for himself in the first league, or any other form of football'.

Like Catton's prediction, that would prove half right. Garbutt reached two FA Cup semi-finals with Arsenal before joining Blackburn, the club Fred Pentland had left two years previously, in 1908. He carved out a decent reputation and represented the Football League in a game against Scotland, but by the time a knee injury ended his career in 1912, even he would have accepted that he had hardly made a great name for himself. Indeed, that summer, his decision to call time on his playing days and take up a post coaching at Genoa warranted just one paragraph in the *Athletic News*. For the next 20-odd years, English readers would barely hear mention of him.

Until, that is, Pozzo's team came to London and journalists started looking into the root of Italy's rapid emergence as Europe's premier superpower. Catton identified 'three Lancastrians who had provided sound foundations' for Italian football's growth: Herbert Burgess, once of both Manchester City and Manchester United, who had managed a 'beautiful young Padova team'; Robert Spottiswood, a 'grafter and splendid help-mate to the forwards' while a player at Crystal Palace, who went on to manage Internazionale; and, most of all, Garbutt, then at Napoli but who had, over the previous two decades, turned Genoa into the country's 'crack club'. He had made a great name for himself after all. Italy's violence and England's fury that night in north London meant that few in his country would be encouraged to hear more about his immense professional success. That, in turn, would condemn him to deep, personal tragedy.

There are competing accounts as to how Garbutt came to be in Genoa. Brian Glanville relates the more compelling story, claiming he was recommended to the club by Vittorio Pozzo, the most powerful man in Italian football for the first half of the 20th century. Pozzo, the tale goes, had watched Garbutt play for Blackburn against Manchester United during his final season as a player and, impressed, saw him as the ideal candidate when Genoa, Italy's oldest team, one with a British identity carved into its very core, was seeking a new coach who might restore them to the pinnacle of the nascent game in the country. The tale contains a kernel of truth – Pozzo did study in England, befriending Steve Bloomer in the process, in the final years of Garbutt's career, and did claim to have seen him playing for Blackburn – but its conclusion appears to be askew. Even Pozzo does not seem to have claimed credit for recommending Garbutt to Genoa, noting only that the two had 'formed an iron friendship when he arrived in Italy'.

The alternative account is less romantic but is supported by a greater weight of evidence. According to Garbutt's obituary in the newspaper *Il Secolo XIX*, the club were alerted to his availability by 'the brother of Thomas Coggins', an Irishman who was running Genoa's youth teams. The problem, here, is quite what the relationship between the Coggins family and Garbutt was. The latter's partner, Anna, was Irish, but that is hardly conclusive proof.

Fortunately, we can at least be sure of why Garbutt accepted the post. He had made his final appearance for Blackburn early in the 1911-12 season – the campaign that brought the club its first league championship – but, by the following summer, he knew his career was over. Like Bloomer and Pentland a couple of years later, he had to find a way to support himself. His need was pressing, too: he and Anna had married only a few months earlier, after she informed him she was pregnant. Garbutt now had his infant son, Stuart, to support. His only previous work experience had been in the army. Football was all he was qualified to do. When a lucrative offer arrived from abroad, he had little choice but to take it.

Similarly, it is not hard to ascertain what it was that appealed to Genoa about a 29-year-old with no background in management.

It was not his experience or his tactical vision: Garbutt would later write that none of the coaches he had worked with had done anything at all to help him develop his understanding of the game or hone his technical ability. Instead, the only qualification Garbutt required was his nationality. In 1912, England was unquestionably the place where the game was at its most advanced. Even the basic training he would have received as a player would have been state of the art to Italian eyes. Likewise the facilities he would have enjoyed. His job would be to turn Genoa into a passable facsimile of a modern English club.

He set about doing so as quickly as he could. In his biography of Garbutt, *The Father of Italian Football*, Paul Edgerton suggests his early training methods concentrated on physical fitness and team unity: that, after all, is what he would have known as a player himself. Others are a little more kind: Gianni Brera, the most influential Italian sportswriter of all time and to some extent a one-man oral history of the Italian game, painted him as focusing on 'team spirit, tactics, passing and tackling'. Garbutt's sides were, he said, 'notoriously virile and quick'. That is not to suggest he ignored technique entirely: he is credited with introducing his players at Genoa – and subsequently the Italian game – to simple exercises like dribbling the ball around poles driven into the ground to hone their touch; another of his favourites involved asking players to head a ball attached to a piece of elastic cord so as to improve their ability in the air. Fitness, though, was paramount.

That interpretation is endorsed by the testimony of one of his former charges, Attila Sallustro, who worked with Garbutt at Napoli. It is, of course, likely that his methods changed the longer he was in Italy and in management. The players he encountered at Genoa in 1912 would have been in need of a very different type of training from those he worked with later on; he would have had to focus much more on the basics of control and passing with footballers who were resolutely amateur and had much less of a grounding in the game. However, by the time he was in charge of Sallustro in the late 1920s and early 1930s, Garbutt's training sessions and his playing philosophy sound resolutely English.

'They followed the same pattern,' wrote Sallustro. 'Ten or 15 laps of the field and then discussing set plays and so on. He was a typical Englishman, very phlegmatic. He was a coach of the highest order, the first to arrive at training in the morning and the last to leave, he never moved far from his bench, not even in the most heated of games. White hair, pipe between teeth, in love with Napoli and Naples, the true style of football, of technique and speed, three passes to the goal!'

Several of those coaches who left England in order to teach the game abroad did so because they envisioned a type of game that the clubs of the Football League would not countenance. They wanted to move away from the blood-and-thunder approach that had come to dominate the game in England. It is hard to include Garbutt in their number. *La Stampa*'s report of a Genovese derby in 1921, against Sampierdarenese – one of the sides that would later become Sampdoria – described it as 'lively and combative', requiring the referee to 'put the brakes on before things got too violent'. Garbutt was no purist and no shrinking violet. His training sessions focused on fitness; according to *La Stampa*, he reserved the ball-work to one training session at the end of the week, 'always behind closed doors'. He left England because his experience counted much more abroad than at home, and he found himself in Italy tasked with bringing that country up to speed with how things were done in his homeland.

As the historian Pierre Lanfranchi puts it, in his paper 'The First European Manager', he was 'representative of the wider pattern by which British technical and practical knowledge was exported by her engineers all over the globe'. England had sent out missionaries to spread the word of the game across the world but, in the early years of the 20th century, the new converts still needed instruction in how to play it. Like the Scot John Madden at Slavia Prague, William Townley in Germany and William Barnes in Spain, Garbutt was one of the second wave of emigres who went abroad to meet that demand.

It is telling that the figure described by both his former players and the likes of Brera is one of almost deliberate Englishness: Lanfranchi describes him as dressing in a three-piece tweed suit, a tie and a hat at all times. He was not yet 30. A devoted pipe smoker, he was reported to carry a set of three or four in his breast pocket at any one time. His demeanour lived up to his image: he was considered polite, a little distant, well mannered. He could not have been more English if he had tried. Given the context, he may well have been trying. After all, his Englishness was the characteristic that gave him his legitimacy. It made sense to play it up.

Confidence trick or not, it worked. Genoa had been Italy's preeminent club in the very earliest days of *calcio*, winning six titles before 1906, but had found themselves surpassed in the period preceding Garbutt's arrival by Pro Vercelli. All of a sudden, they looked like the past: founded by English and Swiss emigres and with a playing squad redolent of that internationalism, they now found themselves overtaken by a resolutely Italian team. Their new stadium, the Marassi, could hold 25,000 people, but the club's hierarchy knew they would struggle to fill it without a competitive side. Garbutt provided one.

In his first two campaigns, he twice brought the club to the regional championships and, with his judicious use of the transfer market, started to build a team capable of challenging for the ultimate honour, the Italian title. In his early years in Italy, he obviously felt fit enough to play, at least occasionally: *La Stampa* records him turning out in a game at Alessandria in 1914. That he still felt compelled to play indicates, perhaps, the standard of the side he had inherited. He knew fresh blood was required, but adding new signings was rather easier said than done: because the game was still amateur, Genoa needed to find creative ways to pay the players they brought in. One, according to Edgerton, became 'the best-paid bank clerk in Italy'. Even Garbutt himself received his salary not for his coaching but for a number of services he theoretically provided to the club, and through an elaborate scheme set up to maximise his expenses. It does not appear to have been a system he was entirely comfortable with, but he was not about to complain: however he got his money, the end result was that he, Anna and Stuart enjoyed a substantially higher standard of living than they might have been able to expect in England.

Everything paid off in his third season. Genoa would regain the Italian championship in 1915, winning the regional championships and then finishing top of the *Girone Finale*. It was a victory that restored them to their place at the pinnacle of the Italian game and ensured Garbutt an unassailable place in history. It was that triumph, more than any other, that secured his professional reputation. The model of management he represented would become a pattern the rest of the country followed; he would form the Italian conception of what a manager was and what a manager did. He had complete autonomy in selecting his team, total control of all football affairs, and a free hand in the transfer market. He might have come from and landed in a football culture where it was far from the norm for a manager to wield such power – trainers were employed to keep the squad fit, and directors often had an input into who played on a Saturday – but Garbutt's success changed all of that. It even changed the language of the game. It was on Garbutt that the title of *Mister* was first bestowed in Italy.

However, given the circumstances of that first championship, Garbutt would have little cause to remember it fondly. Italy
stood apart for most of the first year of the Great War, refusing to
commit to her theoretical allies in the Triple Alliance and conducting negotiations with France and Britain. She joined the conflict
almost a year after it started, on the side of the Allies, after
obtaining concessions over territory as part of the London Pact.
Italy declared war on the Austro-Hungarian Empire on 23 May
1915. There was still one game of the *Girone Finale* to be played.
All football was cancelled as the country mobilised. Genoa would
only be awarded the title in retrospect. By that stage, Garbutt
would have left the country, and would be on his way to war.

None of the characters in this book was quite so influenced by
the tide of history as Garbutt. At every turn, what he achieved is
altered by all that he lived through. The outbreak of World War
I, just as his Genoa team seemed ready to reassert its dominance
on Italian football, is just the first example. When he should have
been plotting to retain the title, he was in Ashton-under-Lyne signing up for military service, eventually joining the 181st Brigade,
a detachment that would form part of the imperial army's 40th
Division.

Garbutt was clearly a fine soldier: within two months, he had
risen through the ranks and been appointed to the post of acting
sergeant. That, as Edgerton notes, makes abundant sense: quite
apart from his previous military experience, he was physically fit,
he had enjoyed a far better diet in Italy than most of his contem-
poraries would have been able to afford, and he was used to taking
charge of men from his life at Genoa's training ground.

That would not be his last promotion. It was not until June
1916, almost a year after he had joined up, that he received
the order to travel to the front. His battalion was posted to the

killing fields of the Somme, but Garbutt had already been identified as possible officer material. He served for six months in the
trenches – according to his friend Pozzo, being sent 'over the top'
twice – before he was ordered to return home for officer training
in February 1917. He was commissioned in August of that year
and was sent back, this time to the mud and slaughter of Passchendaele, in December 1917. In April 1918 he was hit by shrapnel
in his left leg, but he remained in France until the Armistice,
eventually being shipped home on New Year's Eve, 1918. He was
awarded the British War Medal and the Victory Medal for his
service.

Like Fred Pentland and Steve Bloomer before him, Garbutt
returned to a country shattered by war, one that did not seem
to have any obvious place for him. As he wrote to the *Athletic
News*, there were 'none, or very few, coaches employed in England' at the time. Eight months after he was shipped home, he
had been contacted by Genoa once more, wondering if he would
like to resume his work in Italy. Garbutt, it seems, did not leap at
the chance. Quite apart from his complaint to the *Athletic News*
about the lack of opportunities at home, he bargained hard over
his contract. He eventually settled for a salary of 8,000 lire a year
and set sail once more. For all the success he would enjoy, for all
the love that he felt for Italy and all the happiness it brought him,
if he had known how it would all end, he might have preferred to
remain at home.

The Italy Garbutt spent all but one of the next 20 years in was
a country in the grip of a fearsome change. He proved remarkably
immune to it for far longer than he might have expected, but he
would eventually pay the heaviest of prices.

In 1923, he led Genoa to their eighth national title, his second,
and followed that up with another victory in 1924. That came
as no surprise: as early as 1920, *La Stampa*'s match reports of

Genoa's games regularly highlighted his 'deft tactics'. His stock was so high that year that, with a clutch of his players in the Italian national side for the Paris Olympics, he was invited by Vittorio Pozzo to help train the team. Those were the best days of his professional life, but they came as the country descended into darkness. Mussolini's Blackshirts had marched on Rome in October 1922; the Fascist leader had been installed as prime minister a few days later. He would spend the next three years slowly eroding any restraints on his own personal power, altering the country's constitution, combining his Fascist militia with the army and imprisoning or assassinating opponents and dissidents.

Garbutt's relationship with Fascism is hard to unravel. His first encounter with the realities of life in a one-party state, certainly, was not a happy one. In 1925, Genoa once more reached the semi-finals of the *Girone Finale*, where they would face Bologna. After the scores ended level over two legs, the Italian football federation, the FIGC, ordered a third match to be played to separate them. Genoa raced into a 2-0 lead, their place in a third consecutive final seemingly secure. Bologna, though, did not go quietly. When they saw a goal, and a way back into the game, ruled out by the referee, a squadron of Blackshirts invaded the pitch. They were led by Leandro Arpinati, the club's vice president, a personal friend of Mussolini. Arpinati would go on to be mayor of Bologna and head of the FIGC. He was a very powerful man indeed.

For 15 minutes, he and his acolytes berated the referee. Under the sustained, menacing pressure, the goal was awarded. Bologna equalised soon after, taking the game to extra time. Garbutt, furious, refused to allow his players to countenance such an idea, believing the football authorities would award his side a victory because of the pitch invasion. His confidence was misplaced. There would be another replay.

That would not be the end of it. The fourth game ended in

another draw, meaning the two sides would have to meet a fifth time. Garbutt and his club were told the match would, most likely, not be held until September. He allowed his players some time off, to rest and recuperate, and went on a short break himself. In August, though, he was told the game would be happening in just a couple of days in Milan. Bologna, it turned out, had been offered rather more warning. They had remained in training. With their opponents ring rusty, Arpinati's team got the result they wanted. They won 2-1. Garbutt would never win another championship. Nor would Genoa, stuck on nine *Scudetti* even now, the days of their primacy long distant.

That incident suggests Garbutt was a minor victim of the Fascist regime, but the reality is substantially more complicated than that. His unhappiness at the injustice was not, for a start, enough to convince him to leave. Nor did he see the regime's increasing interference in football as reason to call time on his stay in Italy. He remained in Italy for another decade, even as Mussolini tightened his iron grip on every aspect of life in the country in general and on football in particular.

Whereas most dictators shy away from allowing large gatherings of people, Italy's most popular sport was useful for Mussolini. As Simon Martin notes in *Football and Fascism*, the game provided a convenient metaphor not only for the central tenet of Fascism – the triumph of the collective over the individual – but for Mussolini's theories on the supremacy of the Italian race. That is why he became such an ardent supporter of Pozzo's national team. Italy hosted the 1934 World Cup and, with the regime desperate to show off the society it had created, the government offered subsidies to travelling supporters. *Il Duce* was present at all of Italy's games as they won the tournament. That was not enough: Pozzo later insisted Mussolini himself was the driving force behind the meeting with England that year, the dictator determined to prove

Italy could compete with the undisputed masters of the game. In 1938, after Italy had retained the World Cup in France, Mussolini hosted a lavish reception for the team at the Palazzo Venezia in Rome. Giuseppe Meazza, one of the players, remembered him delivering 'an extensive eulogy'. As Bruno Roghi, one of the most prominent sports journalists of the time, suggested: in Fascist thinking, 'beyond the athletic victory [shone] the victory of the race'.

Mussolini's influence extended some way further than the national team, though. In 1926, at the behest of the Fascists, the FIGC enacted the *Carta di Viareggio*, a blueprint for Italian football. Its effect was profound. Not only did it legalise professionalism – putting an end to the need to concoct convoluted ways of paying players – and establish the country's first national league, Serie A, it also banned foreign signings. For the following season, teams would be allowed to have two imports on their books, as long as only one played at any one time. For the start of the 1928 season, there were to be no foreigners at all. The same ruling would apply to managers. By 1928, foreign coaches were only to be hired if 'nobody suitable in the motherland' could be found. The logic was obvious: if football was to be a showcase for the greatness of the Italian nation, then the political message would only be confused by locals being overshadowed by *stranieri*. Even foreign words were to be banned: there was to be no more corner, no more kick-off, no more *Mister*. English was not needed when Italian was so evidently superior. There would be just one exception: Garbutt.

Indeed, the extent to which he was not just tolerated by the Fascists but celebrated became clear in 1927. Another of the effects of the *Carta di Viareggio* was to try to address the imbalance in Italian football between the country's north and south. For 30 years, teams in Milan, Turin, Piedmont and, of course, Genoa had dominated the game, but the Fascists wanted to see a more even spread. In Naples, Florence and Rome, several smaller teams were merged together to create bigger clubs, capable of taking on AC Milan, Ambrosiana (as Internazionale had been renamed), Juventus, Torino, Pro Vercelli and Genoa. The *Carta* marked the birth of Napoli, Fiorentina and, most importantly, AS Roma. The regime felt that the capital needed a strong side, and handed Garbutt the responsibility for creating one. 'The classic *Mister*, after many years with the glorious Genoa club, has come to Rome to dedicate his wisdom to AS Roma,' wrote *La Stampa*.

He would spend two years in the heart of Mussolini's Italy, helping Roma to victory in the Coppa CONI – a forerunner of the Coppa Italia – in their first season in existence and then leading them to third place in Serie A in their second. That success illustrates just how good a manager he was: capable of taking a selection of players from a host of teams and forging from those disparate parts a successful unit, almost immediately. It also hints that his relationship with Fascism was not always as uneasy as the Bologna incident suggested. That his next appointment was with another of the merged clubs, Napoli, simply compounds that impression. His six years there, too, would bolster his reputation: his team finished fifth in his first season and, thanks to third-place finishes in 1933 and 1934, it was the most successful period in the club's history until the arrival of Diego Maradona in the 1980s. For much of his time there, they were invariably described as genuine contenders to win Serie A, even ranked as favourites by *La Stampa* in 1933.

It is at this point that Garbutt's career, and his life, are changed inexorably by events way beyond his control once again. In the summer of 1935, he left Italy. Word of his success had started to spread beyond the peninsula, and he was invited to become manager of Athletic Bilbao, Fred Pentland's old club.

It is not clear why he felt he was ready to move on: his roots, if anything, ran deeper in Naples than they had even in Genoa. He and Anna had moved to the village of Bagnoli Irpino, just outside the city, where the clean air helped Anna cope with her chronic asthma. There, they had effectively adopted a local girl, Maria Concetti, the daughter of one of their neighbours. He had every reason to stay and little cause to leave. What is known, though, is that Vittorio Pozzo offered him a reference – in the most glowing terms – to help him secure new work. It is tempting to think that, after 15 years in an increasingly autocratic state, he was tired of living under Fascist rule. Subsequent events call that assessment into doubt.

He enjoyed his year in Spain, overcoming the shadow of Pentland to win the Spanish title at his very first attempt. In the summer of 1936, he returned to Naples to collect Anna – and presumably Maria – with the intention of settling his family in the Basque Country. He might have been able to build a legacy as lasting as that of his predecessor, strengthening the unlikely bond between Bilbao and Blackburn, the club both men graced as players. He would not have the chance. While he was in Italy, Spain slipped into its bloody civil war. Garbutt was forced to stay, finding work first with AC Milan and then, in 1937, being enticed back to the club he loved more than any other, Genoa. 'After several years of divorce, he has returned to his old love,' wrote *La Stampa*. He would twice go close to winning the club that elusive 10th league championship. It was the missed opportunity to escape Italy, though, which would haunt him most.

The one concrete piece of evidence as to Garbutt's relationship with Fascism dates from the summer of 1940. It was unearthed by Edgerton, who had spoken extensively with his adopted daughter, Maria, before her death. It is the letter written by Anna to the authorities after her husband's arrest and imprisonment as an enemy alien. In it, she pleads for clemency, citing not only his age and his long service to Italian football but also his 'immense sympathy' for Mussolini's regime. Even this, though, is not as straightforward as it might appear. Anna, desperately frightened of what was to become of her husband, would have used any leverage at all to try to secure his release. It is impossible to know whether he truly did sympathise with the Fascists or whether she was simply trying anything she could to get him out.

What is certain is that, after travelling back to Britain to be with their son, Stuart, now enlisted in the army, after the outbreak of war the Garbutts returned to Italy in November 1939. This in itself is a questionable decision: Mussolini and Hitler had, after all, already signed the Pact of Steel. Even when they were advised to get out as soon as they could, when Italy's army joined forces with Germany's in the late spring of 1940, they did not. Edgerton's explanation – centring on Anna's health concerns and their loyalty to Maria, who would have had to stay behind – is convincing, but the basic fact is unavoidable: the Garbutts chose to remain in Fascist Italy, an enemy state, when they could and perhaps should have left.

If Garbutt's previous immunity to the machinations of the Fascists had convinced him he would be safe, he was wrong. The war meant he had been unable to travel to coach Genoa in the cup final in May 1940, consigned as he was to Vara Inferiore, the small town north of the city where the family had made their home, and in June of that year the order went out for his arrest. He gave himself up and was placed in prison for two weeks. His fame, and the affection he engendered in the city, meant he was treated comparatively well, but he nevertheless became emaciated and depressed, before Anna – allowed to live freely on her neutral, Irish passport – finally managed to secure his release. He would not, though, be allowed to work. That August, *La Stampa* labelled him 'the last of the British coaches', admitting that 'after 30 years here, he is more Italian than English, but it is nationality that counts. The war has accounted for him.' In such a climate, it is no wonder that, the following season, as Genoa adopted a more Italian style of play – known as *il sistema* – reverence for Garbutt began to fade. 'Genoa are one of the finest of Italian sides,' ran an analysis of Genoa's new approach. 'The adjective "English" has been taken from them.'

Much more serious than the attempt to deprive him of his significance was the one to remove him from his home. The Fascists did not want him living among his friends in Vara Inferiore; as a British national, he needed to be placed under far stricter surveillance. He and Anna were dispatched to Acerno, a small town in the mountains in Italy's deep south. Maria would join them a few months later, in November 1940, before they moved on again, to the village of Orsogna, not far from the Adriatic coast.

Their lives there were far from easy, but they were shielded from the very worst privations of the war. They had to deal with a curfew and strict limitations on their communication with their friends and family at home. The bitter winters, too, were a challenge, particularly for Anna, and when Garbutt himself suffered a small stroke he took some time to be nursed back to health. They were, make no mistake, poor and hungry, having seen their savings seized by the regime, but they were comforted by the kindness of the communities that took them in. Orsogna, in particular, was filled with refugees and enemy aliens, but the locals did all they could to help the unfortunates suddenly in their midst. Garbutt did his best to build a life for himself in these most extreme of circumstances, even coaching the junior teams of one of the clubs in the town.

They remained there until late in 1943. That was when the

war arrived. Allied troops were pushing north from Sicily, their progress impeded at every turn not only by the dogged resistance of the Wehrmacht in retreat, but by the Germans' determination to lay waste to all territory they lost. Roads, railway lines and bridges were destroyed; every town the Allies liberated lay in ruins. What the Germans could not obliterate, Allied bombing accounted for. The Garbutts, aware of the German troops swarming all over the country, decided to destroy their British passports, knowing that to be caught with one would mean imprisonment or, more likely, death. In the winter of 1943, they fled Orsogna – too close to the Gustav Line, the main German defensive position, to be safe – and headed north to Imola, cloaked in false identities.

It was there, in May 1944, that Anna was killed. According to Edgerton, she and Maria had ventured out to find food – increasingly scarce in a devastated country – when she was caught in an American bombing raid. She was dead before Maria could bring her husband to her side. Garbutt, crippled by grief, buried her under her false name, Giovanna Cota. Italy had given him his life. It had taken away the woman who had shared it with him.

Garbutt never truly recovered from the loss of his wife. It was close to another year before Polish troops marched into Imola, followed a few days later, in April 1945, by the British. Garbutt sought out an officer to explain how a British citizen came to be in this desolate place. Quite what the soldier thought of his story is unclear. It must have seemed a remarkable tale, scarcely believable. He did not know the half of it.

When Garbutt died of leukaemia in 1964, his death passed unnoticed in England. There were no obituaries in the newspapers, no reflections on all that he had done. He was simply an octogenarian living in reduced circumstances in Leamington Spa, tended to his last by his faithful adopted daughter, Maria.

In Italy, the reaction was quite different. In the words of Vittorio Pozzo, this was the country, after all, to which he had 'dedicated his life'. He had given *calcio* its ideal of a player 'somewhere between robust and courageous', one that endured beyond his career and beyond his life. Every newspaper carried a report of his death and a eulogy. He was described as one of the 'first true teachers' of the game. Pozzo called him a 'true pioneer'. 'I have here, on my table, his last letter to me,' he wrote. '[It is] written by the most important man in the history of Italian football. In it, he reproaches me for not replying sooner. I hope that fortune takes me back to England soon, so that I may place two flowers on the grave of a man I will never forget.' Garbutt loved Italy, and Italy loved him back.

Genoa mourned him most. The club had invited him back for one final spell after the war, but by 1948 his spirit had gone. Time had caught up with him and, without Anna by his side, life in Vara Inferiore was full of ghosts. He handed in his resignation after a poor run of form at the start of 1948. The club, out of respect for an association that had lasted nearly 40 years, retained him as a scout for some time before he did what he must have wished he had done earlier and returned to England. Conscious that 'he had not shared their good fortune' after the war, Genoa afforded him a testimonial, attended by some 3,000 fans, in 1950.

During his career, Garbutt had not been exempt from criticism. At Napoli, in his less impressive seasons, there had been rumours that he was drinking rather too much; according to the historian Pierre Lanfranchi, fans had complained that the team might perform better if they had been given a coach who spoke Italian and did not 'fall in love with every glass of good Frascati'. It is hard to know how much truth there was in such tittle-tattle: certainly, when almost any English manager was struggling for form in any country, the whispers of a drinking habit did not take long to surface. The Neapolitan journalist Antonio Ghirelli gave them some credence, though, describing Garbutt as a 'wine specialist' with a penchant for horse racing besides.

Perhaps his death, as often happened, allowed for some perspective. Whatever his flaws, Garbutt could now be seen for what he was: a figure of immense importance in the development of Italian football. Not just for what he did for his clubs, winning three titles at Genoa and helping to establish Roma and Napoli among the greatest sides in Serie A, but for what he did for the game as a whole.

When he arrived, back in the summer of 1912, before the two wars that would shape his life, he was a professional in an amateur world. His job was to pass on his knowledge. By the time he left in the late 1940s, he had done that and more. Italy boasted what was probably the strongest league on the continent. The country was one of football's genuine superpowers, two-time world champions, the first-choice destination for players from across Europe and South America. Its position as one of football's great heartlands was secure. That was, in no small part, Garbutt's doing. England might not have known what he had achieved, but in Italy they mourned their first *Mister*. It had come at enormous personal cost, a pain that eased only with his last breath, but there could be no doubt. He had fulfilled the prediction made all those years previously. He had made a great name for himself indeed.

5

Cassandra

English football cannot say it was not warned. For more than half a century, reports of gathering strength flowed back from Europe telling the motherland that the continent was rising, that 'Jack was becoming just as good as his master' and that to presume that the inventors of the game could count on an innate, everlasting supremacy was nothing but delusion. The message was always the same: through arrogance and ignorance, England is being caught.

The warnings came from some of the earliest coaches employed on foreign shores, the men doing so much to close the gap between the students and the teachers. As early as 1919 – barely more than two decades into the life of organised football in Europe – William Garbutt was writing to the *Athletic News* to suggest that perhaps the refusal of clubs in the Football League to countenance the idea of employing a coach to help improve players was self-defeating. 'The popular opinion was and is, I believe, with trainers, that their work consisted of keeping a player fit,' he wrote from Italy, where football was 'going great guns'. 'I myself never received any tips on how to play from any one of them. I also wonder why one has to come abroad to teach football, when there are none, or very few coaches employed in England, the home of football. I do not think there are many young league players, or old ones for that matter, who would not welcome a coach instead of a trainer.'

Two years later, Fred Pentland offered a similar diagnosis from Spain. The foreigners, he felt, had made 'huge strides' in their football education while England had remained static, the 'tremendous wealth of talent' at the country's disposal ignored because clubs 'would rather pay £3,000 for a new player than pay a coach £500 to churn out many first-teamers'.

'British coaching has brought the continental football practically up to the same standard as the English amateurs in 12 or 15 years,' he wrote in *All Sports Weekly*. 'There was a time when our fellows could have gone to sleep for five years, wakened on the day before the match and beaten any continental team they liked. But those days are past, never to return. I am quite certain our amateurs can still beat the best of them but new methods must be adopted.'

Garbutt and Pentland were far from alone. Tim Coleman, once of Arsenal and later a coach in Holland, predicted that the day was not far off that 'coaches will come from the continent to England' to instruct players. Charles Bunyan, who coached to some considerable success in Belgium, placed the blame firmly on the game's power brokers. 'It would not be possible to obtain a living wage in England' for his services, he wrote, and he worried that 'the big clubs [in the Football League] do not realise the value of coaching and what could be done by placing promising youngsters in the control of a competent coach'.

Herbert Burgess, a contemporary of Garbutt, suggested in 1923 that football in Italy was already on the verge of 'becoming first class'. To William Hibbert, who made his name at Newcastle and later went to work in the United States, it was not so much the clubs at fault as the players themselves. His assessment was a bleak one. 'They know all about [football] in this country,' he wrote, of his decision to pursue a career abroad. 'There is no room for me here. Our young players prefer not to be taught.'

It was not just those involved in the game abroad who saw the future; a handful of those who made a career from observing football also possessed the foresight to understand that England had to rise to the challenge. Prime among them were two of the great founding fathers of football journalism, Ivan Sharpe and James Catton, both pioneering editors of *All Sports Weekly* and consistent voices of dissent against the accepted logic that English players were innately superior to all others.

'Friends who are in close touch with continental teams assure me the Anglo Saxon race will have to be careful of their supremacy,' Catton wrote in 1925, in an article entitled 'How the Game Has Girdled the Globe'. 'My friend, a Belgian and in a position to know what he is talking about, says the Latin races, the Spaniards and Italians, are likely to become the best players in the world. They have a genius for games and are very thorough in all they undertake. He seems to be in love with the Spanish footballer.'

His tone was not always so benevolent. He seems to have become gradually more incensed by the tendency to see football as a game of speed and stamina, rather than skill and subtlety. 'If England is to retain her prestige in the face of the advance of other nations, all players ... must use more intelligence, and by constant practice obtain control of and power over the ball with the inside and outside of each foot,' he wrote. If not, he feared, 'the game will lose its popularity and Great Britain her fame'.

Sharpe – the former amateur international whose connections in Germany had landed Steve Bloomer first his job in Berlin and then four years in Ruhleben – was equally concerned by what he described as the 'win at any costs' mentality of the Football League clubs, something he believed was detracting from football as a spectacle.

'Continental countries still refer to the British as the masters,' he wrote in 1930. '[But] the crowds, the teams and especially the newspapers are of the opinion that now their best sides have nothing to learn from Britain. Strange as the fact may seem, they are practically justified in their opinion. Their technique is excellent, especially in midfield, leading up to a goal by a series of short lateral passes resembling the [famously artistic short-passing] Scottish style. It really is dazzling to watch.'

Sharpe was no blind xenophile: he was sharp in his criticism of the standard of pitches across the continent and equally acerbic when assessing foreign referees, prone to making what he described as 'numerous weird decisions'. But all of that was outweighed by the thirst for knowledge he found, a desire to improve, a belief that talent was a matter of nurture as much as nature, traits that were sadly lacking across the spectrum of English football.

> While in Vienna, I heard the president of the Rapid club observe that, whereas the Austrians knew as much as, if not more than, we did of English soccer, the Britisher knew little or showed but scant attention to their progress. This is unfortunate, but true. Even the small urchins kicking an empty tin can on a dusty heap know our leading players as well as we do ourselves, and quarrel as to who shall be [noted stars David] Jack, [Alex] James and [Alex] Jackson in their little game.

Such criticisms of England's wilful blindness would not end with Catton and Sharpe; their baton would be picked up by two of their heirs at the very pinnacle of sportswriting, Geoffrey Green of *The Times* and Brian Glanville, his counterpart at the *Sunday Times*. Green would warn in his newspaper before the visit of Austria in 1951 that England's unbeaten home record should not be allowed to 'cloud the vision of many who think British football has nothing to learn'. A year after Hungary's Golden Squad had obliterated that point of pride, he would publish *Soccer: The World Game,* insisting that 'now Jack is as good as his master, and sometimes even better', praising 'the high-speed, technical and scientific exposition of ball play, carried out with all the precision and planning of a chess master and all the artistry of a juggler' which characterised much of the continental game. 'It is in this artistic conception that the beauty and the full expansion of the game lies in the future and Britain must be alive to new ideas,' he wrote. Even the very finest British players of the day seemed to recognise that standards were being raised: Stanley Matthews was roused from his isolation by his experiences at the 1950 World Cup, while Bobby Charlton – a member of the fine Manchester United side of the following decade, standard-bearers for English football in the new-fangled European Cup – admitted he was sore amazed by the way the great Real Madrid team played.

Glanville, when he published *Soccer Nemesis* in 1955, was rather blunter. 'British football, in the meanwhile, has degenerated through its incontinence into a premature senility,' he wrote. He saw within it 'a pervasive self-satisfaction: with outmoded training methods, with antediluvian tactics on the field, with a growing series of defeats by foreign clubs and countries'.

All of this, of course, is wearyingly familiar. England's unwillingness to learn from abroad, its inability to change, continues to be something of a defining characteristic, something which lingers even in an era of foreign managers occupying the most illustrious

positions in the Premier League and the Football Association looking across the Channel – to Clairefontaine, to Ajax, to La Masia,
to Germany, in that order – for inspiration in training young
players.

Indeed, flicking through the yellowing pages of *All Sports
Weekly* and the *Athletic News*, it is impossible not to conclude
that nothing has really changed in football since the 1920s. For
example, 1926 was spent discussing whether players should be
allowed to contest refereeing decisions, or whether doing so was
calling into question the very spirit of the sport, all of it in a hec-
toring, despairing tone that would make the *Daily Mail* proud. In
1929, the subject of most concern was whether referees might need
goal judges to help them make decisions – an advancement eventually introduced by Michel Platini and Uefa not far off a century
later – while in 1930 several high-profile figures called for limits on
the number of foreign players each team was allowed to name in
order to stimulate youth development: the only difference here was
that the imports in question came not from Portugal and Poland
but Paisley and Partick.

Fears over England's imperilled place at the apex of the footballing world were just the same. As today, there were concerns
over the way teams on these shores preferred to buy in talent than
develop their own; as today, there was a worry that the emphasis
on the physical elements of the game would lead to a deficit of
technical ability.

And, as today, these expressions of concern did not fall entirely
on deaf ears. As early as 1920, the FA's Frederick Wall sent a
team to the Olympics with the prescient prediction that Great
Britain 'would not have it all our own way': he was right. Norway
knocked them out in the first round. At club level, too, there was
an awareness that the balance was shifting. A.W. Turner, secretary
of Tottenham Hotspur, knew well enough that 'our continental

friends are wide awake', while his Chelsea counterpart, C.D. Crisp, described South American players after the club went on tour there as 'not merely the world's fastest footballers, but very clever lads who can control the ball'. Even in parliament, there was an awareness that British superiority could not be taken for granted. The Reverend Herbert Dunnico, a former player and a Labour MP, penned an article in 1929 asking what England 'can learn from the continent', reserving special praise for the fact that 'every club has its elaborately equipped gymnasium and rigid, systematic year-round training'.

It is not easy, then, to explain why all of these warnings failed to achieve any lasting, noteworthy change. Perhaps those offering the dire warnings were seen as doom-mongers. Perhaps – in the case of the likes of Garbutt and Pentland in particular – their worries were perceived as being the result of self-interest: it is fair to say that their pessimistic prophecies did come laced with the subtext that they were the men to sort things out. Perhaps those in charge of English football did not respond well to being told they were doing things wrong, particularly when, until the 1950s at least, results did little to suggest the motherland had anything to fear from the continent. Perhaps they tired of being criticised. If that was the case, they will have tired of one man more than most. Nobody did more to tell England her day of reckoning was coming than Jimmy Hogan. He, more than anyone, knew how fast the continent was rising. After all, it was him who had set so many of the foreigners on their way.

Of all those coaches who went abroad, the men who became the *Misters*, none had such a seismic impact on the game as Hogan. His fingerprints remain distinct, more than a century on from his first engagement as a coach on foreign soil, on football across Europe and across the world.

Later in his life, Hogan took to carrying with him a business card that bestowed on him the title of 'Football Professor'. He could count among his students the Dutch, the Austrians, the Germans, the French, the Swiss and the Hungarians. He laid the foundations for the Austrian *Wunderteam* of the 1930s, the first continental side truly to capture the imagination of the discerning English public and his first great contribution to the history of the sport to which he dedicated his life. Among the thousands of players who came into contact with him was Helmut Schoen, manager when West Germany won the World Cup in 1974; when Hogan died, the German Football Association wrote to his family describing him as the founder of 'modern football' in the country. It was Hogan, too, who was credited with inspiring Hungary's *Aranycsapat*, the Golden Squad, which crushed England at Wembley in 1953 and again in Budapest a few months later. 'We played football as Jimmy Hogan taught us,' the coach of that team, Gusztav Sebes, said after the 6-3 win in London. 'When our soccer history is told, his name should be written in gold letters.'

Hogan's influence, though, stretches further even than that. They were just his direct pupils. It was Hungarian coaches, men who had taken their principles from Hogan, who first went to Brazil and sowed the seeds of that country's distinctive style. *Il Grande Torino*, the wonderful Italian side that tragically died in the air crash at Superga in 1949, was coached by a Hungarian, Erno Erbstein, who could not fail to have been influenced by Hogan's teaching.

Uniquely among those coaches who struck out from home to teach the game, Hogan can even claim to have had a lasting impact on English football. In 1939, Arthur Rowe, a Tottenham Hotspur stalwart, called time on his playing career. That summer, he was dispatched by the FA on a lecture tour of Hungary. The natives were impressed: they asked him to stay on and coach the country's national team, but the outbreak of World War II prevented him taking up the position. Spurs would benefit: in 1949, he took over as manager at White Hart Lane. He would lead them to promotion and then, the following season, to the league championship.

Rowe's thinking as a coach had been formed by Peter McWilliam, the Scottish manager of Spurs who first gave him his chance as a player in the 1920s. McWilliam preached what was then known as the 'Scottish game', its emphasis on making the ball do the work, rather than the players. But those weeks in Hungary had a lasting impression on Rowe: he met and exchanged ideas with both Gusztav Sebes and Ferenc Puskas, two Hogan loyalists and key figures in the team that would become known as the Magic Magyars. Rowe might have had his ideas about how the game should be played already; it seems reasonable to assume that, at second remove, Hogan's principles helped to sharpen them.

Push-and-run became Tottenham's signature style. It was the founding precept for the Bill Nicholson team that went on to win the double a decade after Rowe had brought the club its first title. It continues to inform the club's identity today, though now it is as much a burden as a blessing. Vic Buckingham, Rowe's former team-mate, took the same ideas to West Bromwich Albion and then on to Ajax and Barcelona. He would go down in history, as we shall see, as the manager who first unearthed Johan Cruyff, as the man who served as midwife to Total Football. Both were inspired by McWilliam, one of those heroes the game has forgotten. But both were connected – albeit indirectly – to Hogan, his style, his beliefs.

The central tenet of his teaching, the one that would ripple so resoundingly around the world, was the primacy of technique. Hogan was a technical fundamentalist. The unorthodox idea that the game could be taught was one he became convinced of as a player. As his biographer, Norman Fox, points out, Hogan was rather more accomplished on the pitch than he is often given credit for: he played for Nelson, Rochdale, Burnley, Fulham and Bolton Wanderers in a career that lasted 13 years. It was, the story goes, while at Burnley as a youngster that he grew frustrated at the inability of his managers to help him address the deficiencies in his game, claiming that he had so little support that he decided to 'fathom things out for himself'. His work paid off: even into his comparative dotage, his technique never left him.

None of the players who experienced one of Hogan's coaching sessions, nor any of the students who attended his lectures, would have been left in any doubt about just how important he felt 'mastery of the ball' was to the prospective player. Both would often start with a demonstration of his own abilities: at one talk in Germany, aware that he was losing his audience, he called for his kit to be brought on stage and proceeded to fire two shots, one with each foot, at a specific panel on the wall. The first one cracked it, the second smashed it in two.

Everyone who came into contact with him would have been aware of his list – presented to all of the players he worked with – of the 11 ways to bring a ball under control, and the techniques involved in doing so, whether it be with the inside or outside of the foot, the head, the chest, the thigh or on the turn. These were the basic building blocks he needed his players to acquire if they were to feel the benefit of his coaching: after all, he did little or nothing that did not involve the ball. He summed up his principles neatly: 'Ball training, ball training and more ball training, until our players are complete masters of the ball.'

From there, he would teach them the finer arts of the game: passing, crossing, dribbling, swerving, feinting. These last two, he said, were 'learned by simple exercises, such as dribbling the ball round sticks and controlling it first with the inside and after with the outside of each foot, coupled with gymnastic exercises to make the body loose at the hips'. He was disdainful of the habit of British teams to restrict training sessions to physical work followed by a spot of 'shooting in', that great cornerstone of the Sunday league warm-up routine, or the most cursory of warm-up games. 'I would,' he wrote in 1930, 'be fired [by a foreign club] if I tried the methods that are used back home.'

Fundamentalist he may have been, but it would be unfair to characterise Hogan as a one-trick pony. He was substantially more holistic than that. Years before Arsene Wenger invented pasta – at least in the collective imagination of English football – Hogan was concerned by players' diets, despairing of the amount of red meat his Austrian players ate as they prepared for the 1912 Olympics and bringing such exotic delights as green vegetables and stewed fruit into their lives while on a special pre-tournament training camp in Salzburg. He would later describe his first job as 'treating their bodies', before he set to work on their minds. 'Once I had set them up physically,' he said, 'treating the mind was an easy matter.'

He was a strict disciplinarian, clashing with one player because he had a habit of spitting after scoring goals, something that contravened his moral code, and a firm believer in what would now be called the theory of marginal gains. He took everything into consideration: the direction of the wind, the position of the sun, the state of the pitch. He would pass that attention to detail on to those coaches who learned at his feet. In 1953, Gusztav Sebes, the man in charge of the Hungarian side due to play at Wembley, travelled to England to watch his forthcoming opponents. He made sure he was there at 3pm, to see what position the sun was in. He took his boots with him, to see what the surface was like. He asked the Football Association – who, rather naively, obliged – if he might take three match balls back to Budapest with him. He missed nothing. That was pure Hogan.

Tactically, throughout his career, he remained wedded to the 2-3-5 system that he had been raised on. He was aware of the development of the WM formation in the late 1920s and early 1930s, the approach pioneered by Arsenal's Herbert Chapman which introduced the game to the 'stopper' centre half, but felt it was too retrograde, too defensive.

His style was less conservative and, he felt, more misunderstood. 'Sometimes I have been accused of being a short-passing expert,' he wrote in *Sport Express* magazine in 1954. 'This is just ridiculous ... we exploited the short pass, the long pass, the cross pass, the through pass, the reverse pass, in fact any other kind of pass which enabled us to keep possession of the ball.' That was key to everything Hogan did: the ball, possession of the ball. He wanted to see what he called 'carpet football' – his version of the famous Brian Clough quote about the absence of grass in the sky – from his teams. Like Fred Pentland before him, he was devoted to something that could be seen as a forerunner of tiki-taka.

This was at odds with the way the game was being played in the Football League, where the belief that fans wanted to watch fast, furious football had given rise to a direct, aerial style, one that Hogan detested. 'Constructive and intelligent football', he believed, was the way the game was supposed to be played. This set him at odds with England's football establishment. Hogan was adamant that both the way the game was coached and the way it was played in his homeland had, as he bluntly put it, 'gone wrong'. He was convinced it was only by teaching the basics correctly, and then moving towards a more expansive, attractive style of play, that Britain would be able to maintain her place at the pinnacle of the world game.

'British training methods are out of date,' he wrote in 1930. 'As boys at school we learnt how to play the game by kicking the ball every day for hours upon hours, and it seems strange to me that when we become first league players the ball work is dropped like hot bricks and we are trained for the game on running tracks or the golf links. I am British and proud of it but I must be candid and express the opinion there is now very little difference between British and foreign football. The secret of this is ball practice and theoretical instruction.' It was not, he said, 'training on the old lines of taking a little country air occasionally, with a little round of golf to relieve the monotony, or breaking records on the track. Ball training, simple gymnastic exercises and football instructions are proving themselves more successful.'

He was even more damning of what he called England's 'big-kicking, get-it-if-you-can game'. 'What, of recent years, has happened to our game of football?' he wrote in the *Daily Dispatch* in 1945. 'My candid opinion is that our game has gone back almost 50 per cent. Gone are the days when the ball went from man to man. What became of our carpet football? We taught the world how to do these things and then flung them away as if they were scrap.' In *Prophet or Traitor?*, Fox recounts him telling a director at Aston Villa, one of the two English clubs to offer him a managerial position, that 'a wild kick up-field is merely inviting the opposition to take possession of the ball'. He wanted the long-ball game 'scrapped'. That nobody appeared willing to listen remained an open sore until his death.

Like Steve Bloomer, in the spring of 1914, Hogan found himself at the Adelphi hotel in Liverpool, anxiously awaiting an interview with Walther Bensemann, German football's emissary in England. His playing career, he knew, was over. An inside forward – widely regarded as the most thoughtful role in any team – he had suffered a knee injury while at Fulham in 1907, one not quite serious enough to stop him playing but one that seemed to hamper his performances to the extent that the club decided to release him. He might have signed for Swindon Town but instead received an offer from Bolton Wanderers. The temptation to move back north, to be closer to his family in Burnley, proved irresistible. It was a decision that set the course for all that was to come.

In 1909, Bolton had gone on a brief post-season tour to Dordrecht, in Holland. They played half a dozen games and won all of them handsomely, but Hogan had been impressed with the raw talent and passion of the natives. A year later, when his close friend, the referee James Howcroft, recommended him for the post of coach at the town's main club, he accepted. Hogan spent two years in Holland, frustrated by the locals' 'primitive' knowledge of the game but the teacher in him was delighted by their ability to grasp the 'science' of it. He was sufficiently well regarded to be invited to help coach the national team in his spare time.

His friendship with Howcroft would bear fruit again in 1912, when he officiated a game between Austria and Hungary. The Austrians were coached by Hugo Meisl, scion of a wealthy Jewish family in Vienna who had turned his back on a business career to indulge his passion for football. Meisl was concerned his team would not fare well at that year's Olympics. He asked Howcroft if there was anyone who might be able to help. Howcroft, once more, suggested Hogan. That was the beginning of the relationship that defined Hogan's career. Quite possibly, it also saved his life.

Hogan spent six weeks working with Meisl to get the Austrian team ready for the Stockholm Games. Powered by all of those green vegetables and lashings of stewed fruit and playing in the Scottish style Hogan so esteemed, they performed relatively well in Sweden, beating Germany before being eliminated by the

red Pentland (fourth from right), in his pre-war Blackburn Rovers days, spent much
of the First World War in a PoW camp, but afterwards could only find work abroad,
and went on to become one of Athletic Bilbao's great managers. *(PA Images/Empics)*

teve Bloomer was one of the most
amous footballers of the Edwardian
ra, but after the war he too had to head
verseas in search of work, joining his
oW friend Pentland in Spain. Both men,
nusually, focused on training with the
all. *(Getty Images)*

Alf Spouncer, formerly of Nottingham
Forest, was another who moved out to
Spain, taking charge of Barcelona in 1923
where he urged his players to play on
the ground and keep the ball in constant
motion – an early version of tiki-taka,
perhaps. *(PA Images/Empics)*

William Garbutt (left) is introduced to one of the players on joining Athletic Bilbao in the summer of 1935, after many successful years in Italy. Following in Pentland's footsteps, he would win the Spanish title at his first attempt. *(Offside)*

Ivan Sharpe, one of the first writers to note how quickly continental football was catching up with the domestic game, hands over the 1948 FWA Footballer of the Year trophy to Stanley Matthews. *(Getty Images)*

By 1946, as the poster says, Jimmy Hogan was a world famous coach, but his message about the threats to England's football supremacy was largely ignored. *(Mirrorpix)*

ust as Hogan had feared, Nandor Hidegkuti puts the finishing touches to Hungary's amous 6-3 victory over England at Wembley in 1953. The coach was watching from he stands and would later assert: 'Our very foundations have gone wrong.' *(Getty Images)*

Sir Stanley Rous in 1961, newly elected as president of FIFA, had worked hard as secretary of the FA to encourage better coaching of the game. *(PA Images)*

One of Rous's key appointments was Walter Winterbottom, the first England team manager, who also headed up England's coaching programme and tried to help spread the word as to how the game should be played. Here he is seen coaching in East Berlin in 1962.

(Getty Images)

esse Carver oversees a training exercise at Coventry City in 1955. He'd had plenty f success in Italy, but the contemporary caption to this photo tells its own story, as hese 'unusual stretching and jumping routines' were part of his 'continental training nethods'. *(Getty Images)*

eorge Raynor would take Sweden to the final of the 1958 World Cup. Here he ctures on tactics to the national team. *(PA Images)*

Vic Buckingham (left) and Spurs manager Arthur Rowe deep in conversation. Rowe's 'push and run' side would influence Buckingham's thinking as manager of Ajax and Barcelona in the 1960s, which helped bring about Dutch Total Football. *(Getty Images)*

A surprise appointment 'off the beach' at Barcelona, Terry Venables became an instant hero when he won La Liga in his first season at the club. *(Getty Images)*

Real Madrid's John Toshack and Johan Cruyff, rival managers in El Clasico in 1989. The Welshman has been one of the most successful of all the *Misters* in recent years. *(Offside)*

...obby Robson celebrates with Frank Arnesen after leading PSV to the Dutch title in ...992. He would win eight trophies with various clubs throughout the 1990s, before ...eturning to Newcastle United at the end of the decade. *(Getty Images)*

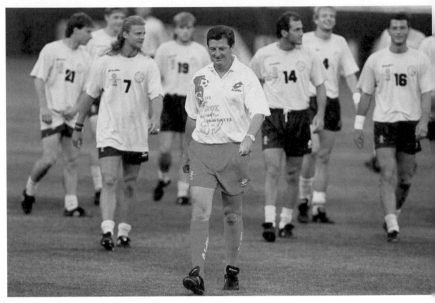

Despite leading Switzerland to the 1994 World Cup finals, many football fans in England took a while to trust in Roy Hodgson's ability, because so much of what he had achieved had been done abroad – it was the curse of the *Mister*. *(Getty Images)*

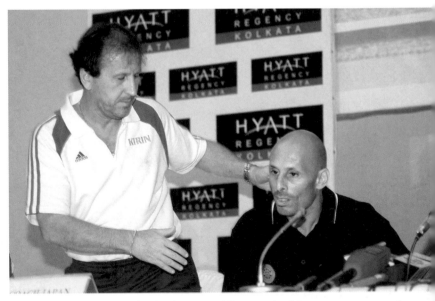

Stephen Constantine, coach of India, meets Zico, coach of Japan, at a press conference in 2004. As footballers they may have been on completely different levels, but now the were on a par. *(Getty Images)*

Dutch – Hogan took credit for their success, too, given his work in the previous two years – but more important was the fact that he and Meisl were bonded by a common vision of how football might be played. The two men dovetailed perfectly, Hogan capable of running the technical training sessions Meisl wanted and his players demanded. The Englishman would return home after the Olympics, going back to Bolton for one final season as a player. Less than two years later, Meisl received a letter that changed the course of his friend's life.

Hogan had been invited to the Adelphi to interview for the same job that Bloomer took. As Fox has it, he was the last candidate Bensemann met as he tried to fill the three positions the German Football Association were offering. Whereas Bloomer would have, naturally, emphasised his playing experience, Hogan no doubt preferred to discuss his work in Holland and Austria. He was never backwards in coming forwards when it came to his achievements. Hogan was no shrinking violet. He would, according to one of the players he encountered later in his career, sign his autograph: 'Best wishes, Jimmy Hogan – the world's number one football coach.' He had never been afraid to advertise his abilities.

For all the bombast, Bensemann does not appear to have been immediately impressed. He sought references to corroborate Hogan's claims. The German Football Association wrote to Meisl to ask him his thoughts on the man he had worked with in Stockholm. Meisl, unwilling to allow a man he deemed such an able coach to be hired by a side he considered a rival for the 1916 Olympics, got in touch with Hogan to offer him the job of coach of the Austrian national side instead. His friend readily accepted. Bloomer got the job in Germany. By the end of the year, he was sleeping under the sackcloth of Ruhleben. Hogan was in Vienna.

That is not to suggest Hogan's war was a happy one and it is

certainly not to give any credence to the idea, which would gain
some traction after the conflict had ended, that he was some sort
of deserter. Like Bloomer, he would spend the years between 1914
and 1918 as a prisoner. It is simply that his cage would be a little
more gilded.

Hogan fell in love with Vienna almost immediately. He
described it as a paradise, a city of 'love, life and laughter',
later ranking it alongside Budapest as the most beautiful he had
known. He loved his work and the knowledge-thirsty football
culture he now found himself in. He coached the Olympic team
twice a week and took on club sessions, too, arranging training at 5.30am because so many sides wanted to benefit from
his wisdom. He was working with players who would absorb
everything he could teach them, players who understood what he
meant when he asked them to 'make friends with the ball'. In the
few weeks he was there, before the world fell apart, he was busy
laying the foundations for the first great side that bore his stamp:
in years to come, the *Wunderteam* he and Meisl constructed
would captivate the world.

It is impossible to know what he might have achieved, how
different the annals of the game might look, had the war not
intervened. Just as Hogan was starting to make an impact, Arch-
duke Franz Ferdinand was assassinated and Europe disintegrated.
Hogan, naturally, was enormously concerned, but was told by the
British consul that there was no immediate cause for despair. But
a matter of days later, in the dead of night, the police knocked on
the door of his apartment in the city. His wife, terrified, answered.
War had been declared and the order had come to round up all
foreign nationals. Hogan was thrown into jail.

He was saved from an internment camp only by the good
graces of the British Blythe brothers, owners of a department store
in the Austrian capital, who offered to vouch for him. He stayed

with them for the next two years, employed as an odd-job man at their family home, teaching their children tennis and looking after their gardens. It is not hard to see why, when he eventually returned to England, there were plenty in football who sneered at his good fortune. If the prisoners at Ruhleben had been considered lucky to avoid the horrors of the Somme and Passchendaele, then fate had smiled on Hogan even more.

He resented that assessment deeply. His family, as he would point out, had been transported back to Britain; he did not see them for four years. His salary from the Austrian Football Association had been cut off; he described himself and his wife as being 'left to starve'. He had to report to police at regular intervals, and was under a strict curfew. When the chance to leave Vienna eventually came, with the war dragging on, he was not even permitted to return to Britain. He was told, instead, that he would be going to Hungary. Hogan would have known that, by the standards of millions, his war was a desirable one. He was fortunate. But that is not the same as easy.

It is not immediately clear quite why the Austrian authorities decided to release Hogan to Budapest. He had never been there before; he had no obvious connections in Hungary. Fox's explanation is that Baron Dirstay, a Hungarian aristocrat and vice president at the MTK club, conspired with Meisl to get him out simply because he felt the Englishman was the best candidate to help fulfil the team's ambition to become the most powerful in Europe. There, too, he would remain under curfew and police supervision. However he came to be there, he was simply glad to be out of Vienna. When he saw what awaited him at MTK, his heart would have soared once more.

The club clearly had big plans. The facilities were the best Hogan had ever seen; he had an office at the stadium and complete control of the team. With most of their senior players away on active service, he was forced to scour the club's youth squads for players. He would unearth two in particular, Gyorgy Orth and Jozsef Braun, whom he ranked among the finest he worked with, both turned into superstars by his relentless technical training. He spent three seasons at MTK. In all three, they won the Hungarian title. Thanks to the foundations laid by Hogan, they would not be dethroned until 1925. That would not be his most lasting legacy, though. It would be almost 30 years later when that was unveiled to the world, on that grey afternoon at Wembley when the *Aranycsapat* shattered England's defence and her illusions. As the rest of world was falling apart, Hogan was slowly, methodically, building something that lasted a century.

For all the satisfaction he took from his work, he returned to England at the very first opportunity, travelling across the continent on a train guarded by British soldiers. He arrived in Burnley almost destitute. He moved his family in with his wife's parents, writing that he was barely able to afford a decent suit. He was forced to apply to the Football Association, asking if he would be eligible for a fund that had been set up to help former players struggling to find work. Frederick Wall not only turned him down, but – according to Fox – offered him only three pairs of woollen socks, the type that had been issued to the soldiers at the front. The inference seemed clear: Hogan was at best a deserter. At worst, a traitor.

That meeting set the tone for much of Hogan's interaction with the FA. His relationship with Stanley Rous, Wall's successor – a man considered dangerously louche by some within the organisation because he only wore a lounge suit, rather than tails, to attend matches – was better than with Wall, but it rarely rose above cool.

Perhaps it was in that conversation, immediately after the end of the war, that it was effectively decided that Hogan, no matter how much success he enjoyed or how many people called for him to be recruited by the game's authorities, would never be given the chance to see if his methods could help the development of the sport in England. More likely and to some extent more significantly, it hints at an institutional suspicion of all those who had gone abroad to work which may explain, at least in part, why so many of them would be ignored in their homeland.

Hogan, then, had little choice but to look further afield for work. He would later insist that his travels were inspired by a boyhood longing to see all of the exotic locations he had read about as a child. There may be some truth in that claim, but certainly his decision – like that of Bloomer and Pentland – to strike out once more immediately after the war was an economic one. He had to work and, thanks to the attitudes of the FA and the Football League clubs, he could not do so at home. Necessity, it is fair to say, was the mother of everything he invented.

Hogan's travels were extensive. His desire to spread the word of the game, to imbue players and coaches across the world with his vision, enabled him to see all of those places he had read about as a boy: 'The daydreams of my youth have been fulfilled,' he would write. 'I have sailed in the Mediterranean, climbed the Swiss Alps, bathed in the blue Danube, [seen] the wonderful cities of Vienna, Budapest, Berlin, Rome, Amsterdam, Zurich and Stockholm.'

He never remained in one place for long. He had three years in Switzerland, between 1922 and 1925, with Young Boys of Berne and Lausanne, another season in Hungary – at Hungaria, as MTK were now known – before moving to Germany in 1926, first as a roving coaching instructor and later as manager of Dresden, with whom he won four consecutive league titles. From there he went to France, and Racing Club in Paris, in 1931, and then back to Austria, reuniting with Meisl to help out with what was becoming known as the *Wunderteam* the following year.

Quite why he was so restless must, necessarily, remain a matter of conjecture, but while the temptation is to assume he was simply a peripatetic character, the likelihood is that there is no single overriding explanation. If he moved to Switzerland, initially, for the benefit of his purse, then leaving for Hungary was seemingly inspired by loyalty and gratitude – as well as, possibly, professional excitement at the prospect of working again with that country's players – for the treatment they afforded him during the war. His appointment in Germany came, again, with extensive remuneration, but his move to France was inspired by something quite different: Meisl seems to have alerted him to the changing mood in Germany, the National Socialist Party growing ever more powerful, and encouraged him to leave. How seriously he took the deteriorating situation in Germany is indicated by the manner of his departure, he and his son, Joe, sewing the family's life savings into their trousers to ensure it was not snatched by customs.

He left France in 1932 in despair, caused not by the ability of the players he was working with but by the culture of the club, which laid on extravagant meals after every match and insisted on hosting their stars in the best class of hotels. To a man of Hogan's almost ascetic tastes, such an environment was deeply undesirable. That, as much as his relationship with Meisl, took him back to Vienna.

The reason his old friend was so desperate for his expert touch was that Austria, that year, were due at Stamford Bridge to face England in a game that had been dressed up as the unofficial championship of the world. The Austrians, inspired by the elfin Matthias Sindelar, were widely held as the best team on the continent. The English, their self-confidence so absolute it appears to have been contagious, were still believed to be the finest on the planet. Two years after neither had turned up to the first edition of the World Cup, dominated by the South Americans and won by the hosts, Uruguay, this was, to European eyes, a real chance to establish football's international pecking order.

Thorough as ever, Hogan and Meisl took their players to Stamford Bridge a week before the game to see Chelsea host Everton. It was a chance to witness two of the era's best forwards in direct competition: Chelsea could call on Hughie Gallacher, while the visitors boasted the prolific Dixie Dean. Hogan left not just unimpressed but a little dejected: not because of the abilities of the two players, but because of the habit of both teams of simply punting long balls in their vague direction, more in hope than expectation. This was not the carpet football he believed in so absolutely; he would have interpreted it as proof of how criminally England was wasting its natural resources.

Austria would deliver much the same assessment with much greater eloquence a week later. In front of a crowd of 42,000, they lost a thrilling game 4-3. England's proud unbeaten record stood unscathed, and there were those, among both players and the press, who saw the victory as proof that, for all the hype about the rise of the continent, the primacy of the motherland should not be doubted. Others were a little more circumspect. The correspondents dispatched to cover the fixture were uniformly charmed by the Austrian performance and, in particular, that of Sindelar, scorer of a goal described as a 'master-piece'. One even went so far as to describe England's win as 'unsettling'. England might have taken the prize, but Austria won all of the plaudits for style. Something, clearly, was happening after all.

That display cannot have hurt Hogan's reputation at home; likewise, Sindelar's insistence afterwards that Hogan had been key in helping develop the game as they played it. It certainly seems too much of a coincidence that, two years later, he was finally given the chance to come back to west London on a permanent basis. In May 1934, he was offered the job of manager at Fulham.

Desperate for recognition at home, he accepted it readily, describing himself as 'honoured and delighted' to be back at one of his former clubs. Indeed, apart from Burnley, he had more affection for Fulham than any other team in England. It was here, after all, as a player, that he had first had the chance to play in a side dominated by Scots, playing in the short-passing style he so adored. It was football as he felt it should be played, and it would influence his thinking as much as his conviction that the game could be taught and refined.

His spell as manager, though, was less happy. His first programme notes, unearthed by Fox in *Prophet or Traitor?*, suggest he is aware that he has something to prove to his new players, directors and fans, with his emphasis on his experience: 'I have managed the international teams of different countries on at least 50 occasions.' They do seem to have needed some convincing. Hogan tried to introduce the methods that had served him so well on the continent, working to improve his players' technique, but the club's hierarchy were unimpressed. Results were hardly disastrous, but he was sacked after just 31 games, while he lay in hospital recovering from a heart operation. 'I was,' he said later, 'sacked for teaching my ideas of playing football in an intelligent manner.'

Disappointed and rejected, he returned first to Lausanne and then to Austria, taking Meisl up on his offer of helping prepare the team for the 1936 Olympics. Once more, their collaboration proved fruitful: despite seeing their quarter-final with Jack Greenwell's Peru end in a brawl that forced its cancellation, the Austrians made the final. They were beaten only by the Italians, coached by Vittorio Pozzo – a man for whom Hogan had a great deal of admiration – in the middle of a glorious spell which saw them crowned world champions in both 1934 and 1938.

Back in England, despite his unhappy experience at Fulham,

his name was starting to carry some weight. He had first encountered Stanley Rous, the new secretary of the FA, when he sought compensation from Craven Cottage for the manner of his dismissal, and in 1936 he was offered the post of instructor at the first ever FA coaching course, a forerunner of the scheme that would be responsible for sending so many coaches to so many corners of the globe in years to come. Rous was hardly bowled over by Hogan, or any of the other coaches he had invited to run a session, claiming that none of them had 'proved expert', but others were more impressed. Those who listened to Hogan that day included Walter Winterbottom, soon to be England coach; Arthur Rowe, the father of push-and-run football; and Alex James, the Arsenal star and one of the most famous players in the world. Previously, he had considered coaching 'moonshine'. Hogan, he said, helped change his mind.

English football, in other words, was no longer ignoring him. In November of that year, he was finally given the chance he had wanted for more than two decades. Alex James was not the only one whose head had been turned by Hogan. The directors of Aston Villa were prepared to make him their manager, despite concerns that, at 54, time was not on his side. Leaving Meisl would not have been a decision he took lightly: Austria remained one of the finest teams on the planet and, with the World Cup less than two years away, he would have known that a chance to record the greatest achievement of his career was round the corner. That he accepted a three-year contract, worth £1,000 a season, at Villa Park can therefore be read as proof of how much the chance to manage in the Football League meant to him, though perhaps politics played their part, too, the worsening situation in Germany and Austria alike prompting him to move.

His tone, upon his arrival, was markedly different from that he had deployed at Fulham. Instead of underlining his qualifications for the job, he admitted that the task awaiting him at Villa Park – taking the club back to the First Division after the first relegation in their history the previous season – was different from much of what he had experienced abroad. 'It will not be [about] manufacturing footballers, as I had to do in my earliest days on the continent,' he said. He was quick to pay tribute to what he believed was 'the best side' the club had ever been able to call on.

His first season saw Villa finish ninth in the Second Division, the club fading into the comfortable embrace of mid-table after a promising start under Hogan's stewardship. There was already a degree of resistance to his methods from above: his refusal to ape much of the rest of the Football League and deploy a 'stopper' centre half, popularised by Herbert Chapman's Arsenal, was a source of some tension, as was his disdain for the 'long-kicking game', which he continued to abhor. Doubtless such troubles dissipated the following year. Finally, Hogan had announced himself to England. Villa won the 1937-38 Second Division title at a canter, finishing four points clear of Manchester United, and made the semi-finals of the FA Cup. He rated the team he had that season as the equal of any he had ever coached; given the results some of his teams had started to record against the English national side, that seems a hopelessly optimistic, and possibly somewhat self-aggrandising, assessment, proof more of his own desire to be a success at home than Villa's actual abilities.

The following year, Villa finished a comfortable 12th in the top flight. In an era when it was entirely plausible to be promoted and morph, almost immediately, into a genuine force, it was no spectacular success, but nor was it any form of failure. It is intriguing to wonder what might have happened had Hogan been given a longer run as a top-flight manager. He had achieved some measure of fame and respect in England, yet the only way, it seems, for him to have changed the minds of the game's establishment about his methods would have been to prove that they worked in the Football League. If he could have turned his Villa team into contenders at the very pinnacle of the English game, perhaps – and it is only perhaps – more clubs would have been willing to adopt his philosophy. Instead, history intervened. As the country again mobilised for war, the 1939-40 season was abandoned after just three games. Villa sat 14th, having beaten Middlesbrough and lost to Everton and Derby. Hogan was dismissed during the conflict, Villa unable to pay his wages. He spent the war as an odd-job man at Burnley, and he found work after it with both Brentford and Celtic, but time was against him. By then, into his sixties, he was too old to be considered for employment. Villa was his chance. At last, the Football Professor had the attention of his homeland. Just as the most advanced students he had ever had were starting to listen, circumstance forced him from the stage.

Hogan was never likely to go quietly. Almost from the moment he went abroad, he had been a consistent and vociferous critic of the English game. He had never tired of telling his countrymen that they must change the way they coached, the way they played and the way they thought about football. He wrote, prolifically, on the subject, whenever his view was sought by the press and often when it was not. He repeated the message being sent by William Garbutt and Fred Pentland. He supported the pleas of Ivan Sharpe and James Catton in the 1920s and 1930s and, a generation later, did the same when the voices of dissent were those of Geoffrey Green and Brian Glanville. For half a century, he told those in power that they should not take their primacy for granted. When the day finally came and the country woke up, he did not rest on his laurels. He simply continued his campaign for change.

As early as 1928, while he was at Dresden, he was pointing out the difference between a coach in Germany and in England:

'the trainer's work here is to teach the game,' he said, rather than 'rubbing down' the players after a match and looking after their boots. In 1929, he warned that teams on the continent were no longer seeking English coaches because they no longer reckoned the motherland had much to teach them. That year, a 'famous coach abroad' wrote anonymously to the *Athletic News* to warn that 'continental football bears no resemblance to pre-war standard and home clubs who nurse the illusion that football can only be played in Britain would speedily be disillusioned by a trip [abroad]'. The *Athletic News*, at that time, was Hogan's publication of choice. It seems fair to suggest that he was the source of the remarks.

In 1930, as England prepared for a tour that would bring them face to face with both Germany and Austria, two teams indelibly stamped by Hogan's authority, he was finally given a sustained opportunity to make his views known to his homeland. He pulled no punches. 'British training methods are out of date,' he said in the *Athletic News*, the cloak of anonymity discarded. 'I am treading on somebody's toes, but my desire is to help, not attack, British football. How do you account for the many reverses sustained by our league teams on continental tours? Further, can anybody explain why clubs from Czechoslovakia, Austria and Hungary, on touring Germany, Italy and Spain, achieve better results and leave a better impression than British teams accomplish?'

The previous year, after all, when Chelsea and Motherwell had failed to beat the mighty Uruguayan team that had just won the Olympics and would soon be crowned world champions, Ferencvaros of Hungary had recorded a victory. 'One gets tired of reading such excuses as tired players, long journeys, hard grounds and bad referees as reasons for British football disasters abroad. There is just a little truth in these explanations, but on the other hand, the continental season is a strenuous all-year-round one [too].

'The progress made in football by Germany, Spain, Italy, Austria, Hungary and Czechoslovakia has been truly remarkable. But the answer to my question is this: continental ball training is more successful than British condition training. The first seeds were sown by British touring sides and trainers. Since then the football training methods have improved and kept pace with the times. Unfortunately, such has not been the case in England.' He found his homeland's emphasis on speed and stamina 'really too absurd for words' and insisted that 'the most famous player or trainer in British football would not be able, as a coach, to obtain a single day's work on the continent unless he were able to teach the game'. His conclusion was stark: 'We are a race of natural football players but we are in danger of losing our supremacy.'

That was not his only attack. 'I have watched continental football grow from a weakling into a strongman,' he said, according to Glanville's *Soccer Nemesis*. 'The question is: Will it reach the stage of full-grown manhood and eventually deprive Britain of her supremacy? When I think of the early days out here, of players who were able to only kick with one foot, afraid of heading the ball and no idea of trapping or ball control ... it makes one rub one's eyes.' The English player, by contrast, was too 'cocky', too guilty of 'thinking they have nothing left to learn'. That is why, he said, as England prepared to face Germany in Berlin, that country and Austria 'had made wonderful strides', while the English were stuck in the past.

His view seemed to be borne out by what happened in Berlin and Vienna, as England failed to win either game. The FA's Arthur Kingscott, one of the most powerful men in the game, described the team sent out for the games as 'the best ... to leave our shores', but accepted that 'Germany have been coached up to our type of football'. Given that Hogan, who was sitting among Germany's football authorities in the crowd in Berlin, had done all of that coaching in the last four years, it would not have been unreasonable for him to assume the FA might have wanted to ask him about – or at least acknowledge – an improvement they themselves had identified.

To Hogan's intense frustration, they did not. Fifteen years later, he would be saying much the same thing. As Britain struggled back to her feet after the war, Dynamo Moscow arrived in London on tour. Few knew what to expect from a team from behind the Iron Curtain, then slowly being drawn across the east of Europe. Once again, despite his admission that he had never coached in Russia – but asserting that he knew 'something of their football' – Hogan's views on what Dynamo would be like made good copy. Once again, he warned England not to assume they would be swatted aside. Once again, even as he was proved correct, nobody thought to ask him any follow-up questions. Dynamo, with their fluid movement, their players comfortable in any position, their technique flawless and their tactics sophisticated, fired the popular imagination in the four games they played on these shores, beating Arsenal, hammering Cardiff and drawing with Chelsea and Rangers. Once again, despite the evidence of their eyes and with the dread predictions of Hogan ringing in their ears, nothing changed.

From Hogan's point of view, though, there can have been no more exquisite annoyance than what happened in 1953. As Fox records, he was present at Wembley to watch Ferenc Puskas, Nandor Hidegkuti and the rest tear England to shreds. He was not a guest of the Hungarian Football Association, but was, instead, present in his role as Villa's youth-team coach. He watched football's world order and England's delusions crumble in the presence of his teenage charges; he had wanted them to watch the Hungarians because he had a feeling they would be impressed. His instincts were correct: he would tell Gusztav Sebes, his one-time protégé, that Hungary had played the type of football he had 'dreamed they might one day produce'. Perhaps wisely, the following day he seemed to decide discretion was the better part of valour and turned down the welter of interview requests that flooded into Villa's offices, spending the morning instead coaching his players. Nor did he glory in the subsequent campaign from certain sections of the media demanding that he be given a role within the FA, a movement destined for failure. However, he did not hold his counsel for long.

'Our very foundations have gone wrong,' he wrote in *Sport Express* in 1954, a thousand-word plea to English football to heed the warnings of Wembley. 'We must have ball training, ball training and more ball training in this country. There are dozens and dozens of ball training exercises which will also get a player into condition. Wake up England, and play the game as it was intended to be played, intelligently, constructively.' Another piece that year articulated who he blamed for England's loss of prestige. 'There are too many men leading the game who have not the foggiest notion of constructive and intelligent football. You know the type of man I mean: the one who walks into the dressing room and gives instructions such as "get stuck in lads, and swing the ball about".'

Even as his reputation started to wane after his active involvement with the game came to its end, he continued writing letters to newspapers and power brokers within football expressing his disdain for the cult of stamina and clamouring for change. His warnings continued into his dotage; they scarcely abated even when England lifted the World Cup in 1966.

Every single one of Hogan's prophecies came to pass. England tumbled, inexorably, from her place at the very summit of the game. The deficit of technical training raised generation after generation of players and sides capable of being outpassed and, crucially, out-thought by teams from across the world. Even now, four decades after his death at the age of 91, England is playing catch-up, able to narrow the knowledge gap but incapable of bridging it completely. Hogan warned them, again and again, what was about to happen. He knew because he had not just seen it, he had started the revolution. Everything he said went unheeded. It is to his credit that he never gave up, that despite all the frustration he never stopped shouting into the void.

6

Prophets Without Honour

Mr P. Coley was not impressed. In the summer of 1954, he led the Luton Town delegation on their post-season tour of Greece and Turkey. Ever since Southampton had struck out more than half a century beforehand, such jaunts had been a regular part of many clubs' calendars. They would spend a few weeks somewhere hot, playing a few exhibition games, seeing a few sights, earning a few pounds in appearance fees. Luton, that year, were paid £150 for each of the seven games they would play in Athens and Istanbul. But this was not just an exotic trip for the players, long before the days when they decamped en masse in the off-season to Las Vegas. There was a worthy purpose to it: it was educational, and not for the upstanding burghers of Bedfordshire.

The trip was not an easy one. Coley found the 'football of the three teams we met in Athens and four in Istanbul surprisingly good'. He was less happy with the time keeping – 'they are very lax in Turkey: the kick-off may be anything up to half an hour over the stated time' – and the quality of his accommodations. Luton's hotel in Istanbul 'would be rated third class in England but was looked upon as first class in Turkey'. So bad were the lodgings, in fact, that the officials did not have a bath until they got to Kifis-sia, their base in Athens. 'It was our first since leaving England, a matter of 14 days.'

Slapdash personal hygiene – a sure-fire sign of any lads' holi-day – was not the only trouble. Mr Coley did take time to admire how 'clever [the Greeks and Turks are] in getting the ball under control very quickly, at whatever height or angle', but that was outweighed by how disenchanted he was with the amount of 'body-checking' he found in Turkish football, in particular, and their desire to 'make another pass' when in shooting positions.

Still, though, he realised that putting up with such frustrations was a necessary evil. 'Unless some teams are prepared to make the effort and show these people the English way of conducting and playing the game, it is difficult to see how their standards are ever going to be brought on a par with our own,' he wrote. 'These tours are of great value, for they give people overseas a chance of seeing our players playing football in a way which for-eign teams must strive to attain: not giving way to sudden, vicious and unwarrantable deliberate kicking on the spur of the moment, not deliberately handling the ball, to accept the referee's decisions without argument [and] general good sportsmanship.'

This, remember, was 1954. It had not yet been a year since the Hungarians had arrived at Wembley and shown England quite how far the continental game had come; it was only six months since the return game in Budapest, when the damage was even greater. England's coaching representatives abroad had been reporting back on the rise of the foreign challenge for more than three decades. Two generations of journalists – from James Catton to Geoffrey Green – had noticed the tide turning. It might have been hoped that, now Puskas, Hidegkuti and the rest had incon-trovertibly proved these men were more than mere doom-mongers, England might have dispensed with its delusions of grandeur. If

Coley's account is anything to go by, the message had not yet got through to the clubs of the Football League.

There is no simple explanation for why that might be, but a number of factors might be relevant. Most immediately, there was no great consensus in the late 1940s and early 1950s that the English game was falling behind. Football seemed to be in rude health: the national team were flying, beating Portugal 10-0 in 1947 – a result that, to some extent, can be explained by the fact that Portuguese sides at the time played with a different size of football – and then, more notably still, winning 4-0 against Italy in Turin the following year. More importantly, to the clubs, more people than ever before were passing through the turnstiles. Some 41.3 million people went to games in the 1948-49 season, the highest number ever recorded. There was no reason for anyone to suspect anything was wrong.

Then there was what Bob Ferrier, in his curious book *Soccer Partnership*, described as the inherent 'resistance to change' within the English game. It is an odd but rewarding work: ostensibly, an essay about the relationship between Billy Wright, the England captain, and the manager, Walter Winterbottom. However, it is at its most interesting when it reaches beyond that and examines the state of the British game on a more fundamental level. Its most important insight is that, for the first half of the 20th century, football in England was an old man's game, run by a class philosophically opposed to anything new.

'Resistance came from almost every quarter,' Ferrier writes. '[It came] from the press and the managers, from former players and also some legislators. There was resistance to the very fact of having an England team manager, there was resistance to pre-match training sessions and meetings of players, there was resistance to the whole, new, ambitious FA plan for a national coaching programme.

'Football is ruled by older men, men who have spent a lifetime in the sport ... and who by that very token assume they have a right to be ruling it. [Change was] impermissible to men who had never been exposed to these things in their own lives ... resistance to change, to new ideas, was inevitable. The resistance was not against the FA. It was simply within the nature and character of the people involved to resist.'

Here, Ferrier believed that England 'suffered because we started the whole thing'. The first generation of players were never coached and the first generation of administrators never had the need to hire coaches. Their assumption was that, because they had taken to football naturally, everyone else would, too. This led to what Ferrier saw as the great misconception: that coaching senior players was to 'teach a tackler how to tackle or a dribbler how to dribble. It is not. Coaching at international level does not consist of teaching players the skills of the game ... it is aimed at blending skills that are already there.' But England had never acquired the habit of learning. It saw football as something that had landed, complete and perfect. It did not see the need to improve it. After the humiliation of the 1950 World Cup, when England were eliminated at the group stage and even managed to lose to the United States, the Football Association had set up an enquiry, stocked by representatives of the clubs, into the causes of the embarrassment. They examined what the Brazilians, among others, were doing that they were not. The turkeys, unsurprisingly, concluded that Christmas was a bad thing. Their report found that Brazilian training methods would not work in England, because English players would not respond to coaching.

This antiquated thinking was not simply evident from how the game was played – scorning new tactics, sticking with the tried and the trusted – but where it was played, too. 'Even with completely new grounds built since the war,' Ferrier wrote, 'instead of building a properly equipped sports stadium, we have reconstructed the old, traditional, rectangular football ground.' Football thought it was being guided by what Ferrier called the 'heavy, burdensome hand of tradition'. In reality, it was being held back.

All of this was compounded by Britain's insistence on living in an echo chamber. Continental Europe had become a hothouse of ideas and innovation before World War II, where new concepts travelled smoothly and easily through contiguous borders. Britain, the Channel becoming a gulf, was not part of that process, locked into what Ferrier saw as the 'self-imposed isolationism' of the Home Championships, only occasionally deigning to face foreign sides, a few times a season at best. By standing apart, the English, the Scots and the rest grew ignorant not only of what was happening beyond their shores but of where they stood in the new world order.

'Nothing is more parochial than the average sports page of the average British newspaper,' wrote George Raynor in 1960. 'The ignorance of football as a world game is abysmal in Britain. It is ignored [there] but in every other part of the world it is reported. This ignoring has done immeasurable harm to football in this country. People are given all sorts of false ideas. They read about false ratings ... [notional] world XIs have at least four Englishmen in them.'

In such an environment, it is not a shock there were some who had not noticed that times were changing. Mr P. Coley was rooted in a past that no longer existed, and had not existed for quite some time. He saw England as the place where all football knowledge resided, the Football League as not just the ultimate but the only proving ground. There were, however, those who were not quite so insular. There were those who had noticed which way the wind was blowing, those who had been trying to modernise England's atrophying football culture for some time. At Manchester United, Matt Busby was fully aware of the need to test his side against the very best, persuading his chairman to lobby for the club to be allowed to enter the European Cup in 1956 after Chelsea had been prevented from doing so the previous year; it is telling that, rather than appealing to his sense of sporting adventure, he informed Harold Hardman, his boss, that playing in Europe would be a profitable enterprise. United were very much the exception, though, not the rule. On the whole, the Football League proved fearsomely resistant to change. The Football Association, on the other hand, was trying to accelerate it.

The walls of the museum at the Estadio Jose Alvalade glisten with trophies. It is here that Sporting Clube de Portugal – Sporting Lisbon, to you and me – parade the spoils they have acquired over more than a century of existence. The vast majority serve as testament to their footballing prowess, but a couple of dozen other sports are represented, too: everything from canoeing to kickboxing, table tennis to taekwondo. In one cabinet, utterly incongruous in the heart of the Portuguese capital, there is even something that looks suspiciously like a snooker waistcoat, in the club colours of green and white, the emblem of a lion rampant covering a pocket.

Tucked away in a corner is a display dedicated to what remains, arguably, the finest side in Sporting's history. Between 1946 and 1954, this was Portugal's premier club. Only once in that period, in 1950, did they fail to win the Primeira Liga title. In 1949, they became the first team to win the title in three successive seasons; in 1954, they went one better, and secured their fourth championship in a row. Their success was built on their forward line. Fernando Peyroteo, Albano, Jesus Correia, Manuel Vasques and Jose Travassos first played together for Sporting in 1946. Each of them would go on to score more than 100 goals for the club; their combined tally, according to some estimates, is beyond 1,000. They became known as *Os Cinco Violinos*: the Five Fiddles.

The five played together for only three years, winning the league every season, before Peyroteo, the most devastating of them all, retired in 1949. When Correia, too, called time on his career, in 1953, leaving just three of the original line-up, Sporting still managed to secure that record-setting fourth championship the following year. They also won the Portuguese Cup that season, the perfect golden swansong. Each of the five has his own profile in Sporting's museum, their place in the most glorious period of the club's history secure. There is room, too, for a brief biography of Jozsef Szabo, the Hungarian coach who was in charge of the club for that final season, the one that brought the double.

Neither Bob Kelly nor Randolph Galloway is afforded the same status. Both appear only fleetingly, in group photographs. There is no mention of the fact that Kelly was in charge for the first of that run of league championships, won in 1947, and nothing to remind anyone that it was Galloway who had led the team to three titles in a row from 1950 to 1953, before being replaced by Szabo. Both should be remembered and celebrated for what they did. Both seem to have been forgotten.

Kelly, at least, has the solace of a relatively high profile in his homeland. Despite seeing his career interrupted by World War I – he served with the Royal Field Artillery – he emerged in the 1920s as one of the outstanding talents in the Football League, first with Burnley and then, after a British record transfer, with Sunderland. He represented his country 14 times between 1920 and 1928. James Catton, the premier football journalist of the time, described him in lavish terms. He was, in turns, 'clever and dashing', 'a quick thinker and very speedy'. 'Originality,' he wrote, 'is a feature of his play.' He was a player 'who did not know one foot from the other' and played 'with an artistry which is delightful . . .

a mystifying swerve when on [the ball] and a shooting power . . . excelled by no-one in the land'.

He was, it seems, just as impressive off the pitch. Catton interviewed him for *All Sports Weekly* in 1924. 'Meeting Kelly, it is obvious that he has a trim, balanced figure and that he has an eye to appearances, for he is always well-dressed. He wears a good suit as if he had been used to the purple from his cradle. I have seen him in an overcoat that, for the fit at the shoulders and the waist, seemed part of him. Any Bond Street dude would have been proud of that coat. Looking through the garments of Kelly, they are unspeakably significant of a young man who respects himself, of one who does not waste his money, of one who has a notion of tidiness, cleanliness and neat living. He has an idea of gracefulness. [He is] a stylish stepper.' He was struck by what 'an intelligent man [he was]; he can, and does, take an interest in general affairs', but he was, also, something of a proto-superstar. 'He likes motoring, whether in a car or on a motor-bicycle, he loves a game at bowls, dabbles with a driver on the links, and knows the points of snooker.' Perhaps he designed the waistcoat that hangs so proudly, and so bizarrely, in Sporting's museum.

Kelly's taste for the finer things in life was not without its drawbacks. Catton's public hagiography of the man detailed how he was allowed by Burnley's directors to live at Ansdell, not far from the beach resort of Lytham St Annes, because they regarded him as 'a credit' to his club. However, his private notes suggest that is not an entirely honest account. As he sought background on Kelly, he received a letter from John Haworth, Burnley's secretary-manager, revealing that the player had 'performed an indiscreet action' with a married woman in his early years at Burnley. According to Haworth, 'motoring in the lady's car' had been the root of the attraction; either that or it was a clever euphemism. He pleaded with Catton not to include the scandal in his story.

When his playing career came to an end, after spells with Huddersfield, Preston and Carlisle, Kelly's reputation was enough to secure a managerial post, first at Carlisle and then Stockport County. He was forced to take a six-year hiatus during the war and, like so many others, found after the conflict that there was considerably more demand for his services abroad than at home. He moved to Portugal, and Sporting, in 1946. He was the first man to take charge of the Five Fiddles. He won the league title at his first and only attempt before moving on to St Gallen, in Switzerland, and the Dutch side Heerenveen.

Galloway's path was different. Born in Sunderland in 1896, he was sent to the local Ragged and Industrial School – a boarding establishment set up to prevent impoverished children sliding into delinquency – as a teenager. A 1929 profile of him in *Mundo Deportivo* suggests he joined the army when he was just 15, serving in India before being deployed in Ireland. British Army records confirm his military background: he served with the Yorkshire Regiment during World War I. It was while with the army that his sporting prowess came to the fore. *Mundo Deportivo* notes that he 'abandoned soccer and joined an Irish rugby team, winning a championship' before being selected to 'represent the Irish army in athletic contests: he went to London and won both the 100 and 250 yard races'. Only now did he return to football, playing for Derby as a centre forward before signing for Nottingham Forest in 1924, for a club record fee. Catton deemed it a wise investment. 'He has a powerful shot and is just the type of leader to give power to the Forest attack,' he wrote. It was not an especially accurate prediction: Galloway scored just eight goals at the City Ground, before enduring brief, unhappy spells at Luton, Coventry and Tottenham. In 1929, just five years after his big move, he retired. He would spend the next quarter century travelling the world as a manager.

His first engagement came with Sporting Gijon in November 1929. His arrival was seen as quite a coup for the Spanish club. *La Prensa*, the local newspaper, described him as 'one of the most well-regarded players the English First Division has had for the last six years', precisely the sort of experience, they were quite sure, that was 'absolutely necessary to have success ... with a club like Sporting'. Their excitement spoke volumes for the esteem in which Spain held not only the English game at the time but English managers, too. 'His name will, in a short time, have the same prestige as [Fred] Pentland's ... [and that which] other compatriots of his have been offered in our most important clubs.'

Galloway's approach was, for its time, advanced. 'A football team has to have a lot of control of the ball and a lot of speed,' he told *Mundo Deportivo* on his arrival. 'It has to have a lot of movement. Players have to be agile and good jumpers. For that, the Basque sport of *pelota* (a version of squash) is a good form of training. It encourages elasticity in the muscles. I will use the modern English style: there has to be depth in attack, movement in the middle and security in defence. The player has to acquire the maximum speed with the ball at his feet, under control, and also has to understand when to get rid of it, either by shooting or passing to a team-mate.' He wanted to create a 'team of young players', explaining that more experienced footballers were less inclined to learn, and was quick to point out that he was not interested in the old-fashioned blood-and-thunder approach *en vogue* in both England and Spain. 'You call it *furia*,' he said. 'That fury is a great advantage when it is married with the technical and the tactical. You have to know when to employ it and when to contain it.'

He found the balance well enough to remain at Gijon for two seasons, before being given the job at Valencia in 1931: a move that can only be interpreted as a promotion. He would spend another two years there before being replaced by Jack Greenwell. Galloway was some 12 years younger than his successor, but the two men cannot fail to have noticed – in the six seasons they spent together in Spain – that they had been born within 20 miles of each other, Greenwell in Crook and Galloway in Sunderland. In 1933, Galloway took the job at another club with a taste for a *Mister*, signing up for two years at Racing Santander, Pentland's first stop in the country more than a decade previously. It is hard to be sure, but Galloway seems to have left Spain in 1935, though he may have done so reluctantly. In January of that year, after his side drew at Barcelona, he told *Mundo Deportivo* that he was confident Racing would be something of a force the following season. 'We will have a [good] team,' he said. 'They are just starting to play.'

He would not be around to see that happen. After six years away, he returned to England with his wife, Mabel, on the steamship *Cordillera* in July 1935. The couple settled in Nottinghamshire – living in West Bridgford and Mapperley – and Galloway seems to have called time on his managerial career, limiting his involvement in football to coaching local boys' teams throughout the war years. By 1946, thanks to either dwindling finances or wanderlust, he struck out again, taking charge of the Costa Rican national team before moving to Uruguay, where was appointed manager of Peñarol, one of Uruguay's twin titans, in 1948. 'He came with a revolutionary tactical system,' one of his players, a Gutierrez, told *Mundo Deportivo* a few years later. 'He established a new style of play, one that caused real surprise when he first introduced it.' He took charge of a number of the players who would win the World Cup with Uruguay in 1950, including the captain, Obdulio Varela, Juan Schiaffino and the man who scored the winner against Brazil, the goal that made a nation cry, Alcides Ghiggia. He would leave after just a few months, an official history of Peñarol eulogising his desire to modernise the club's methods but suggesting that there was a 'failure to extract the benefits of our own characteristics'. He and Mabel returned home from Buenos Aires in 1949, but Galloway was soon on the move again: he pitched up in Switzerland and then, in 1950, in Portugal. That was where he enjoyed his most sustained period of success – winning those three successive championships with the Five Fiddles that are commemorated, without his name, in Sporting's museum – before moving on to Vitoria Guimaraes in 1954, his final post before returning to Mapperley and retirement.

Galloway's story spans two distinct eras. On his first foray abroad, at the end of his playing career, he went as an adventurer, a maverick, forced to seek his fortune on foreign shores because there was no call for his services at home. His story is a remarkable one, in terms of its length and its breadth, but in many ways he was the typical *Mister* of the first half of the 20th century, cast from the same mould as Bloomer, Pentland, Greenwell, Garbutt and Hogan. He left England of his own accord, helping to spread the wisdom of football's motherland but driven to do so, at least initially, by basic economics.

By the time he retired, though, the days of the mavericks were over: the time of the missionaries had begun. After World War II, the Football Association's training courses began to send more and more coaches out from England, specifically tasked with teaching the rest of the world how to play the game. It was by this mechanism that Bob Kelly – relatively experienced in comparison, given that he had already managed at Carlisle and Stockport – found himself at Sporting. Their primary motivation may have been financial, too, but they were no longer on their own. Indeed, by 1951, the FA believed it had sent more than a hundred coaches out across the world to improve the standard of football in all four corners of the globe. They would have counted Galloway among their success stories: they certainly viewed his appointment at

Peñarol as their doing, and it is likely that they recommended him to Sporting in 1950.

This period of sustained and deliberate evangelism is largely forgotten when the relationship between England and the rest of the footballing world is assessed. England is often accused of wilful ignorance; the stories of Pentland, Hogan and the rest illustrate that, during the first half of the 20th century, the charge stuck. The evidence is damning: quite apart from the refusal to engage with Fifa in the 1920s and the decision not to recognise the World Cup until 1950, there is the fact that all of their warnings – and all of their work – on foreign shores went unnoticed. Occasionally, the FA might have offered a recommendation to a foreign club, but there was no organised attempt to help spread the word of the game. It was a piecemeal process. The verdict is one of damaging isolationism; the sentence, still not entirely served, a loss of prestige and primacy that has never been wholly recovered.

Yet what happened in the immediate aftermath of World War II fundamentally undermines this version of history. In those first few years, the FA began to develop coaches in industrial quantities and send them out into the world to dispense their knowledge. This is not isolationism. If anything, what was at play in those years owed far more to the dogmas of colonialism. The sun may have been setting on the empire, but its thinking lingered. Britain still believed herself to be a cultural power, one capable of exporting expertise, of shining light into the darkness. What it failed to realise was that this process was not a one-way street. The reason England fell behind was not because it stood apart, but because it believed it stood above. As Brian Glanville and Geoffrey Green, those esteemed journalists, suggested, the motherland can be accused of an unwillingness to learn, but it most certainly should not be condemned for a refusal to teach.

*

Walter Winterbottom and Stanley Rous first met in 1936, at the Football Association's first ever coaching course. They had both listened to Jimmy Hogan as he gave a demonstration of the techniques that had helped him turn Austria and Hungary into two of Europe's foremost football nations. Within a decade, they would be the two most powerful men in English football. Together, they would set out to stop the country losing its privileged position at the very summit of the game. In that, they would not only fail, but they would have precisely the opposite effect. With the benefit of hindsight, the plan Winterbottom and Rous set out looks like it may have been the final, accidental nail in England's coffin.

Before Rous was appointed as secretary of the FA, he had been employed as a master at Watford Grammar School. His involvement in football had been as a referee. The two roles, combined, influenced the way he saw the game. As a teacher, he was convinced that all things can be learned, including football: if you were taught how to do something properly, you would do it better. If that logic seems obvious now, it was anathema at the time. In 1936, he had not only arranged that first coaching course, but published a pamphlet entitled *First Steps in Playing Football*, designed to help youngsters hone their techniques.

As a referee, he had been given the chance to travel the world to take charge of games. It had, he claimed in his autobiography, opened his mind. 'I was always on the lookout for new ideas that might improve the game,' he wrote. He was, he said, the man who introduced the arc at the edge of the penalty area to Britain, a feature he had first seen in Italy. History has recorded Rous, at least in part because of his repugnant refusal to expel apartheid South Africa from Fifa's ranks, as the very worst sort of reactionary. In some ways, though, he was far less myopic. 'We cling to the myth that our Football League is the best in the world,' he wrote. 'There are others.'

He had seen enough of the growth of the game abroad to believe that England's traditional resistance to coaching was not only holding the country back but allowing the foreigners to catch her up. By 1946, he had managed to convince the ever-conservative FA that the time was ripe for change. He persuaded the organisation that a national Director of Coaching could institute a programme to ensure the game was properly taught and – on the side – might be able to manage the England team. He turned to Winterbottom.

The two had much in common. Winterbottom, too, had been a teacher, at Carnegie College in Leeds. He had, according to his patron, 'the analytical mind of a detached observer and the practical experience to translate that into tactical or coaching methods'. He was convinced that the key to success, at whatever age, was in technical training. He would spend three years writing his guide to the game – the book, *Soccer Coaching*, was described by the *Daily Mirror* on its release as 'the solution to England's soccer future' – and he would travel across the country, visiting schools and clubs and trying to showcase his methods. He had a weakness for jargon, talking of 'peripheral vision' and 'skill acquisition and its environmental application', but if his delivery was imperfect, it is hard to argue with the content of his message. He believed the game could be taught. Rous made it his protégé's job to teach the teachers.

There were some 300 prospective coaches at the first course in 1947, a turnout that suggests an organic change of perspective within English football. That, perhaps, is testament to the effect of the war: not only had clubs seen their ranks decimated by injury and death to a whole generation of young men and their finances ruined by years without gate receipts, leaving them reliant on home-grown youth teamers, but a host of players had spent much of the previous decade working as physical trainers with the army, rearing teams for their regiments. That billet had saved their lives, but it had also given them an insight into the benefits of coaching they might otherwise have been denied. Hundreds more would attend the summer sessions at Bisham Abbey, Lilleshall, Carnegie, Loughborough College and Birmingham University in the coming years. What Rous and Winterbottom hoped to achieve was a steady supply of coaches capable not just of nurturing young players in schools, but making sure their learning did not stop when they reached the professional ranks. They wanted an end to the tyranny of stamina and speed, to encourage a more refined, technical style. Rous, in particular, had seen the direction the European game was taking, and he was keen not to see England left behind.

Although some of Winterbottom's pupils would go on to become household names in their homeland, helping to combat the age-old prejudice against coaching, a considerable proportion ended up venturing further afield. The overwhelming majority left so that they might return, hoping to cut their teeth on the continent and impress prospective employers at home. Most managed only the first part. What Winterbottom had failed to take into account was just how resistant the Football League would be to the idea of change.

Certainly, just as Coley had failed to notice the obvious development of the game on foreign shores, so most Football League clubs were oblivious to the potential benefits of proper coaching. Stan Cullis, the Wolverhampton Wanderers manager, referred darkly to 'funny ideas' taking hold at a time when – as the journalist Barney Ronay has put it – 'any idea was a funny idea'; Tommy Lawton, the England striker, reportedly told Winterbottom his tactical instructions were mere 'guff' during one tempestuous team talk. Winterbottom had become convinced, after the embarassment of the 1950 World Cup, that 'the time for building teams had surely arrived'. At his behest, the FA published a memorandum asking for more help from clubs, demanding that international players be released more frequently to help the national side develop more of an understanding. How successful that request was can be gauged from the fact that, half a century on, the same complaint still echoes. As Brian Glanville wrote at the end of the 1950s: 'The league system, that ever waxing monster, was sufficient unto itself. There and only there was the testing ground.'

Abroad, though, things were quite different. It was not just the FA who had noted how effective the likes of Pentland, Greenwell and Hogan had been. Across Europe, into South America and the Middle East, English coaches were in tremendous demand as clubs sought emissaries of the mother country. Even after 1950, when Winterbottom's side exited the Brazil World Cup at the group stage, cheeks blushing and tails between their legs, it was widely assumed that England represented football's gold standard; that the inventors of the game were its masters, too.

Still, nobody abroad appears to have noticed that the coaches being sent out from England were not wanted in their homeland. In the years after the war, foreign clubs regularly wrote to the FA informing them of available coaching positions. The jobs were then advertised in the *FA News*, the organisation's quarterly newsletter, for candidates to consider.

Some were more attractive than others. In the November 1955 edition, a club in Eastern Province, South Africa, wrote that they were 'considering the employment of a professional coach, from May to July, 1956'. Return sea passage, accommodation and a monthly allowance of £20 were all factored in, but if that was not enticement enough, they were keen to point out 'the coach will be required to work in the afternoons, but could find employment in the morning if he so wishes'. The advert finishes by informing candidates 'the engagement is virtually three months' paid holiday'.

Olympique Marseille were a tad more demanding; their 1952 advert reads a little like the lonely hearts entry of a footloose divorcee. 'A good man required,' the French club wrote. 'Single if possible, with some knowledge of the French language.' Galatasaray were just as picky. 'The club would prefer to engage a bachelor under the age of 40 years.' Given Turkish football's intensity, then as now, presumably GSOH was a must.

The Istanbul club would, however, make it worth the lucky applicant's while, stipulating a stipend of £100 a month; a manager willing to move slightly further afield, to Guatemala, could pick up £75, with his assistant paid £60, both of which sums would be increased by as much as 30 per cent if they stayed in Central America for three years. With such lucrative rewards on offer, it was no surprise that many decided to chance their arm away from home, where the maximum playing wage was, in 1953, just £15 a week. These jobs were a nice way of filling the family purse and, with any luck, proving your credentials to a Football League club into the bargain.

Editions of the *FA News* from those years record countless appointments: Pat Molloy taking the job at Galatasaray in 1947; Michael Keeping going to Real Madrid in January 1948; a D.R. Darling going to Brazil; and an F.R. Limpenny heading to Argentina. Denis Neville and Ron Meades made it to India; Johnny Hancocks to Austria; Frank Hill ended up in Iraq. In the course of just a few years, the FA sent coaches to Kuwait and Nigeria, Iceland and Chile, and in a great flood to every corner of Europe.

Rous and Winterbottom were central to all of this. Both men took an active role in alerting their students to potential vacancies and recommending certain pupils to those clubs that sought the FA's opinion on their appointments. As he had with Alan Rogers, advising him to accept a post in the Philippines, Winterbottom regularly took coaches aside and suggested that a posting abroad might be a quicker way of earning a living than waiting for the Football League's reactionary chairmen to open their eyes and minds. Rous fielded many of the enquiries from abroad. He was quick to point them in the direction of the coaches who had attracted his attention. The two most senior figures at the FA were anything but isolationists, regardless of their original intention. Through their work, hundreds of British coaches found themselves in foreign fields, and hundreds of clubs and national teams found their development stimulated by British ideas. Many of those men irrevocably shaped the game in the post-war years. Rous and Winterbottom set out to help Britain stay ahead of the rest of the world. They ended up having precisely the opposite effect. They did more than most to speed up the chase.

No country benefited more from the work Rous and Winterbottom were doing – as well as the insularity of the Football League – than Italy. The adverts might have flooded in from all over the globe, but the money available in Serie A made the Mediterranean a particularly enticing destination. In the immediate aftermath of World War II, Italy became a prodigious importer of English managers. Almost all of them, as Brian Glanville noted, came with a recommendation from either Rous or Winterbottom. Italian club football would become the strongest in Europe, arguably, because of what these men had learned on the fields of Lilleshall and Carnegie.

There is no more tragic case than that of Leslie Lievesley, the man whose name is inscribed on the monument to commemorate the victims of the Superga air disaster. It was there, on a hill outside Turin, that an Italian Airlines flight carrying the entire Torino team crashed on 4 May 1949. Much as the Munich tragedy would in England nine years later, it devastated the country. Torino were by some distance the best side in Italy at the time. They boasted 10 of the 11 members of the Italian national side. They would have had a claim to be one of the finest sides in Europe. All of their players died, along with five club officials and three journalists. The Italian parliament was suspended. Half a million people attended their funerals. Some 30,000 made a pilgrimage to Superga to pay their respects.

Lievesley was on the flight. Before World War II, he had played for Manchester United – as well as Doncaster Rovers, Chesterfield, Torquay and Crystal Palace – and he had gone to Italy to launch his career in management after the war. He had been appointed by Torino as a youth coach in 1947, but had soon been promoted to first-team duties by the club's manager, the Hungarian Erno Egri Erbstein, who had been impressed by what his biographer, Dominic Bliss, describes as the Englishman's 'disciplined approach and sergeant major demeanour'. Lievesley's speciality was in conditioning, and he fitted perfectly into Erbstein's high-octane approach. He soon settled in the city – joined by his wife, Harriet, in their apartment on Via Moretta and regularly accompanied to training by his son, Bill – and was well regarded, too: he was credited with not simply imposing English training techniques, but adapting his approach so that it was rather better suited to his Italian players, something which a number of his countrymen struggled to do. His engagement with Torino was due to end three weeks after he got on the plane. He was about to be appointed manager of their city rivals, Juventus. He might have gone on to achieve enormous fame and fortune. His journey ended prematurely in the fog at Superga.

In his stead, Juventus' plutocrat backers, the Agnelli family, decided to appoint another Englishman. In 1949, Jesse Carver arrived in Turin. Reading Glanville's account of this 'small, rubicund man who had clearly taken pains to lose his Liverpool accent, which might now be described as semi-genteel', Carver does not emerge as a particularly likeable character.

To Glanville, he was 'closed and complex', unwilling to talk to the press or form a close relationship. Other English coaches in Italy at the time got the same impression. 'I remember him best tightly and symbolically buttoned and belted into his fawn raincoat,' he would write. 'The man himself was buttoned up and closed. His smile was always knowing, rather than amiable.' He was boastful, claiming that a great number of high-class players owed him their careers, leaving Glanville to wonder whether there could 'possibly be so many'. And he was restless, too: after spending two years at Juventus, he would have eight jobs in the course of the following decade – six in Italy, two in England, before seeing out his career in Cyprus – not because of his limitations as a coach but because he was aware of just how good he was. As Glanville put it, Carver was 'forever changing horses', always looking out for a better, more lucrative deal. Apart from Juventus, he never spent more than a season at a club. There were rumours, as well, that he would dispatch his wife to Switzerland with a stash of brown envelopes. Glanville – taking pains not to libel him – admits nobody knew what was contained within them, but it does not take a great detective to work out what he is implying. Carver was in it for the money.

Without question, though, he was a good coach, one far in advance of his time. He worked his players hard, according to the Danish international, John Hansen, but he did not simply let them run. He introduced loosening exercises, encouraging his players to 'walk up and down, vigorously swinging their arms in a way that would have invited scorn at English clubs at the time'. Glanville suggested that he used to practise these on his wife first, to make sure they worked. As with all of those coaches who emerged from the Winterbottom school, he concentrated on ball-work, too, honing his charges' technique, fervently believing that football could be taught and it could always be improved: 'If you don't get the feeling of what you play with, how are you going to command the ball?'

His first appointment abroad had been with the Rotterdam club Xerxes, in 1946. Holland, then, was still recovering from the devastation of Nazi occupation: the house Carver and his wife were given was ravaged by damp, having been unoccupied for years, and players regularly showed up at their door searching for food. They had to make do with a single bar of soap between them every month. Carver endured. His methods were sufficiently successful to take Xerxes to the top of the league and to attract the attention of the Royal Netherlands Football Association, who hired him as manager of the Dutch national side, and Millwall, who appointed him as a coach in 1948. A role with the England B team on their tour of Holland and Finland in 1949 followed, and a permanent post with the FA seemed a possibility. Presumably, the offer from Juventus was just too lucrative to turn down.

Carver won the title in Turin but left after criticising the club's directors in an interview with *Gazzetta dello Sport*. He returned home, for a posting with West Bromwich Albion – where he would be succeeded by another coach who would have an enormous impact on the game, Vic Buckingham – but did not stay long. Carver, like so many, was desperate to prove his credentials in England, but it would be fair to say that was not his highest priority. When Torino sent an emissary three times to try to coax him back to Italy, on each occasion offering an even bigger pay hike, he packed his bags again. By 1954, when he moved to Roma, he was reported to be earning £5,000 a year; Matt Busby, by contrast, was earning around £3,250 a year at the same point. That money enabled him to take an apartment in one of Rome's most exclusive streets, living among both actual and Hollywood royalty.

However, the best example of Carver's approach to his managerial career dates from the end of 1955. He had been at Coventry for just a few months – once again, given a chance to prove himself in the Football League, albeit only in the Third Division – and had generated considerable excitement at the club. He had won the players over by producing the ball on the first day of pre-season training, an unaccustomed treat, and they were pushing for promotion. Carver left. He had two offers from Italy. He flew to Rome to be greeted by officials from Lazio, who believed they had secured his services, only to travel straight to Milan to sign for Internazionale. After a spell at Genoa, Lazio would eventually get their man in 1961. Loyalty does not seem to have been his strong suit.

For all the jobs, though, all of the new contracts and all of the pay packets, Carver only ever won one Italian title – the one he picked up at the first attempt, with Juventus, back in the 1949-50 season. That honour sealed his reputation. It ensured he would never be short of work and never be short of cash. According to Glanville, it may even have been enough to get him the job he wanted more than any other: in 1955, Rous reportedly travelled to Rome to offer him the chance to become England manager, explaining that 'it was time Walter [Winterbottom] was brought into the office'. It never came to pass. Carver's career would be one of gold so abundant that it obscured his pursuit of silver.

Not every English coach who travelled abroad found the experience as rewarding as Carver had. Ted Crawford was a 'tall, gaunt, forthright' Yorkshireman, one Glanville seems to have liked much better on a personal level than Carver. He had played for Halifax, Liverpool and Clapton Orient – spending the last six years of his career with an undiagnosed broken ankle – before embarking on a coaching career, initially in Sweden with

Degerfors and then, in 1949, moving to Bologna. Crawford was unable to save the club from relegation to Serie B and took up another post at Livorno, but could not prevent them sliding from the second to the third tier. He was sacked but remained in the port, waiting for his contract to be paid up. Glanville went to see him there, walking along the promenade with Crawford and his infant son. He was, he wrote, 'bitterly disenchanted' after his time in Italy, thanks both to the prevalence of match-fixing on the pitch – he recalled 'roaring with laughter' during one game as his players grew ever more desperate in their attempts to concede an equaliser – and to the broken promises off it. Livorno had vowed to find him and his family a suitable home. The one they were given upon their arrival, he told Glanville, was 'shit'.

However they fared, though, one thing remained constant: the vast majority went ignored by the clubs of the Football League. In Carver's case, perhaps that was to some extent his fault. He prioritised his pension pot above his *palmares*. Crawford, in truth, never had any great success, although Glanville clearly esteemed him as a coach. He wrote of his time at AEK Athens that Crawford gave 'practical, tactical lessons ... [that were] absorbing and effective'. During training sessions, 'he stationed them around the field in various situations and asked them what they thought they should do'. A brief spell at Barnet and a coaching post at Crewe Alexandra apart, English clubs were not interested, even with that heartfelt recommendation. His time abroad did not count in the Football League, which remained steadfastly content unto itself. He would, according to his friend Glanville, forever remain 'a prophet without honour, who would spend his last working years as a disillusioned store-man'.

More egregious still was the fate of another manager Glanville held in high esteem, another who eventually succumbed to the 'lure of the lira'. There is no story that better encapsulates how all of English football's failings conspired not just to help the world change but to ensure that England did not change along with it. Carver might have blown his big chance because of his greed. Crawford may not have had the CV to earn a job at home. That England somehow contrived to overlook George Raynor, on the other hand, is entirely damning.

7

The Apple at the Top of the Tree

The first edition of *Football Ambassador at Large* is a study in simplicity. It is a slim book, only a little more than 130 pages. Its cover is sea green, unadorned by illustration, save for the gilt outline of a footballer in the bottom right corner. The ball is at his feet, his shirt neatly tucked into baggy shorts. His sleeves are rolled up, his hair a neat, Brylcreem Boy side-parting, his left hip ever so slightly lowered, as though he is about to jink past an opponent. It is almost as if it was designed to be anonymous, to ensure it did not stand out on the shelves. Inside, it is a different story. Inside, it is a book of seismic significance, as important now as it was when it was first published more than half a century ago.

Football Ambassador at Large is George Raynor's autobiography. It tells the story of how a miner's son from South Yorkshire turned Sweden, one of the world's footballing backwaters, into Olympic champions, the 'number one team in Europe' and, then, the crowning glory, World Cup finalists. It details how an unremarkable player, who plied his trade at places like Bury and Aldershot, could eventually lay claim to being the most successful international manager England ever produced.

It is, though, far more than that. Raynor wrote it – with the help of his ghost, the journalist and commentator Kenneth Wolstenholme – in 1960, two years after he had seen his Sweden side beaten to football's greatest prize only by the brilliance of Pele, Garrincha and Vava. He was, at that point, living in Skegness, coaching the local side in the Midland League and applying for jobs as a storeman at Butlin's, the holiday camp. He was happy with his life and he was enjoying his work, but he was frustrated by the fact that he felt he had plenty more to offer football but no opportunity to do so.

That is why his account of his life and career reads, in turn, like an exercise in self-justification, a blueprint for the future and, most of all, like a sales pitch. By publishing the book, he doubtless hoped to raise his profile in his homeland, to alert people to his achievements, and to entice someone – either in the Football League or, better yet, within the Football Association to bring him into the fold. In case anyone was not clear on his underlying intentions, he included chapters on 'Where Britain fails' and 'Britain's future'. These served as Raynor's explanations for where the England team had gone wrong and how it would be put right, ideally by a man with extensive international experience in, for example, a Scandinavian nation. The bulk of the book, his life story, serves as little more than an extended CV.

Raynor's gambit did not work. England had always been deaf to the warnings of those coaches who had worked abroad and blind to their achievements. His sustained assault on her presumed supremacy was not pitched at a sympathetic audience. As he himself admitted, criticising those still in power for their shortsightedness was not a particularly judicious move. If anything, the book achieved the exact opposite of what he had hoped: it ensured he became, if he was not already, persona non grata with the power brokers of the English game. He would have to wait seven

years before a Football League job came up and even then it was
with Doncaster Rovers, in the bottom tier. He would never get the
chance to implement the changes he felt could help make England
an elite force in the modern game.

That is the most obvious significance of *Football Ambassador at Large*. It stands as printed testament to a phenomenon we
have seen before: just how little England wanted to listen. The
improving performances of the continental teams and then the
South Americans did not alert the homeland to how precarious
her perceived place at the summit of the game was. The dire warnings of those coaches, like Fred Pentland and Jimmy Hogan, who
had done so much to help the foreigners catch up went unheeded,
too. That would have been bad enough, but England compounded
those two errors still further.

Presented with a coach who had enjoyed some very obvious
and very recent success abroad and who was more than eager
to pass all that he had learned on to his homeland, it consigned
him to obscurity. Raynor's book was his last desperate plea to be
noticed in the place he most wanted to be noticed, and the place
that he believed most needed to notice him. England's fall from
grace was rooted in twin failures: not only did it send out its best
and brightest to help foreigners improve, it compounded its error
by failing to use the assets it had itself produced.

If that is the most obvious lesson to be learned from the story
told by *Football Ambassador at Large*, there is another docu-
mented inside that simple green cover. Raynor's book is not just
evidence that England failed to exploit a resource it had created,
another staging post on the country's inexorable decline. It does
something else: it provides an explanation as to why it happened,
why its crown slipped, why it did not listen.

One of Raynor's deepest convictions about why English
football was falling behind was summed up in his most eloquent

phrase, referenced at the start of this book. 'Bulldozers,' he wrote, with the assistance of Wolstenholme, 'have become more important than craftsmen.' He was talking, of course, about the tendency of Football League clubs to prioritise physicality, speed and strength and stamina, over skill. He felt that balance needed to be redressed if England was to be able to compete on a technical level with teams in Europe and South America.

The same assessment, it is fair to say, could easily have been applied to managers. Raynor was a gentle man, not inclined to scream and shout at his players. He wanted to guide his charges to becoming better players, not to browbeat and intimidate them into winning matches. Much the same could be said for many of the *Misters*, the men who went abroad. Whatever type of football they preached, they tended to be genial sorts. Pentland was enormously popular with his players. William Garbutt, the 'amiable man with the white hair and the pipe between his teeth', was the same. Hogan called himself a professor, not a sergeant major. Like Raynor, they perceived themselves as craftsmen, their task to mould something from the raw material they were given. The problem was – and is – that English football has always been a place for bulldozers.

Sweden was not impressed with George Raynor, not at the start. When the country's football authorities were looking for a national team coach in 1946, they had done what so many others did and written to the well-connected secretary of the Football Association, Stanley Rous, looking for a recommendation. It was Rous who had, earlier that year, sent 15 coaches out to Scandinavia to help develop the game at a local level. They had done well. It was only natural to seek his advice on who should take charge of the country's side. The name he produced, as Rous acknowledged, was 'something of a surprise'.

The Swedes, doubtless, had been expecting to be sent a famous face, the sort of figure who could galvanise an entire nation. Instead, Rous suggested Raynor, who had hardly enjoyed a stellar playing career: he knew he was 'one of the many, one of the also-rans'. He had spent a year at Sheffield United, another season at Mansfield, before moving on to Rotherham, Bury and Aldershot. Like Pentland and Garbutt before him, he was an outside right, but one of scant reputation and little recognition.

Nevertheless, Rous had been impressed with the work he had done with the army during the war. Like a host of professional players, Raynor spent the first two years of the conflict working as a physical education instructor at Aldershot, turning out as a guest for various teams in London and the Southeast in the local-ised war leagues. Those games had, at last, given him the chance to play alongside some genuine stars: Cliff Bastin, Jimmy Hagan, Stanley Matthews. In 1941, he had been dispatched with the 9th Army to Iraq. They were sent to put down a rebellion that never came and remained as occupation troops. Raynor found himself in Basra and then Baghdad, where he was deputed to take charge of physical training and sport. His most important task was to pick a representative Iraqi side for a tour of the Arab world. His team would lose twice in Beirut before travelling to Damascus, where they won once, lost once and saw a decider abandoned after a riot that ended with one player being shot. The tour was clearly deemed a success: when he returned to London, he did so with two hearty letters of recommendation, including one from the prime minister of Iraq. Rous, suitably convinced, promised to help him find work. He was sure men like him would be needed to help 'rebuild English football' as the country returned to normality.

He was wrong. 'Coaches,' Raynor wrote, 'were [still] regarded as cranks who would soon fade away from the scene so the game could continue.' Raynor found himself in charge of Aldershot's reserve side. It was a deeply frustrating posting: he was convinced of the need for organised coaching, and he had developed a host of 'ideas and principles' for the game that he wanted to pass on. Nobody was listening, not at home, and when Rous first contacted him about the Sweden job, he was hardly enthused. He vacillated over the offer. He wanted to work in England; he was not keen to travel again so soon after the war. He wrote to a number of county associations asking if there might be any interest in his services. The answer was a uniform no: proof, he wrote, 'of the head in the sand attitude that has put the brakes on British football for so long'. Eventually, he decided he had no choice, though the fact he only signed a six-month contract is a measure of how wary he was about taking the position.

He arrived with a glowing reference from Rous, benefactor to him and so many of his peers. The FA's coaching courses had taught the organisation's secretary that 'the best players are not always the best instructors', as he wrote in his autobiography, *Football Worlds*. Rous 'was well aware how dedicated and intelligent a coach George had made himself'. His new employers, though, were cautious. The country's press were not entirely convinced by his appointment. When Birmingham City arrived on tour in 1946, the Swedes were keen 'to show off their new coach'. The fact that none of the visiting players had even heard of Raynor set alarm bells ringing. Putte Kock, the chair of the Swedish FA's selection committee, wondered if Rous had fobbed him off with a nonentity.

Those doubts were assuaged, just a little, when an RAF team came to play in Stockholm later that year. The side boasted both Matthews and George Hardwick, veterans of the same wartime teams as Raynor. That their new manager knew two such important figures in the game helped convince a sceptical press of Raynor's standing; so, too, did his canny decision to allow journalists to attend his early training sessions and team meetings with Sweden's players.

Still, he was well aware of the pressure weighing down on him as he prepared for his second game. Sweden were due to play Switzerland in Stockholm in July 1946. The visitors were managed by Karl Rappan, a visionary himself, the man who had invented the 'Swiss bolt'. This was a resolutely defensive system, relying on both fullbacks playing centrally, and one that would serve as inspiration to Nereo Rocco, the Italian coach who pioneered what would become known as *catenaccio*. Switzerland were seen as one of the world's most obdurate teams. Raynor would have to find a way past them if he was to have a hope of remaining in Sweden for any length of time.

As his biographer, Ashley Hyne, suggests, how he managed it provides the perfect illustration of Raynor's ingenuity. 'Here he was,' Hyne writes in *The Greatest Coach England Never Had*, 'facing a challenge set by one of Europe's foremost football academics and cleverly discarding convention to meet it.' Rappan's system left his team exposed on the left flank, because the fullback played inside; Raynor instructed his forward line to overload that area, remaining high up the pitch, pushing the Swiss back. To ensure they were not isolated, he deployed Bertil Nordahl as what he called a 'G-Man'. His job was to collect the ball from the centre halves and ferry it to the forwards. That may seem uninspired now, with the benefit of hindsight – he was a playmaking midfielder, essentially – but it counted as positively revolutionary in 1946, when positions were so heavily prescribed and football so enslaved by an ancient orthodoxy.

The effect was spectacular: Nordahl ran the game, Sweden won 7-2, an almost unthinkably emphatic scoreline against a side as resolute as the Swiss. Even England, after all, had only managed to put four past Rappan's team that year. 'That victory,' Raynor wrote, 'made me.' One result swept away all the doubts over whether Rous had sent Sweden the right man. When the FA chairman appeared in Stockholm later that year, he described Raynor as one of the 'best coaches in the world', and nobody in Scandinavia was about to contradict him.

For all that Raynor deserves immense praise for his innovation – not to mention his courage in trying out something so unusual in a game of such significance – even he did not pretend it was his invention. It was, instead, something he had picked up from his own playing career. The role had been pioneered by Norman Bullock, as both a player and a manager at Bury, where he worked with Raynor in the 1930s. The G-Man was, as Hyne notes, the forerunner of the deep-lying centre forward, the role Nandor Hidegkuti would use to such devastating effect for Hungary at Wembley in 1953.

That it was in use at Gigg Lane before World War II challenges how that game has long been interpreted: that the Hungarians, influenced by Jimmy Hogan, had developed something England had never seen before. What they had done, in fact, was adopt a system that England had somehow managed to forget. As Raynor wrote, the G-Man was 'regularly used in English football before the war'. It even featured in *Association Football*, a tactical guide published in 1937, along with a diagram of something called the 'double centre forward plan', a spiritual predecessor of what would become 4-4-2.

In the 1930s, in other words, England was refining and adapting how it saw football. For the first time, the game was not just changing, but being allowed to change. Conventions were being challenged, new systems being tested. The previous decade, Peter McWilliam – spiritual antecedent of Arthur Rowe at Tottenham – had popularised the 'Scottish game', the idea of pass-and-move. Across north London, at Arsenal, Herbert Chapman was deploying his third-back system. Lower down the food chain, there were men like Bullock. The orthodoxy of the WM formation, the uncontested idea that there was a single way to play football, was at last under threat.

And then, all of a sudden, it seems to have stopped. It was almost as though someone simply pressed a reset button. Minds, once open, shut down. By the time Raynor was embarking on his coaching career, these advancements had been forgotten.

The temptation is to suggest that this is another side to the 'resistance to change' identified by Bob Ferrier, but the reality is a little different. There can be no question that both world wars hindered the growth of English football. First and foremost, of course, they served to ensure the administration of the game was the preserve of a pensionable class. They remained in power far longer than they might have done had the Great War not occurred, had it not cost so very many lives. When the Football League restarted in 1919, it had no choice but to turn to the people who had been in charge previously. They stood by what had worked for them in the past. That meant, as we have seen, that coaching remained all but taboo.

What happened after World War II is slightly more complicated. Those years of sky-high attendances and thrilling, attacking football are widely seen as some of the most glorious in history. But that golden age may have come at a cost.

The Football League had been cancelled during the war. In its place, special local leagues – those Raynor played in while at Aldershot – were organised to provide the weary public with entertainment. They were expected to give the people relief from their suffering, and that meant all-out attack. Tactics, as Nat Lofthouse once remarked, were not 'what the people wanted'. Anything that compromised the spectacle was rejected. In the years that followed, that attitude lingered. The offensive was fetishised and the defensive demonised. Correlation was taken for causation. Thus, as attendances boomed, it was assumed that dispensing with anything thoughtful, anything patient, was simply meeting popular demand. Yet what may have seemed to be fans responding to the attacking mentality, a more studied interpretation would have taken for a sociological phenomenon, a populace responding to the austerity and suffering of the war years by indulging enthusiastically in the pursuit of pleasure.

The consequence was significant. The teams of the Football League eschewed all of the new ideas that had started to bloom in the 1930s in favour of the spectacle. There were isolated exceptions: in 1954, Manchester City had adopted what was known as the 'Revie Plan', where Don Revie played as a deep-lying centre forward in the style of Nandor Hidegkuti; a few years later, according to Bob Ferrier, they dallied with a system deploying two centre backs, too. At Leicester, first Norman Bullock and then Matt Gillies started to push boundaries. Gillies, a Scot signed as a player by Bullock, was one of the first managers to practise set pieces in training. In an era when players were hidebound to the position associated with their numbers, he regularly switched Frank McLintock and Graham Cross – the right half and inside right – in the middle of games. 'It confused the opposition,' Gillies said. 'Players had not got beyond thinking about numbers then.' At Tottenham and West Bromwich Albion, meanwhile, Arthur Rowe and Vic Buckingham preached the virtues of push-and-run. The vast majority, though, stuck to the tried and trusted. Ferrier believed that was because of the fear induced by the need to win games and the refusal to accept a period of adaptation. 'Far too many try an idea but drop it too quickly because it does not bring immediate results,' he wrote.

On the continent, it was a different matter. The most simplistic analysis of why the foreign game continued to develop would be to say that those nations had an advantage over Britain because they neither had to pause for the wars, nor deal with the loss of almost an entire generation. But that does not stand up to scrutiny. It is true that in Spain and South America, there was no reason to stop playing between 1939 and 1945 – although, as the story of Jack Greenwell alone highlights, that is not to say there was not an effect – but France, Germany, Italy and the rest of continental Europe all suffered just as much, if not more, than Britain during those years. The explanation must be something else, something psychological. Europe approached the game differently: in the absence of an overarching theory as to how it should be played, there was investigation into the many and varied ways as to how it might be. They were open to new ideas, new systems. They had come to the game as students. They were used to the idea of learning. While England stood still and fell back, in those years after the war, as Europe recovered, it picked up where it had left off. And for much of that first decade, before the Hungarians came to prominence, there can be no question: the continent's rising force was Sweden.

Raynor's team went from strength to strength after that G-man inspired victory against Switzerland. He had been rewarded for his impressive start with a two-year contract and tasked with preparing a side that might do well in the 1948 London Olympics. His priority was to address what he felt was the overriding weakness in Swedish football: its lack of bite. 'There seemed to be no hard tacklers,' he wrote. He was delighted by the technical ability of the players he had at his disposal, as well as by their 'thirst for knowledge', their desire to improve, but he knew that without someone to win the ball, their more refined characteristics would count for nothing. Raynor was no fundamentalist. 'To win at football, you must be effective,' he wrote. 'It is all very well to be masters of ball control and accurate passers ... [but] without punch you will get nowhere.' He might have regarded kick-and-rush as 'the greatest sin of the lot' – 'it is not football to boot the ball as hard as you can and run after it' – and he might have been determined not to 'make a fetish out of physical strength', but he demanded his team marry their taste for the short-passing game with a little more directness. 'The clever team,' he said, 'is the one that mixes the short with the long.' Raynor found in Sweden a nation of abundant precision. He was there to add the one ingredient that had always stood England in good stead in her meetings with continental sides: a little power.

That was the characteristic that Bertil Nordahl had provided in the game against Switzerland, and Raynor set about inculcating all of Sweden's players in his philosophy. It was still, then, a resolutely amateur place, so to ensure he had enough time to get his ideas across, he spent weeks and months embedded with clubs the length and breadth of the country, training prospective internationals in what he wanted. That he had a talented crop available to him is not in doubt, but even the very best of his players required a little work. Gunnar Gren, for example, a third of the fabled Gre-No-Li strike force that would soon grace AC Milan, was deemed too self-indulgent. Raynor told him 'not to overdo the tricky stuff' and, after some early resistance, found him a more than willing pupil.

By the time he took his team to London in November 1947 to face England, he felt they were shaping up nicely. He did not expect to win a game against one of the strongest sides his homeland had ever produced – England, of course, were professionals, the Swedes simply gifted amateurs – but he knew it would provide a watermark for their development. Raynor's team lost 4-2, though the scoreline flattered the English, the result only made safe thanks to a late strike on the counterattack from Stan Mortensen. Even

Billy Wright, the England captain, admitted the visitors had given the hosts the runaround in the second half. 'We lost,' Raynor said, 'but we learned.'

Nine months later, they would prove just how much. He prepared his team for the London Olympics by arranging three training camps – in April, May and then again in early July, before they set sail from Gothenburg – and based his own sessions on 'gymnastics and ball practice'. To ensure his team could compete physically, he had them train with some of the country's athletes. He held games in which players were deployed out of position to find the best mix of their talents. When they arrived at their base for the Games in Richmond Park, they were ready. The Swedes eased past Korea, Austria and Denmark in the qualifying rounds before confronting Yugoslavia in the final. Studiously humble, he was confident enough to have a set of commemorative shirts made up and left, with a case of celebratory champagne, in the Swedish dressing room. With good reason, too: his team won 3-1. Less than two years after taking the job, he had won an Olympic gold.

What was happening behind the scenes at that tournament makes his achievement all the more impressive. Sweden's amateur ethos made them ready prey for the magpie eyes and grasping hands of Europe's professional clubs. Raynor had been forced to spend an inordinate amount of time staving off the predations of Italian clubs, eager to sign his stars, the likes of Gren, Bertil and Gunnar Nordahl and Nils Liedholm. Before the semi-final with Denmark, he had to throw two AC Milan representatives out of the team's dressing room. He was offered first £500 and then £1,000 if he could 'persuade' any of his players to move to Italy. He refused on both occasions; when he was sent a telegram asking if he could recommend two inside forwards, he responded with the names of the England stars, David Jack and Alex James. He was, though, fighting back the tide. By 1949, most of Sweden's crown jewels had been ferried to Serie A, the lure of the lira proving too much. The Swedish FA's rules prevented them from playing for their country again. He would have to go to the 1950 World Cup with an almost entirely new side.

He responded by instituting what must, to someone who believed so fervently in the power of coaching, have been the project of a lifetime. He helped to establish coaching courses for schoolteachers to ensure young players received what he felt was the right sort of education. He turned, too, to a programme that became known as 'Stars of the Future'. Using his contacts across the country, he asked local associations to recommend promising players. From the many hundreds of names suggested, he drew around 30 hopefuls together every year, giving them a one-week crash course in technique, tactics, approach to the game and sportsmanship. Those lessons were reinforced by a booklet documenting his '18 commandments of football', which they took home. They ranged from 'when not in possession, get in position' to 'don't be a slave to the orthodox'. His final line asked players to 'aim for the apple at the top of the tree'. These were his guiding principles, the things he needed the replacements for Gren, Liedholm and the rest to understand if he was to build on his success in London.

Such forward thinking ensured an almost seamless transition. In May 1949, Sweden played England in Stockholm. They were 3-0 up at half-time. They beat the Irish in Dublin – rather more of a scalp then than it is now – to confirm their place at the World Cup. Once again, his meticulousness would stand him and his team in good stead in Brazil. Early in 1950, he gathered some 40 players together for a training camp to help choose his World Cup squad. He encouraged them to share their knowledge, to discuss tactics and talk about players they had faced abroad for their club sides. He had a shipment of South American footballs sent to Stockholm, plus 50 pairs of 'featherweight boots'. The grass on their training pitches was cut short, so as to mimic the likely conditions they would find on the other side of the Atlantic. The Swedish FA got in touch with the 'Brazilian office of a famous Swedish firm' to find out about the food, the climate and for advice on a suitable base in the country: Raynor wanted it 'out of town, with plenty of fresh air'.

They would end up on the slopes of Corcovado in Rio de Janeiro, the hill crowned with the statue of Christ the Redeemer. He ran his players up and down the hill as part of their fitness regime, because 'braking in football is as important as acceleration'. This, it is fair to say, was not an exercise his squad enjoyed. They did their technical and tactical work at Fluminense, the oldest and most aristocratic of Brazilian clubs. He tried to make the sessions as light-hearted as possible, 'disguising the drudgery part of training so that everyone enjoyed themselves', with such success that a phalanx of Brazilian journalists, as well as the Spanish and Yugoslav playing squads, came to watch. Each player had a bespoke schedule; some were given vitamin C injections. He asked them to play a more patient style to help them cope with the humidity: there was to be no 'crash and bash'. After their early games, he decided they should not wear shin pads, as they were deemed to be 'unnecessary weight'.

The highest compliment that can be paid to Raynor is that such attention to detail is now typical in elite football. In 1950, it was unusual. In England, it was unheard of: their approach to the tournament, as Raynor himself wrote, was 'pansy' by comparison. The England squad stayed on the beach at Copacabana, in an area that was simultaneously far too noisy to be peaceful and far too dangerous to be relaxing. They found the food too rich, too oily. Still, at least they would not be there for long.

Sweden, by contrast, sailed through their opening group – drawing with Paraguay and, to their immense satisfaction, beating Italy, the country that had deprived them of so many of their best players – and into the final pool. There, they were narrowly beaten by Uruguay, the eventual winners, and humiliated by Brazil, the hosts, but managed to beat Spain to secure third place. Their record of two wins from five might not have been stellar, but in Sweden it was seen as a triumph. This was an amateur side, one stripped to the bones two years previously. Now, as Raynor wrote, they could rightly claim to be 'the number one side in Europe'.

That would prove to be the high point of his first spell in charge of Sweden. His success was a double-edged sword: everything he achieved brought with it the increased risk of seeing yet more players enticed away by professional clubs. After Brazil, he lost no fewer than ten of his team, including the winger Nacka Skoglund, the standard-bearer of the Stars of the Future courses, enticed to Italy by Internazionale. Once again, Raynor had to 'start again at the bottom'.

He managed to do that for the 1952 Olympics. Sweden, their well of young talent not yet dry, took the bronze medal in Helsinki: no little consolation prize, of course, but not quite as much as Raynor felt they might have achieved had they been given just a little dash of good luck in the draw. The Swedes could have faced West Germany or Yugoslavia in the semi-finals, sides their manager felt they could have beaten, but were instead drawn against the Hungarians. They were a different proposition altogether, the nation's Golden Squad starting to glisten. They swept past the Swedes 6-0 and on to the gold medal. Raynor, in hindsight, took the defeat well – 'what team could have coped with Hungary?' – although he may well have been rather less phlegmatic at the time. Both the Hungarians and the Yugoslavs, after all, were widely recognised as being 'shamateurs', players not officially considered professional because of the Communist approach to sport but quite clearly full time in every sense. 'Our match with Germany [for third place] has always been referred to as "the Amateur final", while the Hungary v Yugoslavia game is now known as "the Professional final",' he wrote. The playing field was not entirely level.

That tournament marked the moment when Sweden ineluctably lost her claim to be Europe's best team. The Hungarians, playing the football Jimmy Hogan always dreamed they might, tore through everyone they encountered in the next two years, twice humiliating the English and arriving in Switzerland for the 1954 World Cup as overwhelming favourites to add to their Olympic crown. Their only setback on the way to Bern – where the West Germans would overturn the odds to beat them – came against Sweden. Raynor's team, at that point, were in decline. They did not even manage to qualify for the World Cup, a failure that would temporarily herald the end of a relationship that had been so fruitful for country and manager. They had one last act of defiance in them, though, and it is entirely possible it was the most significant result of Raynor's career.

Sweden travelled to Budapest to face Hungary just a few weeks before the *Aranycsapat* were due at Wembley in November 1953. Unusually, not only did the Football Association dispatch a party, including Walter Winterbottom, to watch the game, but several gentlemen of the press would follow in their wake. They were eager to report back to their readers what could be expected of these supermen from behind the Iron Curtain; as Raynor admitted, they were not much interested in Sweden. If they thought about them at all, it was as lambs to the slaughter.

That misconception would prove fatal. Raynor, more than familiar with the Hungarians, thought he had hit upon a plan to stop them. 'Many people had watched Hungary play and tried to spot the key man in their plan,' he wrote. 'The most popular choices were Jozsef Bozsik, Ferenc Puskas or Sandor Kocsis. I decided the key man was the deep-lying centre forward, Nandor Hidegkuti ... any team that wanted to beat Hungary had to neutralise Hidegkuti.'

The whole Hungarian system relied on other teams' rigidity. It was predicated on their opponents refusing to deviate from football's orthodox thinking. Gusztav Sebes, Hogan's disciple and their coach, would instruct his wingers to drop deep to drag fullbacks away from their comfort zones. Hidegkuti would slip from the forward line and force the centre back to make a choice: leave him be and allow him space, or track him and open up vast tracts behind him. It worked not just because the Hungarians had thought about what they were doing, but because everyone else knew only how to play by rote.

Raynor, as fluid and elastic as ever, decided to dispense with accepted practice. 'I instructed certain players to mark Hidegkuti in certain zones,' he wrote. 'Nobody had to chase him or wander with him. Our players had to stay in their zones and whenever Hidegkuti entered their zones, they were responsible for looking after him.' He was so confident in his plan that he even explained what he was going to do to the visiting members of the press beforehand. He was not disappointed: Hungary dominated the play, but the game was goalless at half-time and finished in a 2-2 draw; the Swedes might even have nicked it at the last, when the winger Kurt Hamrin, yet another prodigy unearthed by the Stars of the Future courses, hit the bar.

Raynor had shown the visiting English delegation the way to stop the Hungarian machine. He thought he had offered them a blueprint that he felt, given his homeland's superior resources, allowed them to 'do the impossible' and beat the *Aranycsapat*. What he had actually done was the exact opposite: his vindication led to their defeat. The pressmen in Budapest decided that if amateur Sweden could hold Hungary to a draw, then maybe Puskas, Kocsis, Hidegkuti and the others were not all they were cracked up to be. Yet another 'false idea' was sown in the English consciousness. The FA were scarcely more willing to listen: Raynor recounted informing an official of the dangers Hungary's wandering wingers could prove to fullbacks lured into their trap. He suggested that the defence should hold their line and ask the English wingers to help cover their defensive duties. The response was dismissive. 'Can you imagine me asking Stanley Matthews to go in and challenge [Zoltan] Czibor?'

The official might well have had a point: in his autobiography, *The Way It Was,* Matthews suggests that 'tracking back, tackling and helping out in defence' were 'not really my game'. Raynor's impression, though, was that England was 'too proud to learn from little Sweden', but that was most likely only half the truth. It was not that the English would not learn from the Swedes, it was that they would not learn from anyone. England played football her way and would not change, particularly not for what even Raynor admitted was a 'negative' approach. 'The traditional dislike of anything tactical,' he wrote, 'was the weapon with which the grave of football in England was being dug.'

The only person who would listen – to his credit – was Walter Winterbottom. Billy Wright, the England captain, recalled the two men sitting down with Raynor in a Vienna coffee shop on the way back from Budapest to discuss how to overcome the Hungarians. None of them would have known the significance of where they held their meeting: it was, after all, in Vienna's coffee shops that Jimmy Hogan and Hugo Meisl had done so much to craft the form of football that Hungary had brought to such a pitch of perfection. Raynor told Winterbottom that his centre back, Harry Johnston, should resist the urge to follow Hidegkuti. Ashley Hyne points out that, watching footage of that game, it is clear that Johnston is doing as Raynor advised: Winterbottom had offered him the choice of whether to man-mark or hold his position. He chose the latter, and yet England still lost 6-3. Matthews recalled that there was 'no discussion about how to stop' Hidegkuti before the game or even at half-time, when he had already done so much damage. There could be no starker, no more direct example of England failing to heed the warnings her own emissaries had offered.

Holding the Hungarians would be Raynor's last contribution – for the time being – to Sweden's reputation. He would have left within a year, finally following in the footsteps of so many of his players to Italy. He had turned down a host of offers in previous years, but by the summer of 1954, he was ready to leave. He had rebuilt his side three times but a fourth, he felt, was beyond him. 'The apple had fallen from the top of the tree,' he wrote. He was approached by an agent, representing Lazio and Torino, to ask his terms. His son, tasked with handling his affairs, replied by telegram that his father would come for the same sum that had been paid by AC Milan to Gunnar Nordahl, their star striker. That did not put the Italians off. They even asked to know which team in Serie A would be most attractive. Raynor suggested Juventus. A few weeks later, the job was his.

Italy, then, must have seemed an alien world. The country's football was 'built on a huge pile of lira notes', Raynor said, startled by the wealth rather than the exchange rate. That it was not a place he ever felt comfortable in should not have been a surprise: after all, he had spent the previous eight years in 'the most amateur soccer nation of the lot [and now] had dived headlong into the midst of the most professional'.

It was not without its advantages, of course. He arrived in Turin to be greeted by Giovanni and Umberto Agnelli, scions of the Fiat empire, and was immediately told to take his pick of the cars rolling off the production line, in addition to his £1,000 signing-on fee. He would not remain at Juventus for long, though. Within three months, after a moderately encouraging start, he was 'loaned' to Lazio, struggling at the foot of the table. This was, it is fair to say, an odd arrangement, particularly because Juventus continued to pay his contract, and Raynor's explanation is that both Agnellis had other things to attend to and wished to help their friend, the Lazio president, Costantino Tessarolo. More likely, given the Italian penchant for hiring and firing coaches, was that they had expected Raynor to have a more immediate impact after all he had done in Sweden.

Lazio was not a happy experience. His team, he found, was an uncomfortable blend of superannuated defenders and international attackers being played out of position. His job was far more complex than it had been in Sweden: Brian Glanville, in his book *Football Memories*, revealed Raynor had been forced to hire a private detective to follow one player who was sampling a little too much of the city's nightlife and threaten to tell his wife if his performances did not improve. Still, Raynor did what he had been hired to do: he helped the team find some balance, eventually comfortably surviving relegation. He was unimpressed by the amount of interference he had to endure from the club's vast array of directors, by a bonus system which he felt encouraged foul play in pursuit of victory and by the temperament of the supporters, 'which can take a man to the heights of enthusiasm and down again to the depths of despair in the space of seconds'.

Most of all, though, he loathed the spectre of bribery. He was warned before a game at Catania that some of his own players were 'selling' the team. He felt moved to replace his goalkeeper with his reserve, 'an old man of something like 35 years of age', clearly because of the suspicion that his first-choice number one had been bought. He was harangued by the newspapers and by the supporters; Tessarolo told him his car had been stoned and a mock gallows set up in case Lazio lost. They did not, but the worry never went away. A game at Pro Patria convinced him the issue was rife. 'We got a penalty kick, and the ball was rolled straight to the goalkeeper,' he remembered. 'To make matters worse, one of their players was sent off the field, so a few minutes later one of our players walked up to an opponent, kicked him and walked off to even up the numbers.' Raynor asked Juventus to release him from his contract and he left after just one season.

Italy did, at least, provide him with one opportunity. While Raynor was at Lazio, Roma were managed by Jesse Carver. Although the two were not natural allies – Carver hostile and suspicious, Raynor regularly inviting Brian Glanville, the British journalist, round to his apartment in Via delle Medaglie d'Oro – the two had a sufficiently cordial relationship to think they could work together. When Coventry, an ambitious side in England's Third Division (South), approached Carver with a view to taking over in 1955, he enlisted the help of Raynor's wife to convince him to become his second-in-command. Eager to escape Italy, he agreed. A touch of Italian glamour would arrive at Highfield Road. Raynor, at last, would have chance to show England what he could do.

The very first line of *Football Ambassador at Large* promises the book will not be 'overloaded with sour grapes'. Raynor will not complain, he says, because 'football clubs at home have never been willing to engage' him. His tone is intended to be light, but it is a thin mask. It is hard to read the book and feel he keeps his promise. What follows is a withering, unflinching critique of all that is wrong with English football.

He draws on the experiences of British sides at international level to condemn the way the country prepares for tournaments, suggesting that if their FAs spent more time making sure their build-up, scouting and accommodation were correct then they would not have to spend quite so much coming up with 'flimsy excuses'. He criticises the absence of long-term planning, describing England, in particular, as 'living from international to international' rather than building towards a tournament. He is no less impressed by the lack of strength shown by directors who claim players cannot go into training camps because they are prone to boredom. He is scathing about the lack of contact the home nations have with continental sides and by the inability to follow and incorporate tactical trends in Europe. He rails against 'narrow-mindedness' and the fetishisation of fighting spirit, praise for the fact that a team had tried its hardest to win a game. 'Any player wearing his national colours will try his heart out,' he wrote.

If anything, he is more contemptuous still of what might be described as Britain's football culture, its policy of philosophical isolationism. 'The average Swedish player knew far more about the game in its wide international sense than the average British player,' he said. 'It would be stupid to deny that Britain lags behind the rest of the world in international football ... these dismal results will continue unless there is a change of heart in Britain. There must be a re-awakening of interest in international football. The average junior player on the continent is encouraged to study the difference between, let's say, the wing play of [Stanley] Matthews and Garrincha. He will read books and articles about the players and have the opportunity of studying film.' He wants to see more 'constructive talking' about the game, with players allowed to contribute, too, rather than simply being forced to listen to old-school managers trotting out the same outdated ideas. He demands more sports schools, on the lines of his Stars of the Future courses, and he is an outspoken advocate, of course, for the benefits of coaching.

If all of that might be laid at the door of the Football Association, he does not spare the clubs of the Football League his arrows. Much of this, doubtless, is coloured by his memories of what happened to him during his time at Coventry.

In truth, Raynor may have been a little rash in agreeing to take up a post with a man as restless as Carver. He should have known he was never likely to stay at Coventry, despite his £3,500-a-year salary, if a better offer came along. It did: he told the club he wanted out as early as December 1955. Raynor was asked to take over as manager of Coventry.

It did not work out; he lasted just a few months in charge before he was replaced and demoted back to his role of coach. Raynor's explanation for that offers another cutting assessment of what is wrong with English football. He was troubled, as he had been in Italy, by interference from above, finding tactics changed when he was absent on a scouting trip and seeing a player he had placed on the transfer list removed from it and given new terms without his permission. He felt undermined when Earl Shanks, the ambitious chairman, broke the wage structure to hand Reg Matthews, the England goalkeeper, a more lucrative contract than the rest of his team-mates. He found that his squad, working under the privations of the maximum wage, were difficult to control, one player telling him that he did not mind being dropped because he would earn more money sweeping a factory floor, another overheard admitting he wanted Coventry to get 'licked' when he was not playing and others concocting 'cock-and-bull stories' to get out of games. Most of all, he despaired at the short-termism of it all. Results were the be-all and end-all. Nobody had any interest whatsoever in his talk of developing coaching structures and building a side. 'The trouble with British football is that everyone is impatient,' he wrote. 'No one is prepared to wait for development. Success must come tomorrow or changes must be made.

There is too much of a "let's get a few points and hang the foot-ball" attitude.'

All of those reasons, doubtless, are valid. But it is worth questioning why it was that Coventry's board, and Shanks in par-ticular, found themselves unable to offer Raynor the support and belief he craved. Lol Harvey, one of the young players he brought through in his time at Highfield Road, offered Raynor's biog-rapher, Ashley Hyne, the likely answer: that Raynor was better suited to life as a coach, rather than a manager, because he could not discipline the players. He was the craftsman, able to improve those he worked with, and he was dedicated to it. He coached the youth teams, he held meetings to plan out sessions, and he made sure that his players were always entertained, that familiar-ity did not breed contempt. 'No true footballer tires of the ball,' Raynor told Glanville. 'What he does tire of is lack of purpose and variation.'

For all his merits, however, even the professionals of the mid-1950s felt they required a bulldozer to get the best out of them. They were used to the sergeant major model that the game had always been run on. They were delighted to see the ball first thing in the morning at training, but they had been conditioned by the environment in which they had been nurtured to expect someone to shout at them if they stepped out of line. They needed to be told to try their hearts out. This is not a condemnation of them, in particular, because they were no more at fault for their upbringing than is a child. But it is a criticism of those who had allowed that climate to develop.

That, too, was why Raynor was left with such a feeling of 'disillusionment' from his long-awaited first taste of the Football League. It also ensured that, his time at Coventry at an end, he found work hard to come by. 'The attitude seemed to be that I was another fellow who had come back from that strange land

that is the continent and had failed dismally in my own country,'
he wrote. It is no surprise he was so angered by England's failure to understand and appreciate the continental game, not just
because it meant that his own achievements there were not celebrated enough but because they were immediately scotched from
the record because of his failure at Coventry. He was a double
victim of English navel-gazing isolationism. He might have won
an Olympic gold and held the mighty Hungarians, but none of
that mattered because he had not won promotion at the first time
of asking from the Third Division. It is an attitude that lingered.
Half a century before it was invented, Raynor had been deemed
to have failed what would become known as the rainy-night-in-
Stoke test. He could do it abroad, but he could not do it at home.
England was no place for a craftsman. Fortunately for him, and
unfortunately for his homeland, Sweden still was.

As contrasts go, it was a sharp one. Soon after leaving Coventry,
Raynor was back home in Lincolnshire, writing letters to the
National Coal Board to volunteer his services to help organise
physical education courses for the scores of Hungarian refugees
who had arrived in Britain in the aftermath of the brutal Soviet
repression of the Budapest uprising in 1956. His outgoing post
went ignored. So, too, for a while, did the letters that dropped
through his mailbox: from his old comrade Putte Kock and from
Holger Bergerus, still two of the most powerful people in Swedish
football. They both wanted him to return to coach the national
side for the 1958 World Cup. He was not keen. 'I did not really
want to go back. I had done my stint of travelling and living
abroad.'

   With little interest in his contribution at home, eventually he
relented. He travelled back in 1957 and set about building his
fourth Sweden side in time for the following year's World Cup,

to be held in the country. The initial signs were not promising. The constant flow of talent to the south of Europe had taken its toll. The national team was filled with second division players. If Sweden were to excel on home soil, he quickly realised that he would have to ask the country's authorities to relax their rules on allowing professionals to play. His pitch was a simple one: that while it was assumed that a team of home-based amateurs was representative of the standard of football in Sweden, permitting those who had gone abroad to join them was a fair example of the players the country had produced. The ploy worked.

Although many dozens of Swedes had gone abroad in the previous decade, Raynor did not want to push his luck. He targeted just five players to bring home from Italy for the tournament, basing the rest of his side around four players from the domestic champions, Norrkoping. First on the list was Nils Liedholm, veteran of his Olympic team a decade previously, now 35 and at AC Milan. Then came Nacka Skoglund, at Inter, whom he had first discovered before Brazil 1950. Atalanta's Bengt Gustavsson and Padova's Kurt Hamrin – both given one-to-one tuition by Raynor while working for AIK – he had nurtured after that tournament. Arne Selmosson, a striker with Lazio poetically known in Italy as the 'Ray of Moonlight', completed the quintet.

The circumstances, still, were not ideal. The Italian clubs would only release their highly paid stars a few days before the tournament started, which meant Raynor would be denied the chance to arrange the training camps that had been so effective in forging his previous teams. He would have to live on his wits a little more than he would have liked, but he did not seem to have been disheartened. His players recalled that he would wake them every morning by singing to them.

Sweden sailed through their group, beating a much-diminished Hungary and Mexico and playing out a 'rather boring' goalless draw with the Welsh in which, already qualified, Raynor had given a run-out to his second string. That set up a game with the Soviet Union, conquerors of England, in the quarter-finals. The hosts won through thanks to the combination of Raynor's two greatest gifts as a manager: his meticulousness and his flexibility. He had travelled to watch their meeting with Walter Winterbottom's side and noted that Yuri Voinov, the Soviets' best player, had been used to man-mark England's star playmaker, Johnny Haynes. He was deeply unimpressed by the way the English could not work out that Haynes was being scientifically removed from the game by Voinov's preternatural positional sense – he commented that he continually intercepted passes just before they reached Haynes – but he was inspired by the approach. He shifted his pack and told Liedholm to do to Voinov what the Dynamo Kiev inside right had done to Haynes. Voinov was neutralised, and Sweden won 2-0.

West Germany, the reigning champions, were swatted aside 3-1 in the semi-final, teeing up a meeting with Brazil in the final. Raynor had seen just how good Didi, Vava, Garrincha, Pele and the rest had been throughout the tournament, but he still harboured hopes of claiming football's greatest prize, especially when Liedholm put the hosts ahead after less than five minutes into the game at the packed Rasunda Stadium. Though few had given Sweden a 'ghost of a chance', Raynor believed that his team could win if they scored early. 'South American footballers, with their highly strung temperament, are likely to get flustered when their opponents go in front so quickly,' he wrote. Liedholm's goal gave him hope. The sensation did not last. 'Instead of looking dejected, the Brazilians were calling for the ball to be returned so they could restart the game. If that was the Brazilian attitude, we were heading for trouble.'

They were. Brazil ran out 5-2 winners and Pele announced himself to an enthralled world. Raynor, though, 'felt no sense of failure'. Just as in 1952, when his team lost to Hungary in the Olympic semi-final, he felt 'not one team in the world could have beaten the Brazil of that day'. They produced 'a superb exhibition of football that was just too good for us'. Even in defeat, Raynor recognised that game as the finest moment of his career. He had come within touching distance of the ultimate honour, and only been denied grasping it by one of the finest sides ever to grace a pitch.

If he thought that, finally, would grant him authority in his homeland, he was wrong. The postscript to his story is an undeniably melancholy one. Within a year, he was back in his bungalow outside Skegness, a knight of the kingdom of Sweden reduced to working with Skegness Town, a team whose ambition stretched no further than getting out of the Midland League, the place where his career had started. It was as far from the world he inhabited for so long, the world of Puskas and Pele, as it was possible to be.

Naturally, that intrigued the English press. In the immediate aftermath of the World Cup, a steady flow of journalists beat a path to his door. He was a figure of sufficient interest to the general public to be sought out for interview when Sweden played at Wembley in 1959 and to be offered a deal for the publication of his autobiography in 1960. He made no secret at any point that he wanted to 'work in England, for England'.

The chance never came. England's clubs were not interested, his failure in a few months at Coventry evidently deemed more important than his ability to reach a World Cup final, his reputation for being too indulgent with his players influencing their thinking. He may have been considered for the national team job, the one he craved above all, but the FA, stung by the criticism in Raynor's book, plumped for Alf Ramsey, and would not regret their choice, at least in the short term. Sweden remained close to his heart, and he to theirs. A steady stream of players made the journey to Skegness to work with him. He was invited back on a regular basis and was hired, without success, to help them qualify for the 1962 World Cup. He always returned to Skegness, though, working with the local club until 1965 and retiring from football, once and for all, after an abortive couple of months at Doncaster in 1967.

Hyne, his biographer, is inclined to feel he was not unhappy with the way it all turned out. A detached bungalow with a sea view and a top-of-the-range Saab did not represent a bad life's work for a miner's son from Wombwell, after all. However, it is hard to believe that he did not harbour some resentment at being so consistently scorned by the country that he felt needed his help more than any other. He had done so much to turn Sweden from a backwater into a first-rate football nation. In many ways, through isolation and ignorance, England had allowed herself to make the opposite journey. Raynor was precisely the sort of man she required.

Her eyes, though, were blind and her ears deaf. No wonder Raynor seemed so angry, in *Football Ambassador at Large*, at all of England's enduring errors, at seeing her fall from the top of the tree. Most of all, he was angry at how self-inflicted it had all been. He knew it did not have to be as it was. The penultimate line between that sea-green cover is the most perceptive. It is the most heartfelt. 'Britain has the greatest potential for success in world soccer,' Raynor writes. 'But Britain misuses her assets.'

8

Curious Harry

Harry Game stares at the fire. He is an old man now, but still a vital one. His voice is firm. His body, clad in a green woollen jumper, is still strong. As he casts his mind back over a career that took him from his home in the East End to Greece and to Belgium, that brought him face to face with the Real Madrid team of Alfredo Di Stefano and Francisco Gento and saw him stand as an equal with Ferenc Puskas, he is warm, friendly.

He is quick, though, to dismiss questions he deems foolish. It is easy to see why he was successful as a manager. He must have cut an imposing, mildly intimidating, figure to his players. He would have inspired respect, and more than a little fear. You get the impression that he does not suffer fools gladly, and never has. He served as a physical education instructor in the RAF during the war. He would have fitted the role quite well. He is, even now, a tough man.

In the course of six hours in his company, there is only one brief instant where that image falters. He is still passionate about football: that much is clear. He grows animated when he talks about 'the clique' of managers who dominated the game in England when he was in his prime, the group he feels denied him the chance to work in his homeland. His disdain for the people who run the sport today, the owners and executives he sees wasting obscene amounts of money in a vainglorious chase for trophies, is equally obvious. He is fiercely defensive of those who helped him, but fearsomely critical of those who did not.

Now, though, he is silent. It is the only moment when he seems to be overwhelmed by emotion. It is not one that has been brought on by the pain of remembering, a recollection of something or someone that he has lost. No, it is quite the opposite. He is undone by the joy of being remembered.

A few weeks before we met, in the spring of 2014, I had attended the Fifa World Player of the Year gala in Zurich, that annual festival of glad-handing held to honour whichever of Cristiano Ronaldo and Lionel Messi has scored the most goals in the last three months. In the interminable hours before the ceremony started, I found myself sitting next to a Greek journalist. He turned out to be a Panathinaikos fan. Knowing of my appointment with Harry, I asked him whether he knew the name.

'Yes, of course,' came the response. 'Everyone at Panathinaikos remembers κυριος Harry.'

Κυριος is the Greek word for leader. That was the title afforded to Game when he arrived in Athens, in the summer of 1950, to manage Panathinaikos. He was only 27, younger than many of the players he would be coaching. Harry's Greek is still excellent, but his accent lets him down just a little on that one word. It should be pronounced 'kurios', with a hard 'k' and a hard 'u', but the way Harry has it sounds more like 'curious'.

It is when I tell Harry of that snatched conversation in Zurich that he catches his breath. The journalist's final sentence, delivered with absolute certainty, as though the very idea that the opposite might be true is quite ridiculous – 'everyone remembers κυριος

Harry' – hangs in the air. Harry turns away. There is, I think, a glimmer of a tear in his eye.

All of the managers who travelled abroad – either on their own initiative or at the behest of the Football Association – eventually had little choice but to accept that they were out of sight, out of mind. Harry himself readily acknowledges that. 'I was in pretty regular contact with the FA, but nobody from England took any interest in what I was doing,' he says. Those managers knew all too well that the game's motherland was happy to teach, but not nearly so willing to learn. Harry does not betray so much as a scintilla of bitterness about it.

He has got used to not being remembered, not being known. At the start of our interview, he had leaned across from his seat by the fire and handed me a double-sided, cream-coloured business card. His name is set in bold on one side. **Harry Game**. On the other is a run-down of the clubs he managed, together with a list of his achievements, the league titles and the national cups he picked up.

His eldest daughter, Carole, had them printed a few years ago. They function, partly, as an aide-memoire for him, a way to cut through time's muddling haze, to get his thoughts in order, but also as a testament to where he has been and all that he has done. They are a simple, defiant declaration of his quiet uniqueness in a country that remains blissfully unaware of his career. They are not the sort of thing he would need if he had been celebrated as perhaps he – and so many of his peers – should have been.

There are places, though, where his name alone would be enough. Greece is one, Belgium another. He won championships in both places. In Norway, too, there are those who have not forgotten his contribution. One of them, indeed, went on to carve his own place in history.

Towards the end of his career, after an unhappy spell in charge of the National Oil Company's side in an Iran festering with oppression and revolution, Harry was contacted by a team called Clausenengen, based in Kristiansund, on Norway's Baltic coast. He took the job because he needed to 'make as much money as possible' for his impending retirement. He was there for five years. Part of his remit was to establish a youth academy. A few years later, that school took charge of a young player with a baby's face and an assassin's instinct: Ole Gunnar Solskjaer.

It was at Clausenengen, according to Solskjaer himself, that he learned the principles that would propel him to Manchester United, and to glory. 'It has always been my background that we play technical football,' he told the excellent Norwegian magazine *Josimar* when he was still manager of Molde, Kristiansund's top-flight team. 'There was an Englishman who came to Clausenengen in the mid-1970s. Harry Game was his name. He set up the junior department at Clausenengen. It became very technical [in its style]. The football education I got there is what made me what I was.'

English football might have ignored Harry Game. It might not know what he did. But Solskjaer does, and so too Panathinaikos. And as Harry stares at the fire, composing himself, you see just how much that means. That is all he wanted: not fame, or fortune, but simply to know that he was remembered, that he has not been forgotten.

Harry Game was one of Walter Winterbottom's boys. His life was shaped, irrevocably, by the man he refers to as 'the father of football coaching'. In the same way as George Raynor owed everything he did to that first recommendation from Stanley Rous, Game became who he was, who he is, because of Winterbottom. His story can never be described as typical – he was too extra-ordinary for that – but in one key sense it is symbolic of the stories of many of those who emerged from the coaching courses the

Football Association established to try to teach the teachers: it all starts with Winterbottom.

It is not that Harry's memories have started to fade, more that they have run into one another. As he starts down one path, he veers on to another. A story that starts in Athens might end in Antwerp, or Cape Town, or Israel. There is more than half a century between him and the events he is trying to recall. It is no surprise that occasionally he loses his way, but it frustrates him. He shakes his head, as if trying to retune his mind, a violent shudder of annoyance at the passing of time.

Just occasionally, though, he remembers a conversation almost word for word. One stands out because it may have saved his life; because it meant that he spent World War II at the RAF base at Padgate, putting pilots through their paces; because it was the moment that his privileged status as a professional footballer helped him avoid a far more dangerous fate.

'When I went into the RAF, they asked me what I wanted to do,' he says. 'I said that I wanted to take physical training. It seemed like the right sort of thing at the time. They gave me a piece of paper, and told me to go to the gym and see the squadron leader.

'I walked in as smartly as I could and introduced myself. He barked: "Name?" I said: "Game". He said: "Do you play sport? Who do you play for?" I told him football, cricket, athletics: people like me, no matter what kind of thing you want us to play, you can do it. I said I was playing for Millwall. He asked me straightaway: "Are you a professional?" I said yes.'

Harry smiles. 'When he heard that, he said: "Oh, sit down, have a cigarette." He asked if I wanted to stay at this station, told me they had plenty of professional players there, promised to arrange a 48-hour leave pass so I could play at the weekends. Then he said that if there was anything else he could do for me, he would arrange it. So I thought I'd probably better stay.'

The other conversation that he can recall almost verbatim – well enough to play both parts in the drama – dates to the summer of 1950. That he can remember it is testament to just how important it was; perhaps not quite as significant, in terms of his life, as the one that saved him from the war, but as far as his destiny goes, not far off.

Harry's career, by that stage, was over. He had first learned his craft at West Ham United – his local side and 'one of the best schoolboy teams in the country' – and then, after the war robbed him of those years in which he might have hoped to make a name for himself, played at senior level for Millwall and Crystal Palace. Throughout, he was plagued by a knee injury. By the time he was 26, it was too much to bear. 'I could run around and enjoy myself, but a little twist and I was gone,' he says.

He knew his time as a player was up, but he wanted to stay in football. His experiences in the RAF meant that coaching seemed like a natural fit. He signed up for the FA coaching course at Carnegie College in Leeds. 'There was a guy there called Bill Flatley,' he says. 'He came to me and asked where I was playing. He was coaching abroad as well. I said I was at Millwall. He said he was working in Italy, and that there was quite a call over there to encourage coaches to come over from England. This is when English coaches were in demand. He said he would have a word with Walter Winterbottom for me because there were always vacancies coming up.'

Even now, a note of reverence comes into Harry's voice when Winterbottom's name is mentioned. He refers to him, throughout, by his full name – *he said he would have a word with Walter Winterbottom* – and the awe in which Harry held him is clear from the fact that it took some time before he had the nerve to approach him.

'At the end of the course, he knew enough to recognise me,

if not to call me Harry. I cornered him one day and asked if he thought there was a possibility of me getting a job. He said he would recommend me, but that unfortunately the chances of me getting any recognition in this country were nil. "They want people in their thirties and forties," he said. I was only 26.

'He said he would see if he could get me fixed up. He told me that if I got 10 years' experience abroad, then I would have something to back me up. I would be able to say I had been there and done it. He made it clear it would depend on my success and how I went about it, but that he would get his secretary to put my name forward for any positions that came in. A few weeks later I got a letter from the FA. There was a job in Hong Kong, one in Switzerland, and one at Panathinaikos. Maybe one other, too.'

Winterbottom set up his coaching course to try to change the way England thought about football. His ultimate aim was not, it is fair to say, to improve the game abroad: it was to get coaches into Football League clubs. Harry's account of his meeting with him, though, suggests he was well aware – three years after he had welcomed his first batch of students – where the majority of them would end up, at least at first. It hints, too, at a frustration at how resistant most of the clubs in the Football League were to the idea of coaching. Most importantly, it serves as proof that, with the help of the FA, he actively assisted in finding work for his protégés in foreign countries. The process by which England dispensed her wisdom, by 1950, had drastically changed. No longer was it piecemeal, reliant on an individual's spirit of adventure. It was organised, and it was deliberate.

Still, of course, it helped if the coach in question was willing to take a risk. Taking Winterbottom's advice on board, Harry Game decided he was. 'My wife Joan and I had not been married long. We were very young,' he says. 'I was 26, she was five years younger than me. I told her what the situation was. We talked about it and

I said I remember my history, what wonderful people the Greeks were, the Spartans and all that, and that I thought it would be a good place to go. I asked her what she thought, whether we should chance our arm. She told me to choose, but I was no wiser than she was. I wrote back and the next thing I knew there was an offer for me to be coach of Panathinaikos. It was nerve-wracking, but it depends where you're coming from. Sometimes if you face up to things, they are not nearly as scary as they seem to be.'

Harry and Joan had just a few weeks to pack up their lives and arrange their passage to Greece. They had to explain their decision to leave England, when such an idea was almost anathema, to his mother and her parents. Harry still has the ticket that took them to Paris and Rome, where they were allowed off the plane for an hour as it refuelled, and on to Athens. They were greeted at the airport by Panathinaikos and then taken to meet a full delegation of directors. 'We went down by the sea, at Phalerum,' he says. 'There were quite a few of the Greek people from the club there. It was wonderful. They came to greet me, but they did not know me from Adam. I could have been the biggest mug.' Harry remembers the date. There is a reason that one sticks in his mind. It was his 27th birthday.

The Greece the couple discovered was still struggling to its feet after the devastating effects not just of German occupation, but the brutal civil war against Communist partisans that had left the country in ruins. It was a fractious, tense place, one in which Harry learned it was safer to discuss neither religion nor politics, where occasional skirmishes with remnants of the rebel forces still scarred the north of the country. It was a place dominated by the black market, where prices varied depending on the nationality of the person doing the bartering. 'I was quite lucky,' Harry smiles. 'There were a number of fans who worked on the black market.

They would see me food. Sometimes, you would even get butter. But, as it always is in places where there have been problems, it was a hard life.'

Certainly, adapting was not easy for a young couple who did not speak the language and who had never previously left their homeland. Panathinaikos did what they could to help their new manager and his wife settle in, putting them up in a hotel in the centre of the city as they searched for a home, and laying on a translator to help Harry, in particular, acclimatise. Even then, though, there were examples of his naivety, not least on his very first day.

'I was told to take the tram to the stadium from right outside,' Harry says, laughing at what is coming. 'I didn't think, and they didn't warn me, that everything worked on the other side of the road. So I set off in plenty of time on this tram that supposedly stopped right outside the stadium.

'Anyway, it seemed to go on for an awful long time, on and on. It broke out into the back of beyond, no sign of civilisation. I spoke no Greek. I couldn't say a word. I somehow made the driver understand I was going to the football ground. I mimed kicking a ball. It turned out, I had gone the wrong way. He got me on the right tram to where I wanted to be. I got there and explained what had happened. They laughed. I always got the right tram after that.'

Things were no easier when he eventually arrived at training. Harry had been expecting to have to choose a first-team squad from, at most, a pool of a couple of dozen players. 'There were four or five hundred people on the pitch when I arrived. And two or three thousand had turned up just to watch. I just thought: "How the hell do I get out of this one?"' He organised brief games, designed to see who might be of interest and who was, as he puts it, 'any old Tom, Dick or Harry', and slowly whittled the hopefuls down.

There was, it turned out, some considerable talent at his disposal. To his relief, Panathinaikos could call on a host of Greek internationals, though many of them were approaching the autumn of their careers. That came at a cost. The club's directors might have determined only an Englishman could whip them into shape, but that does not mean the players saw it that way. 'It was difficult. I was just a 27-year-old, and I had very limited experience. There were times when people would have a go at me, but the people at the top of the club shielded me from it as best they could.'

The criticism centred, not least, on Harry's training regime. He admits that his players found out, pretty quickly, that he could be 'a bit of a bastard'. As a schoolboy at West Ham, he had been given an early introduction to the importance of physical fitness. 'They placed tremendous stress on being fit,' he remembers now. His weekly sessions at the club's gym were, essentially, a 'thrashing'. It was that fitness which enabled him to turn professional; it was that fitness, presumably, that he passed on to the pilots who came under his care and control in those years spent at Padgate; and it was that fitness that he recognised his players would need to succeed.

'My training was very physical,' he says. 'The biggest emphasis was the physical side of it, because if you're not fit, you can't be a good footballer. Those that train hard, in the last part of the game, have an advantage.

'Years after I left, I had gone back to Athens and I was walking along the street and one of my former players, a postman, recognised me. He rushed up to me, asked why I was here, what I was doing in Athens, where I was staying. He told me that the rest of the team would want to see me. The next night, they took me up to this taverna in the hills. In the space of 24 hours, they had got all of my old players together. We all met at this taverna. It was marvellous.

'One of them, Giorgos Kourtzidis, called me over. He said to me: "Κυριος Harry, when you started training us, you nearly killed us. We wanted to get at you. We wanted to kill you, every single one of us. But then we saw that you were right and we were wrong."'

There were three separate threads that seem to have led to that realisation and prevented a wide-scale mutiny. The first was that Harry insisted on leading by example. 'I had a good thing on them: I would say to them that this is what we had to do, but that if I couldn't do it, then they didn't have to. But if I could do it, they had to do it.

'I had a guy interpreting when I first started. It seemed to me pretty strange, after a while, that the messages didn't seem to be coming out as they should. I mentioned it to someone I was friends with. They said that I was saying one thing, the interpreter was translating: "He says do this, do that, but I think it is better if you do it like this." Eventually, I would use a stick of chalk and a board to explain things and then I would demonstrate them myself. I would do the exercise and they would do it after me.'

There is an echo, here, of Jimmy Hogan, another who based much of his teaching on practical demonstration. The second strand of Harry's success – that his methods were not based entirely on running, that he believed in the primacy of the ball – is by now familiar, too: this was the common philosophy of all of his predecessors as English coaches on foreign shores, from Fred Pentland to George Raynor, and the most consistent complaint of all of those in England, like the journalists Ivan Sharpe and James Catton, who felt the country would fall behind unless technique stood at the centre of all training. Whether they were aware of it or not, it became dogma among Winterbottom's disciples. The ball came first.

That was the lesson Harry had been taught at Carnegie, and it was one that chimed with his own experiences of the game. It lent his coaching a technical edge that would have been heretical in England but worked perfectly in Greece, where the emphasis of the game was on individual ability.

'There was one thing I couldn't make out when I turned professional,' he says. 'The players did what they wanted. At school and in the air force, training was organised. But in the clubs, you did what you wanted. Players were categorised either as good trainers or bad trainers. We used to get the ball on a Thursday morning. Once a week, the ball came out. They would shout: "balls, boys, balls!" The idea was that you would be hungry for it at the weekend, but you were hungry for it every day. I learned from that.

'My training was based on the use of the football. I did what they used to do to us at West Ham, but always with a football. If you are chasing a ball, you'll run more than when you aren't. You will run across a field all day, as long as you are running after a ball. Your mind is focused on the ball, just as it should be during the game.

'What I had learned, at school and in the short time I was professional, was that you have to work with the ball. The more you work with the ball, the better a player you will be. It is the ball that does the work. Football is kick and run, but it is a matter of how you kick and where you run. I always worked with the ball in training. I tried to make sessions as interesting as I could, and by and large it must have worked.'

That is the third strand of Harry's success: results. In England, the importance of victory was often seen as holding the game back; in Harry's case, it served to allow his methods to flourish. As Kourtzidis said to him that night, high in the hills above Athens, as he and his players reminisced about all they had achieved: 'We began to realise that the longer and harder a game was, the better we were. The other teams could not keep up with us. We kept going and going and going, and in the last half hour, we scored goals.'

It is only the highlights that remain. The three years of that first spell in Athens culminated in Harry winning the Greek championship in 1953, more than enough to vindicate his decision to leave his homeland and Panathinaikos' to appoint a 27-year-old coach with no experience. Harry does not dwell on what he won. History, as he says, speaks for itself. The stories that animate him most are not those that celebrate his success but, rather, those that affected him most personally.

He still recalls, in high definition, his first visit to the club's 15,000-capacity stadium. 'We got there, and there was no grass. It was all sand. Around the premises of the field were these big wire cages, all the way around the pitch. I was shocked. I didn't much fancy it. I asked why they had the cages: they told me there was a friendly game that night, and I would find out.

'There was a bit of scepticism, an attitude that there was a new manager, a youngster, and that he probably didn't know anything. The game kicks off and after a few minutes, there is this sudden yelling, real screaming and bawling, and all of the fans, 15,000 of them, are clambering up the wire. I asked what was going on, but they told me not to worry, that it would be over in a minute.

'The outside left, Yannis Baba, was a great favourite, a real individual. His greatest enemy was playing right back for the opponents. Something had obviously been said, and this guy had had a kick. Before you knew it, my player was chasing their player round the perimeter of the pitch. Everything stopped: the players, the referee. Nobody did anything. We all just stood there, watching these buggers run after each other. What on earth goes on here, I thought. It took a minute or two – they ran out of puff, stopped, and then the game carried on. I have no idea what the score was.'

Then there was the time he was given a lift to a game by one of his directors. Panathinaikos were to play Olympiacos, their fierce rivals from Piraeus, Athens' port. Only in Greece, where they aren't bad at mythology, could it be known as the Derby of the Immortal Enemies; hyperbole aside, it is, without question, one of the most fraught rivalries in world football, the green of Panathinaikos eternally opposed to the red of Olympiacos.

'You have to be careful,' Harry says. 'We were driving to the game. It was in Piraeus. The director picked me up, and as we were driving, we came to some lights. They were on red. He did not stop. He did not even slow down. He just went zoom, straight across. I said: "Yannis, what are you doing?" He said: "Today, I do not stop, not for red."'

As he casts his mind back over those three years, it is easy to imagine that Harry would, given the choice, have remained in Athens. The club's precarious finances – and the uncertainty of Greece's post-war economy – precluded that. Fresh from their championship victory, Panathinaikos wanted to keep him, but informed him they simply could not afford to renew his contract. The drachma had tumbled in value compared to the pound. Harry's contract was in sterling; they could not continue on this basis, but to switch to drachmae would have entailed 'paying him more than the prime minister'. Harry returned to England.

That should have been the ideal opportunity, of course, for a young English manager with a gleaming record abroad – and a glowing reference from Panathinaikos – to be given his chance in his homeland. At the very summit of the Football Association, Stanley Rous and Walter Winterbottom were starting to implement genuine change. Their coaching course had by now been running for seven years. One edition of the *FA News* from around that time bemoans 'the amount of ball play' foreign players were given in comparison with the English. 'With constant practice, they aim to be as little worried about the whereabouts of the ball as they are the [pedals of the] bicycle they ride,' the correspondent wrote.

However, when Harry landed back in England he found that Winterbottom's gloomy prediction still held true. The Football League's clubs were content unto themselves, locked in a self-imposed catch-22 where the only experience that counted was experience in England, where you could only get a job if you had already had one before. There was still little demand for the fruits of Winterbottom's labours. The Football League remained deaf to the claims of those men who had worked abroad. Perhaps, despite his tender age, Harry would have found work easier to come by had he returned home *after* the defeat to Hungary. Perhaps, in the bout of soul-searching that followed, he might have found an environment more open to taking a risk. Alas, he was home a few months beforehand. Even with a Greek title to his name, there were no takers.

'Nobody from the Football Association said I was ready to coach in England,' says Harry. There is a trace of annoyance, more than bitterness, in his voice. 'I did not go drinking with the boys. I have always been a virtual teetotaller – I'll have a glass of beer if I feel like it – but I never tried to push my way into their circles. They had their little group. I was in touch with the FA pretty regularly, but nobody in England took any notice. I think there was still a suspicion of coaches. Those that had big names got jobs, not those who were coaches.'

In the absence of interest at home and out of work, Harry was forced to head abroad once more. Offers for his services came in from two Belgian clubs: Racing Mechelen and Royal

Antwerp. The former arrived first, but the latter proved more tempting: Panathinaikos had played both on tours under Harry's guidance, and he felt Antwerp, regarded as the best team in the country, to be the better side. In 1953, just a few months before the Hungarians exposed the folly of England's supposed superiority, one of the country's brightest young coaches would move away again.

He finished seventh in his first season in Belgium – winning the country's cup for good measure – but soon hit his stride. Over the next three years, he would win one league title and come within a whisker of landing three. His side was built around Vic Mees, captain of the Belgian national team, and his international colleague Bob Maertens. In his second year, his team finished three points behind the eventual champions, Anderlecht. Antwerp more than made up for that the following campaign. They won the title with two games to spare, eventually seeing off Anderlecht by six points. The next year, they finished joint top with Standard Liege, but failed to retain their crown by virtue of having lost one more game than their rivals.

Despite that disappointment, the 1957-58 season brought what may well have been the most high-profile moment of Harry's career. Their title the previous season allowed them to enter the still relatively new-fangled European Cup. The rather antiquated draw system meant that Antwerp were given a bye into the first round proper, while the likes of Manchester United, Benfica and Saint-Etienne were forced to take part in a play-off. That was roughly as far as Harry's luck went. They were drawn to face the great Real Madrid side of Alfredo Di Stefano, Raymond Kopa and Francisco Gento. It was not a fixture he was likely to forget.

The first leg was to be held at Antwerp's Stade Bosuil. In front of 45,000 fans, Real took the lead through Di Stefano after 15 minutes, but the hosts struck back before the hour. For three minutes, thanks to Constant de Backer, the Belgians were level. Then Di Stefano pounced again. 'It was a really good game,' says Harry. 'We played probably the best football we ever played. We held them to a single-goal lead. Fantastic. They had been told before the game they would beat us easily. But I always remember that, when they were being interviewed after the game, they were kind enough to say what a good side we were and that we were not to be underestimated.'

More than half a century on, quite how much that means to the coach who oversaw it is evident and understandable. The pride he can still take from earning the respect of the greatest club side ever to grace a pitch almost – but only almost – makes up for what happened in the return.

'In the last two minutes of our training session, Vic Mees went to kick a ball and slipped. He had pulled a muscle. Real Madrid really were a nice group of people, and they did all they could to get him fit to play against them, but everything they did was not enough. He could not play. Losing a player like Mees at that time was not something we could overcome. My team's strength was the starting XI, but they were the best we had by a distance. We did not have a player to step in and take his place.

'We chose Eddie Wauters – who would later be the president of the club – and the game started. My players touched the ball three times in the first four minutes. All three were kick-offs.' Two goals from Hector Rial gave Real a two-goal lead. They were three up at half-time, and added three more after the break. 'They could have run up a cricket score,' says Harry. 'Maybe a low cricket score. I don't know if they were being kind or not, but they did not take advantage as they might have done. They thrashed us, but they did the same to the rest of Europe. They scored fives and sixes all the time.'

The sadness has long since dissipated, of course, to be replaced by something between admiration and awe. No coach would describe a 6-0 defeat as the highlight of their career. Yet Harry talks about that game less as if it was a humiliation and more as if it was an honour simply to watch them up close. 'They were the best football team I have ever seen. And that was the team before they had signed Ferenc Puskas. There were 80 or 90,000 people there. As a manager, you try not to lose in that sort of situation, because they had players who were superior to the rest of the world. In a pure football sense, though, you just stood and admired it.'

By the end of 1958, Harry had won league championships in two countries, plus a cup. He had gone toe to toe with the great Real Madrid. The Football Association, five years on from the debacle against Hungary, had long since accepted that there was much to learn from the way the game was played on the continent and further afield. Not once, though, did anyone consider asking a 35-year-old from the East End, who had witnessed that development at first hand, for the benefit of his experience. There were still no job offers from the Football League. Walter Winterbottom had trained Harry and his peers and sent them out to teach foreigners how to play. Even when England started to accept that the foreigners might be able to offer a lesson or two in return, there was no attempt to tap into a resource they themselves had created. Harry stands as testament to the 'double loss' described by Brian Glanville: England suffered twice, failing to use its own coaching talent and allowing others to benefit from it.

'Was anyone in England following me? No. I was outside. I was in Europe. The powers that be – the press, the hangers-on – had no idea who I was. Nobody said I was ready to coach in England. Nobody took any interest.'

*

There were others, though, who were tracking his career keenly. Harry's last two seasons in Belgium, after the high of facing Real Madrid, were disappointing. Antwerp finished sixth and eighth, and, by the summer of 1960, it felt like a change might be beneficial for all concerned. Fortunately, his stock remained high at his former club, Panathinaikos. 'One or two of the board members told me, years later, they had kept in touch with my career, reading the papers, seeing who was doing what,' Harry explains. 'I was still only 37 in 1960. They said they had experience of me for three years and would like me to come and help out again.'

It was the start of a pattern. Wherever Harry went, he tended to get invited back. As he says, slightly bashfully, he must have been doing something right. It started with Athens: another three years at Panathinaikos, another two championships. He left, in 1963, for a season in Israel, with Hapoel Tel Aviv, where he managed to finish fourth despite having to quell a player strike. From there, he went back to Antwerp for another three-year stint. In 1971, after a spell at Hellenic Cape Town, Hapoel called again, where he would take charge of a gifted player by the name of Rifaat Turk. Turk would become the first Arab player to represent the state of Israel. Harry nicknamed him 'Jimmy'.

By this stage, as Harry openly admits, he was not only motivated by a desire to coach. He was not, he says, a 'grab-all' for money in his younger days. When he returned to Antwerp in 1965, he did not negotiate a contract: he simply told his president that he wished to be given what would be regarded as a competitive salary. When, in 1968, a power struggle with one of his players left him feeling his position was untenable, he did not haggle over compensation. He simply walked away.

But while his career had given him plenty of adventure and a comfortable life, it had not been inordinately lucrative. He acknowledges that he became rather more conscious of his

earnings as his life wore on, with a family to support and a retirement to plan. Still, it would be unfair to characterise him as a
mercenary. He remained in Tel Aviv, working, even as the Yom
Kippur War of 1973 raged just a few miles from the city.

'I saw the match delegate, the man who helped me with the
team, one weekend,' he says. 'Trouble had been brewing. It was
imminent. I had been to the embassy and spoke to the people I
knew there and they said no, nothing to worry about, just the
usual. Of course, they're saying that as their families are being
ushered back to Britain.

'I asked my delegate, and he said it was nothing to worry
about, too. He said when he was not there, that was the time to
worry. I did not see him again for about five months. He was on
the reserve list and he had been called up. Everyone was on the
front line. It was 20 miles or so away. You could cycle there and
back in a day. Some of them would come back for training sessions, because it was so close and because, as sportsmen often are
in these situations, they had special privileges. It was impossible
to get them all together, though, because they were all in different
areas and they all had different functions. But yes, we stayed.'

His memories of Israel, war and all, are rather fonder than
those of the final club posting he took: with the side representing the National Oil Company in Iran. He had been head-hunted
because of his experience in Israel, the familiarity he had with
the working conditions to be found in the Middle East. However,
nothing he had seen or heard in Tel Aviv prepared him for what he
found in the oil fields of Abadan.

'You could not trust anybody,' he says. He had taken the job
because of the money on offer and, principally, because he was
hoping to buy a house in England for his retirement. The club
agreed to provide a loan to cover it. Their generosity came at a
price.

'It was the last couple of years of the Shah. It was very sticky, because if you made any remark that was said to be anti-Shah you could be kicked out. There were a couple of Englishmen thrown out of the country for a joke, nothing major. Half the population were his informers. You never, ever knew. You had to be careful how you breathed.

'My job was to talk to players, privately, but within three minutes, every time, a bell would sound and I would be asked to go and see the big boss. He was in charge of the marketing and public relations and the football team was part of his remit. There would always be a roundabout question and then he would ask what he really wanted to know: what were you talking to that player about? He was the boss, but I would not accept his views on football.'

His stay did not last. It was his success in Israel that had tempted his prospective employers, but as revolution started to ferment, his past in Tel Aviv began to prove a problem. He left in 1976. There was one final offer for his services submitted to the Football Association, one that Harry obliquely refers to as 'from an Arabian country', but his experiences in Abadan had been so bitter that he informed them he did not intend to take it. Instead, his final stop would be Norway, and Clausenengen, and the school that first unearthed Solskjaer.

In the course of a little more than 25 years since Walter Winterbottom sent him on his way, Harry had coached in six countries. He had won championships and cups in Greece, in Belgium and Israel. He had taught hundreds of players, emphasising the importance of physical fitness but never losing sight of the ball.

He had experienced, he says, nothing but respect, to such an extent that on the eve of the 1971 European Cup final – between Ajax and Panathinaikos – he had been invited to his former club's team hotel and introduced, not the other way round, to the current manager: Ferenc Puskas. 'We had a small conversation,' he says, beaming with pride. 'It was just a few minutes, but I appreciated it. I had spent a few years there and then he came along to put the polish on it, and take them to the biggest game in European football.'

For those brief moments, he and the Galloping Major stood as equals: one man who had, back in 1953, shown how far England had fallen, and another who might have helped arrest the decline, if only anyone had thought to ask, if only someone had remembered him.

9

Billy Smart's Circus

Vic Buckingham was not an easy man to ignore. He was the sort to dress to impress: a pocket square emerging ostentatiously from his tweed jacket, a tie of purest silk, a trilby perched raffishly on his head. He moved in the most glamorous of circles, attended the most exclusive of parties. He counted the singers Lulu and Frankie Vaughan as friends, and was even on first-name terms with James Bond himself, Sean Connery. As a manager, there was a touch of showbiz to everything he did: he asked his players to abandon their usual warm-ups and go through dance routines instead; he rewarded them with trips to London's most star-studded variety shows. He was, in a far broader sense than just football, a man ahead of his time. In the black-and-white, austere, buttoned-up 1950s, he was a shot of colour, the spirit of the Swinging Sixties made flesh.

In the vernacular of English football, Buckingham was a character. He liked to talk to his players in convoluted cricketing metaphors: one goalkeeper, having developed an alarming tendency to misjudge the flight of crosses, was told that if a batsman is bamboozled by a ball once, it can be ascribed to bad luck, but if he made the mistake again and again, it rather suggested he was not learning his lesson. He encouraged displays of trickery and ball mastery: inviting a gymnast to perform in front of his baffled squad, instituting a daily ball-juggling competition. English football, as a rule, loves characters, but it pigeonholes them, consigns them to the role of comic relief. It does not take them seriously.

Buckingham, for all his flamboyance, deserved more. At the time, he should have been esteemed for the work he did at West Bromwich Albion, taking the club to within a whisker of what would have been England's first league and cup double of the 20th century, and at Sheffield Wednesday, where he spent three seasons, twice taking them into Europe and never finishing outside of the top six in the top flight of the Football League. He was not. Just when his reputation should have soared, he was cast aside. It is only now that we can say, without exaggeration, that Buckingham ranks as one of the key figures in the game's history. He is the manager who took the past and turned it into the present, the man who developed the football envisaged by the early pioneers, by Jimmy Hogan, and the football taught by Walter Winterbottom and his protégés, by George Raynor, and helped it become the football espoused first by the Dutch school of Rinus Michels and Johan Cruyff and then by Barcelona and by Spain. Vic Buckingham is the man on which it all turns. He is the final link in the chain.

The thread runs like this. Buckingham spent his playing days at Tottenham Hotspur. He counted Bill Nicholson and, just as importantly, Arthur Rowe as team-mates. It was Rowe, of course, who went to Hungary in 1939 to coach the country's national team, where he was first exposed to the teachings of Hogan. He combined what he learned there with what both he and Buckingham had been taught by Peter McWilliam, the visionary Spurs manager of the 1920s and 1930s. Rowe's ideas crystallised into

what became known as 'push-and-run', the style of play he introduced to White Hart Lane when he took charge as coach in 1949.
Four years later, when Buckingham became coach at West Brom,
he did precisely the same. He had been to the same finishing
school, after all: like Rowe, like Alan Rogers, like Harry Game,
Buckingham attended one of Winterbottom's coaching courses.
'On the first day, he got the ball out,' says Brian Whitehouse,
one of his players at the Hawthorns. 'You knew then that he was
different.'

   He spent six years at West Brom, to no little acclaim. He might
have thought that would have been enough to earn him a chance
in the mainstream, away from one of England's comparative backwaters, particularly given his timing. He left the club in 1959, the
year in which George Raynor was busily drafting *Football Ambassador at Large*, adding to a literary canon that already included
Geoffrey Green's *Soccer: The World Game* and Brian Glanville's
Soccer Nemesis. It was a year after England had returned home
from Sweden, unceremoniously dumped out of the World Cup; at
the end of a decade in which the motherland's outdated methods
had been ruthlessly, undeniably exposed, the Football Association had taken measures to try to arrest the decline and Britain
as a whole was waking up to the idea that its place in the world
was changing. Its attitude to football, its belated realisation that
perhaps having 'invented the thing' was no longer enough, seemed
to reflect its changing status in a broader sense. The Suez Crisis
in 1956 drove home to the British public that the days of empire
were over. A third of the world was no longer coloured pink. All
that was left was the game of football and the phrase 'fuck off'. It
was a time not just of change, but of the awareness of change and
the need for it. Up and down the country, clubs should have been
coveting Buckingham and his ultra-modern methods, his counter-
cultural viewpoint.

They were not. Out of work, he moved not to Old Trafford or to Highbury but to Holland, to Ajax of Amsterdam. Their name then was not as famous as it is now. They were one of the pre-eminent forces in the Dutch game, winning the first edition of the national championship a couple of years previously, but how competitive they were can be seen from their first venture in the new European Cup. They lost 6-2 to the Hungarian side Vasas in the quarter-finals. They played in a league that was not yet fully professional. Buckingham had gone from a backwater to a nursery pond. There, he set about passing on his style to a young, ambitious team, one brimming with players thirsty for knowledge. He taught them about push-and-run, about moving with freedom and fluidity, about his vision of a game where players were not shackled to their nominal positions, where everyone could do everything. He found a willing audience. Among those who absorbed all he had to say was a skinny teenager with long hair and an independent mind. He took Johan Cruyff under his wing and crafted him in his image. Buckingham would go back to Holland, in the mid-1960s, for another two years. He would be succeeded, then, by Michels. A couple of years after he left, the movement that would become known as Total Football, the set of principles that would later be revived at Cruyff's instigation at La Masia and refined as tiki-taka, was born.

Buckingham would precede Michels at Barcelona, too. He took the job in Catalonia in 1969. Norman Fox, confirming his appointment in *The Times*, revealed that there had been two English candidates for the post. Buckingham edged out his opponent not simply because of his work at Ajax but because Barcelona's directors had been impressed by his Sheffield Wednesday side when the two clubs had met in the Fairs Cup – the forerunner of the Europa League – not far off ten years previously. They had remembered, and that was enough to convince them. Besides, the other contender was something of a firebrand, and one who was not yet entirely proven at the very highest level. The other contender, according to Fox, was Brian Clough.

To most, that would appear to be a serious error of judgement. Buckingham, after all, lasted only two years at Camp Nou, eventually forced out of his job by a chronic back complaint. Clough, meanwhile, went on to become arguably the finest English manager of all time. He would lead a club of Nottingham Forest's limited stature and narrow horizons to glory both at home and abroad, turning them into champions of not just England but Europe, too. Barcelona, at a cursory glance, missed the boat. Their history would have been very different, if only they had decided to go with Clough and not with Buckingham.

It may not, though, have been better. It was Buckingham who left Catalonia in January 1970 for a whistle-stop tour of two cities to see if he could entice a world-class player to return to Spain with him. His trip to England was a bust. His attempts to take one of the household names from the Football League to foreign shores failed. His detour to Amsterdam was more successful. He spent only a couple of days in the Dutch capital, but while he was there, he was the first man to float to Cruyff the idea of moving to Spain. It took three more years to persuade the ever wilful Dutchman that the time was right but, in 1973, he took the plunge. Even if the decisive factor was that he felt Ajax had acted inappropriately by selling him to Real Madrid, he acknowledged that Buckingham played his part in convincing him to move to Barcelona. 'I knew Rinus Michels and I knew Buckingham, so there was a relationship,' Cruyff told Sid Lowe in *Fear and Loathing in La Liga*.

That was the start of a relationship between player and club that had an indelible impact on the game. Cruyff would grace Barcelona as a player and then, later, as a manager. He laid the foundations for the club's academy, the institution that gave the world Xavi Hernandez and Andres Iniesta and, most of all, Lionel Messi. He laced his principles into every strand of the club's DNA. He would be hailed as the spiritual father of everything that followed, all of the beauty and all of the brilliance. It would all have been very different, though, if it were not for Buckingham. He was there at the start of it all, the man standing at the junction between football's past and its present, at the crossroads between where it came from and where it would go.

'There was a phrase he always used,' says Graham Williams, casting his mind back to the four years he spent playing under and marvelling at Vic Buckingham. He is 77 now. It is more than 60 years since Buckingham first plucked him from obscurity and threw him, still a teenager, into the greatest side West Bromwich Albion ever had, but the stories pour out of him at a great rate of knots. Age has done nothing to dampen his enthusiasm. The Hawthorns dressing room, at the time, was 'mega'. Buckingham's career was 'mega'. His affection and admiration for the man who gave him his chance and his career are crystal clear.

'He was all about pass and move. He wasn't interested in defending. He wanted to see tricks and goals and push-and-run. He said he didn't want us to go "da di da di da", passing for the sake of passing. He always said he wanted us to play like ice cream and chocolate. That was his phrase. Just flow, like ice cream and chocolate.'

Speaking to those players who worked with Buckingham in his first high-profile managerial job – he had previously coached Pegasus, the combined Oxford and Cambridge University side, and Bradford Park Avenue, in the Third Division (North) – there are echoes of every one of the *Misters* who struck out before him. There was, evidently, a type of coach who might go abroad. Buckingham was very much cast from their mould.

Like Jimmy Hogan, he centred all of his work around the ball. He was a coach, not a mere trainer, concerned with making sure his players were physically fit. 'There were a lot of long walks and hill climbs in pre-season,' says Williams. 'But the rest of it, you always ended up with the ball. He didn't want you being tired. We did a bit of boxing when he was manager, and we did some weights, but the ball always came first.' Like Fred Pentland – with whom he shared an avowed penchant for hats – Buckingham wanted to see football played on the floor. 'There were no long balls from defence,' says Williams. 'The defenders would fetch it down and we would play it out.'

Like all of those men – managers and journalists alike – who had warned the English that the day of reckoning was coming, he recognised there was much to be learned from how the continentals played the game. He arranged for the likes of Honved and CSKA Moscow to visit West Brom, aiming to expand his players' horizons, to expose them to new methods and different styles. But his greatest coup came while he was in charge at Sheffield Wednesday, when he managed to secure the ultimate glamour tie: an exhibition game at Hillsborough against the mighty Brazilian side Santos, with Pele in their ranks.

Like George Raynor, he eschewed the traditional autocratic style of most of his peers, preferring a more collegiate approach, happily soliciting the views of his players during team talks, allowing the senior members of his squad – men like Ray Barlow and Ronnie Allen, ranked among the finest players the decade produced – to do much of the pastoral work, charging them with pointing out the mistakes made by their less refined team-mates. 'He gave the players responsibility,' says Alec Jackson, another youngster Buckingham drafted into that side. 'He would leave the dressing room before games, telling us he had somewhere to go or something to do. He was giving the impression he wasn't going to watch the match. He was telling the players that he could trust us; he could leave everything in our hands. It was an education to play under him.'

Neither man remembers him as a screamer and a bawler; both recall his gentle, personal touch. 'My first game at fullback was at Aston Villa, a derby at Villa Park,' says Williams. He would have been a callow teenager then. 'I was only called up at the last minute, because Don Howe had an ulcer. After the game, he came up to me in the dressing room. He walked across and said: "That is the best display of fullback play I have ever seen. I am very happy, and you should be too." I was delighted. Then he walked five or six yards away and turned back. "Of course, if you can't play at fullback behind Ray Barlow, you never can." He knocked me straight flat.'

Jackson agrees he was 'an exceptional psychologist. He was like nobody else. He would call you over in training and invite you to have a walk with him around the pitch. He would ask if this, that or the other was OK away from football. He wanted to know about your outside life, to make sure you were all right and that nothing was troubling you. He saw you as a person, not just a player.'

Buckingham was, though, far more than simply an amalgam of his predecessors. He might have built on what others believed, but in giving it his own personal touch, he turned it into something else entirely. The greatest influence on how he worked was not necessarily the coaches he learned from – though he unmistakably bore the stamp of Arthur Rowe and Peter McWilliam – but the circles he moved in. Buckingham, friend of the stars, invited Frankie Vaughan into his dressing room and arranged for Ronnie Allen, a dead ringer for the singer, to join him on stage. He regularly spent his Sunday evenings at the London Palladium watching the variety shows, and would return to training the next day brimming with new ideas.

'If he'd been down in London on a Sunday, we would be doing whatever he had seen on stage,' says Williams. 'We would be warming up by doing the cancan, all of us in a line, holding hands. We thoroughly enjoyed it. You were always trying to guess what he was going to do next. But there was a method to it: dancing gives you rhythm, and you have to play to a rhythm: slow slow quick quick slow slow quick. [Mario] Zagallo trained to music with Brazil [in 1970]. Vic had us doing it more than ten years before that.

'He loved tricks. He got a gymnast in to do head springs and hand springs in front of the players. We all gathered round to watch and then he asked us if any of us could do the same. We had a player called David Burnside, who'd turned down a lot of money to join Billy Smart's Circus. They wanted him as a ball-juggler. He could keep the ball up 10,000 times in a row. When we played CSKA Moscow, at half-time he got Davie to come out and juggle the ball for the crowd. That made him famous, but he loved Davie. We would have a keepy-uppy competition every day in training.'

Buckingham, in other words, saw football as just another branch of entertainment, something most others would not realise for several more decades, until the Premier League came along and packaged it into a product, all bite-sized vignettes and pounding music. In many ways, it was this that marked him out as far in advance of his time, but it had a more immediate impact, too: how he saw the game altered the way he wanted to see it played. It was his love of entertainment, the hold the glamour of show business had over him, which encouraged him to tell his players to flow, like ice cream and chocolate. He did not want just to win trophies, he wanted to put bums on seats, and for that he required a side that would capture the imagination.

He recoiled at anything he saw as reductive. Maurice Setters, later of Manchester United, was one of his senior players in those years at West Brom. He was, as Jackson puts it, something of a 'nutter', a hard-man, bites-yer-legs sort of a player. 'We had a cup game at Nottingham Forest,' Jackson says. 'Maurice was talking, Vic was taking a back seat. Maurice started saying that we had to get into them, to kick them into touch if necessary. You could see Vic couldn't stand it. Eventually, he stood up and just said: "Maurice, please. I am concerned with the living, not the dead."'

Instead, he encouraged his team to express themselves, not to be hidebound by convention. As we have seen, accepted wisdom, in the 1950s, had it that players should stick rigorously to their nominal positions. Much of the success enjoyed by the Hungarians, and later the Brazilians, came from their willingness to challenge that dogma. Buckingham did precisely the same.

'One of the things that really helped the way we played was that Vic believed you should play the game as you saw it,' says Williams. 'I was a fullback, but if I found myself in the position of the winger, then he told me to play as a winger. If you went further forward and suddenly discovered you had become the centre forward, then go and be the centre forward. [He told us to] play the game as you think it should be played, to play the position you found yourself in, and rely on others to go and fill in your position. He made it all easy.'

In West Bromwich, in the middle of the 1950s, Buckingham was teaching his players the same set of principles that would, eventually, become famous as Total Football. He had taken the values of Hogan, Raynor and the rest, given them a sprinkling of *Sunday Night at the London Palladium* pizzazz, and created something that would change the way football was played forever.

And – most remarkable of all – it worked. West Brom won the FA Cup in 1954 and finished second in the First Division the same year, missing out on the first double since Aston Villa the previous century by a mere four points. They spent the next three seasons mired in mid-table, but recovered in his final two campaigns to finish fourth and fifth in the First Division. By 1959, it seemed Buckingham might have achieved what so many others – Raynor, Jesse Carver, Hogan himself – had failed to do, and proved to the elite of English football that there was another way. His legacy was so great that Williams, now, firmly believes that West Brom's self-perception as an attractive footballing side can be traced directly to Buckingham. 'He set the style that fans have come to expect,' he says. 'It all goes back to him.' So why, when he came to leave, was he not given the chance to continue his work? Here, again, there is an echo of what happened to all of those men whose work he – consciously or not – was building on. 'People thought,' says Williams, 'that Vic could not do discipline. They never realised it was because he didn't have to.'

That impression seemed to be confirmed when, on tour in Canada at the end of the 1958-59 season, his relationship with Maurice Setters collapsed. Setters was sent home and he promptly put in a transfer request. The club's directors evidently decided he was too valuable to be allowed to leave. They sacked Buckingham instead. He was informed he was no longer in work when he returned from the other side of the Atlantic. The gamble did not pay off for West Brom – Setters fell out with the physical trainer Dick Graham in pre-season, put in another transfer request, and was eventually sold to a Manchester United still recovering from the Munich air disaster – but it did substantially more damage to Buckingham. No matter what he did from that point on, English football seemed to have made up its mind. It lost one of the greatest thinkers it has ever produced because it thought he was soft, a craftsman in a bulldozers' world.

*

There is a stark contrast in how Buckingham and his ideas were received at his next two jobs: at Ajax in 1959, and at Sheffield Wednesday in 1961. At Hillsborough, it is fair to say, he did not find a particularly enthusiastic audience. 'He was a flamboyant character who used to flick the brim of his trilby as he put it on,' wrote Peter Swan, his captain at the club, in his autobiography, *Setting the Record Straight*. 'He would sit on the table in the dressing room and flick his trilby so it tilted to the back of his head. When we went down to London, there was always one of his showbiz friends coming into the dressing room. He would greet them with a kiss, whether they were male or female. We players weren't used to that sort of theatrical behaviour. We would look at each other and say: "He's a fucking poof, he's definitely queer."'

Swan's career is most notable for its lowest moment: his involvement in the great match-fixing scandal of 1964, in which he and two team-mates, Tony Kay and David Layne, were found to have bet against Wednesday in a game at Ipswich two years previously. He was eventually sentenced to four months in prison and banned from football for eight years; that one wager ultimately cost him his place in England's 1966 World Cup squad. His book is, by and large, a protestation of his innocence, though he does not appear to deny putting money on his own team to lose.

However, the picture he paints of his relationship – and that of his team-mates – with the dapper, cultured Buckingham is fascinating. Some elements of his approach, Swan admits, were refreshing. As captain, he appreciated being asked to contribute his ideas on tactics and team selection. He admits that Buckingham was 'so far ahead in his thinking, he wanted us to play like they do today'. He suggests that if Wednesday's players had been able to 'play how he wanted us to play, all would have worked well'. Swan comes across as a fairly bluff Yorkshireman, all holidays at Filey and suspicion of outsiders, but he does seem to have developed a rapport with his manager, despite their differences in outlook.

For all that, the criticism is never far away. Swan's footballing principles are best summed up by his assessment of the 1962 visit of Santos. The Brazilians might have had Pele in their ranks, but Swan picks out David Layne, his co-conspirator, as the standout performer. 'They did not,' he intones, 'know how to handle big lads.'

It is no great surprise, then, that he was a little befuddled by Buckingham's demands. He seems to have had no problem with the approach to training adopted by Harry Catterick, the Wednesday manager Buckingham replaced, despite the fact that it was 'the same as when I was a part-timer, doing laps around the pitch. Then we went on to sprinting before finishing the session with a game ... we did very little with the ball.' He found Buckingham's ideas, on the other hand, a little too 'foreign'. 'We had previously concentrated on our fitness in training. Vic got us to work with the ball all the time.' He is similarly conflicted by the difference in how Catterick and Buckingham got their ideas across: it is not hard to discern that he preferred the former's more dictatorial style to the latter's 'more relaxed' approach. 'Harry Catterick would give you a good bollocking if he felt you deserved it; Vic couldn't do that.' There was no attempt to 'rule by fear', and in all honesty, Swan does not seem to have liked it.

His gravest doubts, though, coalesced around the type of football Buckingham asked his team to play. His vision of Total Football might have been proven in the Football League – his results at West Bromwich Albion were more than good enough to suggest as much – but the message had not seeped out. He still found English football resistant to his way of thinking. 'He would try to get Keith Ellis, who was a big, bustling centre forward, to lay the ball off,' Swan writes. 'That was not Keith's style: he was a gangly lad who lacked finesse ... I think Buckingham was trying to get him to play in a way that did not suit him ... If I broke up an attack in my half, I had always knocked the ball long, but Vic wanted it played out instead. You could play a long ball on occasions when you found yourself under pressure, but otherwise it had to be played out. I think the mistake he made was to try and change our style overnight, which was asking too much.'

To the modern mind, there is something odd about these complaints, and not just because Swan seems to be attributing the blame to the flaws in the system and not to the limitations of his team-mates. Players, even hard-bitten northern central defenders, are far more likely to carp when asked by a manager to restrain their imaginative instincts; they talk of being liberated and invigorated by those coaches who want them to take risks. That Swan's reaction was the polar opposite encapsulates perfectly not just the way English football thought in the early 1960s, but the restrictive, brutalist philosophy that held it back for so long. Buckingham existed in an era in which players were reared on the creed of *if in doubt, kick it out*. He could not overturn that by himself, not even when results bore him out. What is most remarkable about Swan's assessment of his three seasons in South Yorkshire is that he remains so unconvinced despite the fact that Wednesday finished in the top six in each of Buckingham's campaigns. Twice, they found themselves in Europe. Swan and the rest did learn how to play Buckingham's way. They just do not seem to believe that they did.

The environment at Ajax was considerably more fertile. Where Wednesday's players were resistant, sceptical, in Amsterdam his charges could not have been more receptive. For that, he owed a debt of gratitude to another Englishman, Jack Reynolds, who had spent some three decades at the club, teaching them, in his own words, that 'the best form of defence is the attack'. In Buckingham's own estimation, that was not the only difference: the stage of development of the Dutch game when he arrived was crucial. They did not have the 'rough, tough, got-to-win-things mentality' that was prevalent in England, where you could take a club into the top six three seasons in a row and still be deemed a failure.

'Their skills were different, their intellect was different,' Buckingham told David Winner in an interview in 1993, reproduced in the journalist's excellent history of Dutch football, *Brilliant Orange*. 'They were gentlemen. They played proper football. Possession football is the thing, not kick-and-rush. Long ball football is too risky. If you've got the ball, keep it ... football is a serious game, but an elegant game. They did not get [their ideas] from me: it was there, waiting to be stirred up. It was just a case of telling them to keep more possession. It was lovely. I just used to sit back and relax. It was real stingo stuff. I influenced them, but then they went and did things that delighted me, [things] I had never seen done before. You only had to give them an idea: they added skills, movement and combinations. They were playing habit football, and habit football was star football.'

It is important, firstly, to note that there were still whispers of a lack of discipline, rumours of arguments that Buckingham lacked the authority to control. It is key, too, not to be taken in by Buckingham's modesty. His timing, of course, was impeccable: had he gone to another club, he would not have found himself working with the likes of Sjaak Swart, Bobby Haarms, Bennie Muller and the Groot brothers, Henk and Cees. He would not have had chance to give Piet Keizer, a player of such lavish gifts that he was eclipsed only by Johan Cruyff, his debut for the club. It is true that any manager who went to Ajax when Buckingham did would have benefited from the tremendous raw material waiting to be unearthed in the Dutch capital.

But it is equally true that not every coach would have taught them to play as Buckingham did. As he himself admitted, much of their brilliance lay in their interpretation of his message, but that does not mean the message in the first place was not of primary importance. That team, that Ajax school of thought, would have looked very different if the job had gone not to Buckingham but to, say, Catterick. They might still have won the Dutch title, as they did under Buckingham, but whether they would have done it in the same way, in the same style, is debatable, and whether they would have gone on to redefine the game even more so. Buckingham found, at Ajax, a team capable of playing the football he dreamed about. In Cruyff, whom he came to regard as a 'son' during his first spell in Holland and whom he introduced to first-team football at the age of 17 in his second, he found a player capable of things he could not even have imagined. But it is just as true that, in Buckingham, Cruyff and Ajax found a coach who encouraged them to play the football their talents demanded, who taught them to play the football they deserved to play. It all flowed together, perfectly. Like ice cream and chocolate.

It was the scale of Barcelona that first struck Buckingham. 'It is difficult for anyone who hasn't been here to imagine the set-up,' he told *The Times* a few weeks after he and his trainer, Ted Drake, had taken on the job at Camp Nou. His first task, as he saw it, was 'to do a bit of reorganising'. The club had spent the previous few months in the grip of an almost constant crisis. When the Englishman – chosen ahead of Brian Clough – arrived in December 1969, he was their third coach of the season. They were sitting just four points off the foot of the table. It did not take long for him to work out why. There were some '300 players, from infants around 10 years old to the first team' at the club, far too many to be manageable. They had finished third the previous year – a success for most but unacceptable in Catalonia even at that time – and had not won the Spanish title for almost a decade. Buckingham was aware that it was 'hard to lose the smell of failure'. The sheer size of the place, though, captivated him. 'It's a tremendous club,' he said, over a phone line 'as noisy as a flamenco festival'. 'It is vast. We get up to 100,000 for home matches. The club even has its own chapel. It is bloody marvellous. There is a trophy room with enough cups to sink a battleship.'

In the course of his season and a half at the club, Buckingham added one Copa del Generalisimo (what the Copa del Rey had become) to that collection – beating Valencia in the 1971 final on enemy territory, at the Bernabeu, Catalan glee only heightened by the sight of General Franco being forced to hand over the trophy – and might have added a second, had he not found himself embroiled in one of the most controversial moments in the history of Spanish football. On 6 June 1970, Barcelona faced Real Madrid in the second leg of the Copa quarter-finals. Real had won the first game, on home turf, by two goals, but when Carles Rexach reduced the deficit early on, Catalan hopes soared. They pinned Real back, pressing for the goal that would level the tie on aggregate. Real broke. Rife, the Barcelona fullback, brought down Manolo Velazquez. A foul, certainly, but outside the box. Emilio Guruceta, the 28-year-old Basque referee, 30 yards behind play, awarded a penalty. Camp Nou seethed. One Barcelona player was sent off for contesting the decision, Amancio converted the spot-kick and mayhem broke out. Police records would estimate that 238 seats were damaged, 11 windows broken and five benches burned as Barcelona's fans made their displeasure felt. Guruceta's report claimed 30,000 cushions had been hurled on to the pitch in protest, and that Miguel Muñoz, the Real coach, had been struck on the head with a bottle.

A man down and raging at the injustice, Barcelona lost the tie. That they completed the game is testament to Buckingham: it was the Englishman who persuaded his incensed players to return to the pitch, to finish a match that has gone down as perhaps the moment the rivalry between the two clubs mutated from enmity to something deeper, something more visceral, something more like genuine hatred. In that instant, though, Buckingham sealed his reputation as a gentleman, as a calm head in a crisis. His performances in the league served to cement that impression. He transformed Barcelona from relegation candidates into European contenders in his first few months – they finished fourth – and then took them to within a whisker of the title in 1971. Barcelona finished level on points with Valencia that year, and with a superior goal difference to boot, but missed out by virtue of their head-to-head record.

His legacy, though, extended beyond what he achieved on the pitch. At Barcelona, as at Ajax, even a comparatively brief encounter with Buckingham was enough to change something about how the club thought about itself. Rexach told Jimmy Burns, in a conversation recounted in *Barça: A People's Passion*, that it was Buckingham who passed on the importance of having 'discipline in the changing room, having a game plan'. Josep Maria Minguella, a man who would go on to become one of the most powerful agents in the world, remembered him saying 'things that would become commonplace in modern football'. Buckingham 'managed to convey to the players the sense that they were in a big club'.

That change manifested most notably in the way his team played. Just as he had in England, Buckingham encouraged his players to play fluid, expansive football, to express themselves. He asked them to entertain him. He instilled in them a relentlessly attacking attitude. 'When they had possession of the ball, they had to completely forget about the opposition,' Minguella told Burns. 'Only if a player lost the ball should he think about defending.' Buckingham had to stand down after 18 months at the club, thanks to a chronic back problem that required surgery. Just as he had at Ajax, he left his successor a squad ready to play the sort of football he would ask of them. Just as he had at Ajax, he laid the foundations of what Rinus Michels – helped by Johan Cruyff – would go on to build.

That was Buckingham's fate, forever destined to be the one before the one. His work at Barcelona secured his reputation in Spain sufficiently for him to be welcomed as a hero when he took his final job in the country, at Sevilla, in 1972. It ended sourly – he could not save them from relegation in his handful of games in charge – but his reception in the city was telling. When he was first spotted in the directors' box during a friendly against the Danish side Randers in March of that year, the night before he took the job, 'his presence attracted all of the attention of the spectators', according to the newspaper *ABC*. He has since been bestowed the mantle of one of football's eternal bridesmaids, something that would have been a source of great pride but perhaps, too, great frustration. He might have laid the foundations, but the credit always went to the man who finished the building.

It was not just Michels, though, who benefited from his work. Buckingham was more than the conduit who helped funnel Jimmy Hogan's ideas to Johan Cruyff and on to Pep Guardiola. He was a trailblazer in another sense, too, one which means that an entire class of coaches owe some part of their career to him.

All of those English coaches who set off for foreign shores before Buckingham made his way to Amsterdam in 1959 – everyone from Jack Greenwell to Harry Game – had one thing in common. Whether they were proven stars as players, who had been coaxed abroad to pass on their knowledge to nations eager to learn, or whether they were, as Fred Pentland put it, 'very ordinary' players who happened to discover they had a gift for coaching, they were all ignored in their homeland. English football's awakening was so glacial in its pace that, while it dismissed the early coaching pioneers as practitioners of an art that they did not require, it overlooked those who came later simply because they had only ever worked abroad and that, as everyone knew, did not count. Until Buckingham, all of the men who became *Misters* had been deemed surplus to requirements at home. Those few of them who were given the chance to test their mettle in the Football League were either forced to do so at its very depths, like George Raynor and Jesse Carver at Coventry City, or were given little or no time to implement their ideas.

Buckingham, on the other hand, had spent much of the first 15 years of his coaching career working with no little success in England; his two spells at Ajax served as a lacuna of less than four seasons. He never quite returned to the peak he ascended at West Bromwich Albion, but the 1960s brought him those consecutive top six finishes at Sheffield Wednesday and then, between 1965 and 1968, three seasons helping Fulham stave off relegation. On the surface, Craven Cottage should have been the perfect home for Buckingham: a glamorous club in his beloved London, a favourite of the celebrities of the day, run by the eccentric showman Tommy Trinder and graced by the sort of maverick players who should have responded keenly to his methods.

It did not quite work like that. He found a squad just as resistant to his more unusual coaching techniques as Peter Swan and Sheffield Wednesday had been, most famously illustrated by the defender Bobby Keetch responding to Buckingham's demands that he learn a tap-dance routine to improve his balance with an expletive-laden reply so explosive he was sold immediately. That was a rare instance of ruthlessness. Buckingham seemed reluctant to take the sergeant major approach so many English players of the day felt they needed. He fell out with Rodney Marsh – the sort of magician Buckingham ought to have adored – and indulged Johnny Haynes, his aura hardly fading with age. The journalist David Lacey, in his obituary of the former England player, recalled a night in Sheffield when Fulham had lost an FA Cup tie against Sheffield United. All of the players were ordered to bed by Buckingham. Haynes wandered out on the town with a local actress, his manager turning a blind eye. For two years, Fulham managed to avoid the drop and Buckingham managed to keep his job. Neither would survive a third.

So far, so typical: the story of a visionary English coach deemed too soft is one we have heard before. However, what indicates that Buckingham's case was different, what shows that it signposted a shift in the dynamic of the relationship between England and the continent, was how he responded. He was a coach of quite some experience. He also had a reputation at home, as demonstrated by the grand proclamation Trinder had afforded him upon his arrival in west London, declaring Buckingham the only man 'big enough to speak up' for Fulham. Most managers at the time – and, indeed, now – would have been content to wait for the next opportunity to arise in the Football League, confident that at some point they would encounter a club of sufficient imagination or desperation to employ them. Buckingham did not. He upped and left: first for Ethnikos Piraeus, in Greece, and then answering the clarion call of Catalonia. There, he found a club of such magnitude that he believed nobody in England would be able to grasp it without witnessing it at first hand.

This marks two key shifts. The first lies in how England was starting to perceive the foreign game: Buckingham did not travel abroad with the almost colonial mind-set that had been commonplace up to the 1950s. He did not see the continental game as a sapling. He felt, at the end of the 1960s, three years after England had seemingly been restored to her perch by winning the World

Cup, as though he was walking into something that was bigger than could be conceived of at home, something that anyone who had not been there could not grasp, something 'with enough cups to sink a battleship'.

The second, though, is even more significant, and it is to do with how the foreign game perceived England. Not all continental clubs still felt moved to write to the Football Association to ask if they might be so gracious as to suggest to them a coach. They no longer felt compelled to take the cast-offs; or saw themselves as a proving ground on which ambitious young Englishmen might cut their teeth on their way to somewhere else. At some point in the 1960s, across the powerhouse leagues of Europe, there remained an intense, undimmed affection for English football, one that continues to this day and can be witnessed every week in the popularity of the Premier League. But where there had once been a sense of awe, a feeling that there were the masters and here were the pupils, there was now a very different dynamic. England was no longer the source of all wisdom and the font of all knowledge, spreading its expertise to the grateful ingenues. It would be too much to say that the view in Europe was that it had become superior, but the feeling was certainly one of equality. If a foreign side was in need of a coach, then they felt able to go and get one from the Football League, just as they might take one from Germany or Portugal or Belgium. The only obstacle was whether the candidate in question was sufficiently adventurous.

The flow of bright young things – untried and untested at home – did not stop, of course, though they tended more often to head to what might be termed second-wave nations, as was the case with Bob Houghton and, soon after, his close friend Roy Hodgson, who made the move to Sweden. Coaches trained by the Football Association still went out to the United States, Australia and South Africa for their first taste of life in management.

But Buckingham was no less a trailblazer off the pitch than he was on it. When he beat Brian Clough to the Barcelona job in 1969, it demonstrated conclusively that Britain's relationship with the rest of the footballing world was no longer one based on the old rules of colonialism, but something more modern. The empire was no more. Four years before Ted Heath took the country into what would become the European Union, Buckingham's move to Spain marked the point at which Britain joined football's Common Market. Over the next two decades, a select handful of others would follow the path he had set. These were no anonymous hopefuls but a cluster of genuine stars. Among them would be one of the Football League's most promising coaches, one of the British game's most familiar names and, eventually, a man who studied Buckingham at close quarters at both West Bromwich Albion and at Fulham. By 1990, the balance between England and the rest of the world had reversed so completely that Bobby Robson saw joining PSV Eindhoven as the best way to continue his career after the head-shrinking pressure of leading his country into two World Cups. That the continental game had become so sophisticated owed much to the work of all of those who had gone abroad before him, stretching right back to Hogan. That the most famous manager in English football felt going abroad was an option was down in no small part to Buckingham, the man in the trilby who spent his life blazing the trail.

10

Welcome to Paradise

Fernando Ochoa's first call was to Anfield. Athletic Bilbao's general manager was in the market for a new coach, and Liverpool seemed a good place to start. Not only was there a connection with Britain burrowed into Athletic's identity, dating back to the days of Fred Pentland and William Garbutt, but he had known Peter Robinson, the English side's well-regarded chief executive, ever since their clubs had first met in the European Cup in the autumn of 1983. They had struck up a cordial relationship over the course of those two ties as Liverpool had won through, going on to lift their fourth continental crown in Rome.

Four years later, in the spring of 1987, Ochoa decided to see if he could use that link to pull off something of a coup. He picked up the phone to Robinson, exchanged pleasantries and then asked him how much it would cost to make Kenny Dalglish the new manager of Athletic Bilbao. The answer was a polite, but firm, no. A year after he had led Liverpool to the first ever league and cup double in their history, the Scot would not be allowed to leave Anfield at any price.

Robinson, however, was as cunning an operator as English football has ever produced. He apologised to his friend for having to dash his hopes but, eager to help, volunteered to recommend someone who might be just what Athletic were looking for, a bright young thing on the verge of claiming the Division One title for the second time in three years. He was precisely the sort of coach who could revitalise Athletic. Why, said Robinson, did Ochoa not see if he could persuade Everton to part with Howard Kendall? 'Peter realised,' according to one member of the Anfield hierarchy at the time, 'that Everton were getting a little bit too good under Howard.'

A few weeks later, Kendall landed in Madrid, where he was due to meet Ochoa to discuss the terms of his contract. He travelled to one of the Spanish capital's finest hotels and approached reception to try to check in. 'Name?' asked the receptionist. 'Kendall,' he replied. There was no booking under that name. 'Holmes,' he suggested: the name of his agent, Jonathan. No luck. 'Ochoa?' Again, the receptionist shook her head. 'I was perplexed,' writes Kendall in his autobiography. 'But then I was struck with a brainwave. I said the name of an executive at Liverpool Football Club, and the receptionist smiled. "Here is your room key, sir," she said. "Please enjoy your stay."' Robinson had taken every care to ensure Athletic got their new manager, and to make certain Everton lost theirs.

The story of how Kendall came to be in Bilbao underlines more than just how shrewd an executive Robinson was. It encapsulates, perfectly, where English and European football stood in relation to each other in the late 1980s. Athletic were a historic club, of course, but they were also a mid-table one, their ability to compete with the multinational, glamorous squads at Real Madrid and Barcelona reduced by their long-standing policy of only using Basque players. And yet, once Ochoa had been pointed in his direction, they proved irresistibly attractive to the manager of the champions of England. This was a world inverted, the polar opposite of how things had been for the first century of football's history.

In part, that change can be attributed to the dual process of continental education and English ignorance which started with those first explorers and accelerated with Buckingham: as the foreigners constantly tinkered with ideas in the hope of moving the game forward, England remained wedded to outmoded concepts and misleading preconceptions, unable to shake off the heavy hand of tradition even when it became clear that English football had been caught and overtaken. There was always, it seemed, a reason not to change: just as, in the immediate aftermath of World War II, fans had come in record numbers to watch the Football League, what spark of innovation there might have been trampled by the football, so too in the late 1970s the achievements of England's clubs masked the reality of a fading league.

Between 1977 and 1982, English teams won six European Cups in a row. Liverpool made it seven in eight years with their penalty shoot-out victory against Roma in 1984. Never mind that many of those successes belonged to one club – Liverpool's four trophies were proof of the excellence of Liverpool, not of anybody else; the same can be said of Nottingham Forest – the Football League, it was held, was in rude health. England's national team might not have qualified for either the 1974 or 1978 World Cups, but her club sides were more than a match for anyone on the planet. There was no groundswell of opinion at home demanding an on-pitch revolution.

And yet, had anyone taken the time to notice, there was something strange afoot. Although the Scot John Fox Watson had joined Real Madrid in 1948, it was not until the 1950s and 1960s that high-profile British players had started moving abroad, firstly hoping to escape the privations of the maximum wage and then, after its abolition in January 1961, for the very simple reason that the money to be made outside Britain – and in particular in Italy – far outstripped what was on offer at home. John Charles went to Juventus in 1957. He was followed in 1961 by Jimmy Greaves, Denis Law, Gerry Hitchens and Joe Baker. When he joined AC Milan in April 1961, Greaves was paid £140 a week, and given a £15,000 signing-on fee. The maximum wage had been just £20 a week in the Football League.

Their experiences, it is fair to say, were mixed: Charles was known as *Il Gigante Buono*, the Gentle Giant, in his adopted homeland, and his death in 2004 was felt more keenly at Juventus than anywhere else. 'We cry for a great champion, and a great man,' said Roberto Bettega, then the club's president, upon hearing of his passing. Greaves, on the other hand, fell into a deep depression and returned home after just a few months. Law and Baker, both at Torino, did not last much longer, though they are remembered for vastly different reasons: the former for his performances on the pitch, the latter because he once knocked a photographer into a canal and because of the car crash that almost cost him his life. Neither settled in Turin. Both spent most of their time holed up in their apartment.

Their difficulties in adapting to life abroad seemed to serve as a warning – to British players and to continental clubs – that perhaps recruiting from the Football League was not worth the risk. The mutual suspicion lasted until 1977, when Kevin Keegan, Liverpool's dynamic forward, surprised the world by agreeing to move to Hamburg. His departure seemed to break down the wall of doubt that had built up over the intervening 15 years or so. A handful – including Dave Watson and Tony Woodcock – soon made the same journey as Keegan to West Germany, while in

1979 Laurie Cunningham became surely the only man who will ever go directly from West Bromwich Albion to Real Madrid. Once again, though, it was Italy that proved most magnetic: in 1980, Liam Brady swapped Arsenal for Juventus. A dozen or so others followed. Some, like Trevor Francis, Joe Jordan and Graeme Souness, can be counted as successes. AC Milan, who brought in Ray Wilkins, Luther Blissett and Mark Hateley, had a rather more mixed record.

What this roll call makes clear is that, even as English clubs dominated the European Cup, seemingly marking out the Football League as the best in Europe, a steady stream of its best players – and also Blissett – were being coaxed away. Whether their motivations were sporting or financial, a whole generation of players seemed to have come to the same conclusion as Vic Buckingham almost a decade beforehand: English football was not the be-all and end-all.

Nevertheless, that does not adequately explain quite how it came to be that in 1987, a Spanish side in need of a revamp might be able to snatch the manager of the English champions. Such a dramatic shift was only possible because of what happened on the night of 29 May 1985, when the dark horror of Heysel cast a pall over the English game. It was the death of those 39 Juventus supporters, as Liverpool fans charged across the stadium's crumbling terraces, which changed everything.

Two days later, as Italy was mourning its dead and the *Daily Mirror* was publishing photographs of the Liverpool fans wanted in connection with the riot, the Football Association announced outside Number 10, Downing Street that English clubs would not be permitted to compete in European competitions the following season. Uefa would extend that ban to five years. Liverpool, for their role in the disaster, would not be allowed to return for six.

It is impossible, at every turn, to separate the diverging stories of English and European football from their social contexts. England's initial evangelism of the game was rooted in a mind-set developed by colonialism. Its soul-searching of the 1950s was played out against a backdrop of the loss of empire and uncertainty over its role in the world. In the 1970s and 1980s, the shame and stain of hooliganism – culminating in Heysel – seemed a physical manifestation of the troubles that had made the country the sick man of Europe. For so long, the home of the game had served as its fountainhead, disseminating its expertise and its knowledge to all four corners of the globe. Heysel definitively marked the end of that era. That was the point at which Europe broke, once and for all, from the old teacher–pupil relationship. It had long since decided it had nothing left to learn; or, rather, that England had nothing left to teach. Now it determined that the price of having the English involved at all was not worth the cost. England had given the Europeans the ball. Heysel convinced the continentals that they should take it home.

In the misery of their self-inflicted ostracism, English football stagnated. The wellspring became a backwater. In 1986, Barcelona took Gary Lineker, England's golden boy, from Everton. Glenn Hoddle and Chris Waddle, two more of its stars, would soon be in France, at Monaco and Marseille. And in 1987, Fernando Ochoa phoned Liverpool because he truly believed his Athletic Bilbao side could recruit their manager. He was fobbed off, and promptly snapped up the man who had just made Everton champions. The fall of the masters was complete.

At first, Terry Venables thought it was a joke. Jim Gregory assumed it was something more Machiavellian, an underhand negotiating ploy. In the spring of 1984, the two men were locked in talks to extend Venables' contract at Queens Park Rangers. The club, perennially unfashionable, had just finished fifth in the First Division. A couple of years beforehand, their bright, ambitious young coach had taken them to an FA Cup final. He was, clearly, a manager of some considerable promise. But what he told Gregory on the afternoon of 23 May rather exceeded the bounds of likelihood. Venables had, he informed his chairman, just taken a call from a man by the name of Joan Gaspart. He was being offered the chance to take over as Barcelona manager. Gregory, in a series of colourful colloquialisms, indicated his belief that this was probably not true. Venables, affronted, stormed out of the meeting. A few weeks later, he touched down in Catalonia and took over at Camp Nou.

In fairness to Gregory, Venables was equally bemused at the thought of being coveted by one of the world's biggest clubs. Even in his autobiography, written almost 30 years after he took the job, he confessed he was still not entirely sure how he had attracted Barcelona's attention. He guesses that perhaps the agent Dennis Roach, the Aston Villa chairman, Doug Ellis, the England manager, Bobby Robson, and the journalist Jeff Powell might have had something to do with it. One of them was right. In 1982, Barcelona had approached Robson to see if he might be interested in the post. He turned it down, but suggested they take a look at Venables instead, describing him as a 'young, thinking, English coach'. His word carried weight, and the recommendation stuck. Two years later, they followed his advice.

Not everyone was impressed with the appointment. Bernd Schuster, that Barcelona team's troublesome playmaker, wondered if the club's board had just plucked the first Englishman off the city's beach. The man Venables was replacing, the Argentine World Cup-winning coach Cesar Luis Menotti, summed up eloquently not just what Barcelona's fans thought of the choice but how world football's sophisticates now viewed the English game: 'I wouldn't have this guy from England. They can't play football.' Venables had been one of three candidates to replace him: the others were Helmut Benthaus, who had just won the German title with Stuttgart, and Michel Hidalgo, about to turn France into European champions. The Englishman, by contrast, had 'no reputation in Spain. My arrival did not fill the fans with excitement, or a belief the good times were about to return.' He won out because he had the support of Gaspart, president Josep Lluis Nuñez's key adjutant. In his interview, Gaspart acted as a translator. Venables was asked a host of questions 'more about ethics and discipline than tactics and systems of play ... Gaspart knew the answers, even if I did not.'

Eager to hit the ground running, aware he had no other choice, Venables sought out the advice of everyone he could. Buckingham told him that 'if you win here, you're a king. If you lose, they'll set fire to your car.' Menotti was rather less helpful: 'If you like beautiful women, welcome to paradise.' His first task was to deal with the impending sale of the world's best, most expensive, player. After two years of injuries, hepatitis, disgruntlement, cocaine and occasional magic, Diego Maradona wanted out: Venables believed the debts he and his entourage had run up in the city meant he needed a transfer to pay the bills. Nuñez volunteered to sign the Mexican striker, Hugo Sanchez, as the Argentine's replacement. Venables stood firm and demanded the club bring in Steve Archibald from Tottenham Hotspur instead. 'They were none too impressed,' he said. Archibald admitted he felt everyone at the club was looking at the man bought to take Maradona's place and thinking: 'Who the fuck are you?'

For all the doubts over his ability to do the job, and for all the 'stomach-churning' nerves Venables felt on taking over, that first season proved to be an overwhelming success. There are two very clear explanations for that: the first is that the Englishman did his due diligence. He locked himself away in 'solitary confinement', watching videos of Menotti's teams to work out where they were going wrong; he pumped his predecessor for information; he rescinded many of the Argentine's diktats – such as afternoon training sessions, introduced largely so that Maradona could sleep off the previous night – which had proved unpopular; he studied the youth teams and plucked three of the best young prospects for his senior side. Venables found a club 'in crisis' and, through sheer hard work, turned it around.

More significant, though, was what he did to change the style of play. 'In those first few weeks, he made us run like horses,' laughs Pichi Alonso, the winger. Venables described the players as the fittest he had ever seen, but he pushed them way beyond anything they had experienced before. 'The sprint training in particular' was hard-core, he wrote. He would make his players race 'flat out over 220 yards, rest, and then go again. They would go to considerable lengths to get out of it, but when I started pinning their times on to the board [of the changing room], that made them competitive and they wanted to do well.'

There was a method to his madness. Alonso is quick to point out that Venables made Barcelona much more threatening from set pieces – a very English trait – and there was a lot of time spent in training on fine-tuning the team's defensive system. 'He taught us to push the wide man inside, rather than letting him go down the wing,' says Alonso. 'We had never done that before.' Venables was laying a trap. 'You get his head down, and then this man comes in from here and this one from here, and he's dead,' Archibald recalled. By far his greatest contribution, though, the most enduring gift he gave Barcelona, was that he taught them how to press. That, says Alonso, was Venables' 'great innovation, his little revolution' in Barcelona's DNA, one that remains crucial to their style to this day. According to

Archibald, it was Venables and his team that 'brought Barcelona out of the darkness'.

'This was in the time when the goalkeeper could still have the ball in his hands [before the back-pass rule was changed] so it was not as easy to press,' says Alonso. 'But Terry studied the opposition teams. He identified the weakest player in possession. So when the opposition fullback had the ball, a striker would cut off the pass to the goalkeeper and then a winger and another forward, or a midfielder, would close the ball down. We worked on that a lot: a lot of physical work. But we won a lot of balls that way.' Venables was determined his team 'were going to outrun and outplay any team we met'.

They did just that. Venables' first game was away at Real Madrid. Archibald scored; so did Ramon Caldere, one of the youth players he had promoted. They won 3-0. That victory set the tone as Barcelona stormed to the title that year, their first for 11 seasons, clinching the championship as early as March. They were ten points clear of their nearest rivals: no mean feat now, but exceptional when just two points were awarded for a win. They secured it in Valladolid and returned to Barcelona for the party. Millions piled on to the streets. It took five hours to make the 25-minute journey from the city's airport to the stadium. Venables described the experience as 'humbling'. The gamble had paid off. The Englishman off the beach would take Barcelona into the European Cup.

That immediate success caught the eye across Spain. Marco Antonio Boronat, assistant manager of Real Sociedad, had long been obsessed with English football. He was a regular visitor to Melwood, Liverpool's training ground, in the early 1980s. He would stand on the sidelines during training, furiously scribbling notes, trying to work out what made Europe's dominant club tick. Then he would retire to the inner sanctum, where he would exchange ideas and observations with Ronnie Moran, Joe Fagan and Roy Evans, the club's coaching staff. He reported back what he picked up, though he would not have discovered anything desperately revelatory. 'Everything we did was very straightforward,' says Evans. 'A good warm-up, a bit of work on the attack or defence, depending on what we thought we needed to improve that day, and then we would always finish with a game. It worked because it was simple: good players doing things well.'

When Venables proved that English coaches could succeed in Spain, *La Real* decided they should follow Barcelona's lead. 'We respected Venables,' says Joaquin Aperribay, then a vice president at Real Sociedad and the father of the club's current president, Jokin. 'He did well at Barcelona and so we asked him if there was a British coach he would recommend.' Just as Robson had paved the way for Venables' move, so Venables, in 1985, paid the favour forward. He advised Aperribay and his president, Iñaki Alkiza, to look at John Toshack, the former Liverpool striker who had taken Swansea City from the Fourth Division to the First in just four seasons and was now working at Sporting Lisbon. Boronat would serve as his assistant. The plan was to take the principles of Melwood to San Sebastian. Kendall would join them in Spain in 1987; Ron Atkinson would take over at Atletico Madrid, albeit briefly, in 1988.

Barcelona made the final of the 1986 European Cup – the first since Heysel, the first without English clubs – after a run of nerve-shredding drama: beating Sparta Prague and Porto on away goals, edging past Juventus in the quarter-finals and then losing the first leg of the semi-finals 3-0 to IFK Gothenburg. Pichi Alonso's hat-trick in Camp Nou completed the greatest comeback in the club's history; a penalty shoot-out took them past the Swedes. Steaua Bucharest awaited in the final. The game

would be played in Seville, virtually home territory for Venables'
side. Few doubted their long wait to be crowned champions of
Europe was at an end. Tens of thousands of Catalans made the
journey to the banks of the Guadalquivir. The Romanians – who
are alleged to have volunteered to throw the game – sat and
defended. Barcelona could not find a way through. Alonso, the
hero of the semi-finals, waited on the bench until extra time,
despite the fact that Archibald was carrying an injury and struggling to last. 'When I eventually came on, I'd been warming up
for so long that I was exhausted,' he says. Alonso was asked to
take a penalty. He was tempted to refuse. He did not. He missed.
So did all three of his team-mates who took the long walk to face
Helmuth Duckadam. Steaua, against all odds, won. A vast ban-
quet had been arranged for Barcelona's players in one of Seville's
grandest hotels, so certain had they been of victory. There were
300 people in the room. It was almost silent. Alonso summed it
up in one phrase: *se acabó el mundo*. It was the end of the world.

Although, that summer, Venables was allowed to recruit
heavily – he added Andoni Zubizarreta, the goalkeeper, and
returned to England to sign both Mark Hughes and Gary
Lineker – both he and Barcelona struggled to cope with the
intense disappointment of Seville. 'That had left a real malaise,'
says Lineker. 'They had not won the league the previous season,
so there was no European Cup the following year. Everyone was
in a deep depression, and Terry suffered badly for it.' He would
see out the season, but lasted just a few games of the 1987-88
campaign. He harboured no resentment. 'I'd had the thrill of a
lifetime,' Venables remembered. 'I take pride in being considered
by some as modern Barcelona's enabler, and appreciate the Catalans who say I started the ball rolling towards a new era. I would
love to think I had, indeed, put down a marker for them.'

*

Life in Spain for the growing community of expats was not always easy. Venables demanded his regular stream of visitors from England provide him with a steady supply of home comforts – he turned Malcolm Allison into little more than a sausage mule – while Gary Lineker remembers the hotel where he was first installed by Barcelona as being distinctly pokey. 'It was an absurdly small room,' he says. 'I'd moved across to set up a new life. I asked if I could have the room next door as well, just to store my things. Mark Hughes was just down the corridor. We were there, in these tiny rooms, for four or five months. The way they looked after their players, back then, was massively behind what you would expect in England.' On the pitch, it was just as difficult. Spain, then, was no artistic enclave. 'It was very defensive, teams sat very deep, and it was very difficult to score,' the former England captain says. 'They did not play the game like they do now.' It was an era of brutal tackles, permissive refereeing. If the idolisation of Xavi is a symbol of what Spanish football represents now, the prominence of the fearsome Andoni Goikoetxea, the 'Butcher of Bilbao', best summed up what it was then.

Lineker thrived briefly, before Venables and his replacement, Luis Aragonés, left and Johan Cruyff came in. He was suddenly surplus to requirements. 'He wanted me to play as a winger,' he says. 'I thought he was trying to wind me up.' He would be reunited with Venables at Tottenham in 1989. Hughes did not even last that long. Venables felt there was an 'immaturity' to the Welshman that prevented him settling, though he did, at least, manage to do what few others could and stand up to Goikoetxea during a game with Athletic Bilbao. 'He worked out Mark was a player to be left alone.' He went on loan to Bayern Munich in 1987, and returned to Manchester United a year later.

Many of the managers went the same way. Kendall managed two years at Athletic Bilbao; Ron Atkinson and Jock

Wallace a season apiece at Atletico Madrid and Sevilla. By those standards, Venables did well to survive for more than three campaigns, testament to his immediate impact. It would be Toshack, though, who proved the most long-lasting, the best suited to life abroad.

He had already left Britain for Lisbon when Venables pointed Real Sociedad in his direction in 1985. With the exception of two spells – one very brief, one rather longer – in charge of Wales, he has not stopped moving since. He has worked in each of Europe's biggest leagues, Germany apart. He has developed a reputation, as Ian Hawkey wrote in the *Sunday Times*, as 'a specialist in crises, a sheriff to police a difficult dressing room'. He was drafted in to firefight at Saint-Etienne and to keep Catania in Italy's second tier, where he decided to resign midway through the campaign because he was sick of the club's president interfering in team selection. The next night, he was summoned from his hotel by a group of fans, led by a Sicilian with business connections in Miami. Sicilians with business connections in Miami tend to get their own way. The mob wanted Toshack to stay. Toshack stood his ground. He is a man of principle. 'On more than one occasion, it might have cost me,' he told Hawkey.

In recent years, his travels have taken him to clubs as far afield as Azerbaijan and Morocco. Toshack is cut from the same cloth as those great pioneers of football's early years, possessed of the same adventurous spirit that took Jack Greenwell to Peru and to Colombia, though he is probably significantly better rewarded. Like Greenwell, it was in Spain that the great nomad found a home. He became known for his waspish one-liners: upon taking charge at Deportivo La Coruña, when his predecessor boasted that he had left the Welshman an appealing team, he responded: 'Yes, like yesterday's bread.' Then there was the time, years later, when he found himself at loggerheads with the

management of Real Madrid over a comment he had made criticising the board. He was asked if he might apologise. 'You have
more chance of seeing pigs fly,' he said, making a point of translating the English idiom directly into Spanish: *cerdos volando*.
Marca, the newspaper, had never heard the phrase before. Their
front page the next day had a swarm of swine aloft over the Bernabeu. Toshack was sacked within hours.

It was in San Sebastian, though, where he always felt most
settled. He lived in the city during his first, four-year spell there,
between 1985 and 1989, among the *fin de siècle* grandeur and
pintxo bars. He developed such affection for it that he returned
in 1991 for another three seasons. When the club needed him to
stave off relegation in 2001, he could hardly say no. Long after
his final departure, he kept a house just along the coast in the
beach resort of Zarautz. He was accepted by the Basques as one
of their own. 'He has never been short of friends here,' says Aperribay. 'He likes to live well, to eat well.' There is no better place
for that than the southern shore of the Bay of Biscay.

But it would be grossly unfair to dismiss Toshack as nothing
more than a tourist, to dismiss his work as a litany of sunshine
sinecures and fleeting patch-up jobs. Aperribay credits him with
having just as transformative an effect on Real Sociedad's style
of play as Venables had on Barcelona's. 'Before he came, our play
was quite static,' he says. 'The defenders did not go into midfield.
He brought us more mobility. He wanted players to run, to be
more free. He took Jose Maria Bakero, a great right winger, and
turned him into a number 10, a playmaker. He was a very intelligent, a very urbane man, but he had a great vision for football.'

That vision, the Welshman has always insisted, harked back
to his playing career. He has never pretended to be a great revolutionary. 'Everything I have done in management ... has been
down to the basic stuff I learned under Bill Shankly and Bob

Paisley at Liverpool,' he said. 'The things that are important in football now were important 50 years ago and they will be important in 50 years' time.' The word Aperribay uses most often to describe him is *exigente*: demanding. He was not a hard man, not a bulldozer, but he expected his players to live up to his standards, just as Shankly and Paisley had. 'I remember we lost a cup game in Madrid, and he was very disappointed with the way we had played,' says Aperribay. 'The players all went to sleep. And then at 4am, John Benjamin [as Toshack is known in Spain] woke everybody up, forced them to get on the bus, and we drove back through the night. Yes, he could be hard when he wanted to be.'

At Real Sociedad, his tried-and-tested methods worked spectacularly. Toshack led the club not only to second place in La Liga in 1987 but to success in the Copa del Rey, beating Atletico Madrid on penalties, before coming close to retaining the trophy the following year. Sociedad were due to face Barcelona in the final in Madrid in late March. The week beforehand, the Catalan side approached them to buy three of their star players: Bakero, Txiki Begiristain and the fullback Luis Lopez Rekarte. 'We were in a position when we needed money,' says Aperribay. The offers were accepted. Toshack selected all three for the final, but the feeling in San Sebastian was that their heads had been turned, that something had been broken. 'These are things we cannot change,' says Aperribay, a tinge of regret in his voice.

Toshack left San Sebastian in 1989 – just before John Aldridge, another former Liverpool striker, became the first non-Basque to represent the club, perhaps a further legacy of his time there – for Real Madrid. Here, too, his Melwood methods bore spectacular fruit. He had a wonderfully talented set of players at his disposal, including four members of the original *Quinta del Buitre* – the Vulture Squad – and Hugo Sanchez, the Mexican striker Venables had deemed inferior to Steve Archibald at Barcelona. Real won the title by nine points and set a goalscoring record in the process: the 107 they scored in picking up the championship was more than the famous side of Di Stefano, Gento and Puskas had ever managed, and more than the original set of *Galácticos* would be able to produce. It was only in 2012, with Cristiano Ronaldo rampant, that Real finally beat the mark set by Toshack's side.

Although he is reluctant to admit it in public, those who know him well say there has always been a part of Toshack that feels his success abroad has been too easily dismissed back home. He has been overlooked in favour of managers whose CVs pale in comparison to his, a victim of English club football's self-satisfied, isolationist navel-gazing every bit as much as Jimmy Hogan and George Raynor before him. What went on tour, stayed on tour, well into the 1990s. There is, however, a crucial difference between Toshack and his predecessors: whereas they craved a return to the league that was widely regarded as the finest in the world, he felt Spain, where he spent so much of his career, represented the zenith of the game. He was working with the world's best players, at some of the world's biggest clubs, and he was amply rewarded for it. While Hogan, Raynor and the others would have taken – and, indeed, did take – the slightest chance to prove themselves in England, Toshack's circumstances were sufficiently beneficial that he needed the opportunity to be right. To some extent, he was able to dictate his terms.

Sadly – for him, for English football – the timing was never quite right. He might have taken charge at Liverpool in the early 1980s, going as far as meeting the club's board, only for Paisley's side to storm to the title after Christmas, prompting his former mentor to decide to stay on. The chance came again in 1991. He had been sacked by Real Madrid, just months after winning the title, in November 1990. The following February, the emotional burden he had carried since the Hillsborough disaster became too much for Kenny Dalglish to bear. The Scot stepped down as manager of Liverpool. Toshack was identified as one of his possible replacements. He ticked all the boxes: a former player, steeped in Boot Room tradition, a spiritual descendant of Shankly and Paisley. It was the job he had always wanted: 'I learned my trade there and one day I wanted to come back and manage them.' This time, though, it did not quite work for him. 'I was settled in my new life, and had moved on to other things,' he said. The job went to Graeme Souness instead. Toshack, in the summer of 1991, returned to San Sebastian. 'He had missed the club, and he had missed the city,' says Aperribay. 'This was his home.' He would be there for three years more, before embarking on his odyssey: Deportivo La Coruña, Besiktas, Real again, Saint-Etienne, Catania, Real Murcia, Khazar Lankaran, Wydad Casablanca. He would spend six years as Wales manager, too, but he would never be given a chance at an English club.

Not all of Toshack's appointments were happy. He remembered the dressing room in his second spell at Real Madrid as being 'like Baghdad', the 'Ferrari boys' culture of Clarence Seedorf, Davor Suker and Predrag Mijatovic completely at odds with the values he had always been taught. It took him several months of a court battle to get his compensation payment from the club that time around. He kept on travelling, though, kept on moving, every inch the modern *Mister*, a fusion of the English manager and the continental coach. He has never articulated quite what it is that inspired him to set out abroad, exactly what his motivations were. His hero as a child had been John Charles. He remembered being impressed by hearing him 'pick up the phone and speak Italian'. Perhaps that stirred something. Or perhaps it was always there, a desire to use his trade to see the world, a

yearning for adventure, for expanded horizons. 'Apart from anything, it's been a marvellous cultural experience for me,' he said.
'All the things I've seen.'

Two men came to Portela airport to greet Bobby Robson. One
was Sousa Cintra, the bombastic, volatile president of Sporting Lisbon, wearing a sharp grey suit, a rather lurid green and
white tie, bald as a coot. He was the man who had identified the
former England manager as his club's next coach. Standing next
to him, in the sort of green jacket that would normally single
him out as a recent winner of the US Masters, was a darkly
handsome younger man. In impeccable English, he explained he
was a teacher, an aspiring coach and, most immediately, Cintra's
translator. Over the next five years, he would become Robson's
trusted lieutenant and his carefully nurtured protégé. He would
accompany him from Lisbon to FC Porto and on to Barcelona,
the Englishman so admiring of his abilities that he made it a condition of accepting the job at Camp Nou that he be allowed to
join him. That meeting at the airport was the start of a relationship that would not only help Jose Mourinho's career take flight,
but would add the two most revered managers of the modern era
to the tangled branches of English football's conceptual family
tree.

Robson learned his managerial craft at the knee of Vic
Buckingham. He was his captain at West Bromwich Albion in
the 1950s and would join him again as a player at Fulham the
following decade. In his autobiography, *Farewell but not Goodbye*, he is fulsome in his praise of his mentor. He describes him
as an intellectual, a gentleman, an inspiration. He remembers
how precise, how perfect his team talks were, and how total
his dedication to the right sort of football. Robson recalls him
screaming at players who dared to walk on the pitch as they left

training: '"You do not walk on this pitch. This pitch is invio-
late." I would think: "What colour did he say the pitch was? It
looks green to me."'

Buckingham passed on to Robson the principles he had
shared with Arthur Rowe, Jimmy Hogan's unofficial emissary
in England. He groomed him in the art of push-and-run. It was
not, as Robson acknowledged, the sort of football it was possible
to play every minute of every game, but with a little refinement,
a little shot of Durham pragmatism, it formed the philosophical basis for the style Robson would espouse during a coaching
career that spanned four decades and two centuries, starting
with his wonderful Ipswich side of the 1970s and ending with
his beloved Newcastle in 2004. That may not have been Buckingham's only influence on his star pupil. By deed, if not necessarily
by word, he may have helped persuade him that there was more
to life than the Football League.

Robson was not, it is reasonable to surmise, a natural traveller. He had first ventured abroad at the end of his playing career,
moving to the Vancouver Royals in the nascent North American
Soccer League in 1967, but he had done so with a fair degree
of trepidation. He was 'tormented' to see the shore of England
recede as he left. What he found in Canada hardly served to calm
his fears: his experiences taught him 'hard lessons about the vul-
nerability of the wandering coach'. The Royals were owned by
the same group that ran the NASL franchise in San Francisco,
where Ferenc Puskas was coaching. Weeks after Robson arrived,
they decided to conflate the two outfits, with the Magic Magyar
as manager and the Englishman as his assistant. Robson not
only felt Puskas was no manager – 'he joined in the training
games' but thought nothing of systems and tactics – but had a
contract that gave him control of his own team. He left at the
first opportunity.

By 1990, though, he had little choice but to put those memories to one side. He had been in charge of the England team for eight years, leading them to the quarter-finals of the 1986 World Cup and the semi-finals in Italy four years later. His reign has, in truth, been judged rather more kindly by posterity than it was at the time. Robson went into Italia '90 feeling hunted by a cadre of football writers who had been 'trying to lever him' out of a job for some time, their efforts redoubled by the country's failure to make any significant impact on the 1988 European Championships. The Football Association had taken the criticisms on board. Bert Millichip, the organisation's chairman, told Robson before the tournament that it would be his last, no matter how England fared. His contract would not be renewed, and he was free to consider other offers.

The news that he had agreed a deal with PSV Eindhoven, commencing immediately after the World Cup, was nevertheless greeted with fury. Robson was described as a 'traitor' to his team and to his country, standing accused of being less than fully committed to England's cause in Italy. It was a charge he rejected out of hand; the country's performance that summer more than justified his fury at the way he had been portrayed. However, more interesting than the kneejerk response of the British media at the height of the super, soar-away tabloid era was precisely what convinced Robson his future lay abroad. His relationship with Buckingham – who, of course, had also worked in Holland – may have helped. So, too, the fact that so many of England's best and brightest had left home in recent years, principally for Spain, as well as the lingering effects of the Heysel ban, due to be lifted on everyone but Liverpool for the following season. Most of all, though, after almost a decade in the unforgiving glare of the England job, Robson longed to escape for more peaceful surrounds. This time, he wrote, he was 'glad to see the shore of England recede'. His decision to strike out from domestic football would set a trend that would last for more than two decades. For good and for bad, thanks to his example, the continent would come to be seen as a refuge for the damned and the drained.

Robson chose his first club well. His first glimpse of PSV Eindhoven convinced him this was a 'nice club in a pleasant city'. He was impressed by the gentlemanly approach of Jacques Ruts, the president, and the studious professionalism of his assistant, Hans Dorjee, relieved to discover his number two did not harbour designs on his job. He discovered, too, a gifted young coach in the marketing department: it was at Robson's PSV that Frank Arnesen, later technical director at Tottenham and Chelsea, first cut his teeth. Philips, the electrical giant, provided both the funding and the sensible, long-term business planning: Robson was just as pleased by the way the club did not gamble with its future as he was by his wage, which was 'twice as much as I was earning managing England'.

He would win two league titles in two seasons in Holland, though it should be pointed out that not all was plain sailing. If the tactical discussions the Dutch players insisted on holding after every game were new to him, his star striker, Romario, was an even more troublesome case. He was not a drinker – that would have been a familiar problem to Robson – but he was a dilettante. 'Alcohol was not the problem,' Robson wrote. 'He was a Coca-Cola guy. Friday night was party night, even if we had a game the next day.' The club would regularly receive calls telling them the Brazilian striker had 'been out all night, leaving [this or that club] at four in the morning'. 'He would dance, chat, meet a local lady, carouse with her and then sleep all day to be "fresh" for the game,' said Robson, presumably aware that neither 'carouse' nor 'sleep' were quite the right words for what Romario was doing.

The forward's active social life, of course, affected his training. Robson and Arnesen had to sit him down and explain that he was not allowed to walk off the training pitch just because he was tired, no matter how many times he cited spurious injury complaints. He did not respond well. 'All he did was stare, like a cobra, straight into Arnesen's eyes.' His team-mates appreciated his talent. They understood that he was 'a special case, a lethal weapon, the star of the team', but they did not feel so fondly about his lack of appetite. Eric Gerets, a sturdy Belgian defender, was particularly unimpressed by Romario's approach to his work. All Robson could do was manage the resentment. 'Nobody,' he said, 'could bring Romario to heel.'

To win two league titles in such circumstances underlined Robson's gifts as a coach. It would be easy to say his success in Holland rehabilitated his reputation in England, but in truth he needed no such thing: his performances in the World Cup meant that when he walked away from the national team, he did so held in the highest esteem back home. When he was told, in 1992, that he would not be kept on at Eindhoven – partly because his PSV team had 'not made the expected headway in European competition' and partly, he felt, because the club's board had been spooked after he missed a portion of his second season while he was being treated for cancer of the colon – he did not attempt to return to England. His indulgent, understanding wife, Elsie, consented once more to continue their travels, to 'sustain his addiction to football management'. She yearned for a return home, for retirement. 'Do we have to?' she said, when he mentioned that Sporting Lisbon were looking for an English coach. He promised her 'a nice life for a year or two' and then promised they would head back to England. Robson flew to Portugal, to Sousa Cintra, and to Jose Mourinho.

He would spend the next four years in Portugal, first at

Sporting and then at FC Porto. He found both clubs in 'a terrible state'. Sporting were hamstrung by Sousa Cintra, 'a loose cannon, emotional and volatile'. He finished third in his first season and took the club to the top of the table at the start of his next, but was sacked in December 1993, just 18 months into his spell in Lisbon, after being eliminated from the Uefa Cup by Casino Salzburg. His exit was typically messy: on the plane home from Austria, the president took to the intercom to express his unhappiness. Robson asked Mourinho, seated next to him, what he was saying. His loyal assistant had to explain that Sousa Cintra was describing the defeat as a 'disgrace' to the club and promising to speak to Robson as soon as they were home. He was sacked the next day, on the pitch, in front of his staff and his squad.

He was not out of work for long. Robson decided to remain in Lisbon while he waited for Sousa Cintra to pay up his contract – he was convinced the debt would never be settled if he returned to England – and it was while he was there that Pinto da Costa, Porto's equally firebrand chairman, got in touch. He offered to send his limousine to the capital to collect Robson. He wanted him to come to his villa on the coast to discuss the managerial position at Porto. 'We can make the third club in Portugal the king of the hill,' ran the sales pitch. Robson assented. He took Mourinho with him. He and Elsie moved into an apartment block in the city, where one of his well-to-do young neighbours had a particular passion for football. The 16-year-old, still at school, even went as far as to prepare a dossier for *Mister* Robson explaining why he should give the striker Domingos Paciencia more of a chance in the side. Robson asked for data to support the argument. The teenager returned with a raft of statistics. Robson was so impressed that he gave Andre Villas-Boas a role in the club's scouting department, the start of a meteoric rise to managerial stardom that would land him the Chelsea job by the age of 33.

Despite finding himself at a club where attendances had dwindled to around 10,000, Robson guided Porto to the Portuguese Cup in his first season and league championships in the two that followed. His success did not go unnoticed: he would end up, in 1996, taking charge of Barcelona, just like Buckingham, his old friend Joan Gaspart finally landing his man, more than a decade after he first tried. Robson did not last any longer than his mentor, enduring the intensely political environment of Camp Nou for just a year before allowing himself to be shunted upstairs in favour of Louis van Gaal, the thrusting young coach of Ajax. It was long enough to leave his mark: Robson brought Mourinho with him as a condition of his employment, despite the club's reluctance, the final post in the Portuguese's long apprenticeship; he personally intervened to help Barcelona capture Ronaldo, the Brazilian striker, from PSV Eindhoven; in his sinecure year, when he was really little more than a glorified scout, he recommended the club sign Rivaldo – Toshack's discovery at Deportivo La Coruña – ahead of Steve McManaman. He was, as he always had been, a popular figure with his players. He found a young Pep Guardiola to be particularly bright, always willing to learn. He even managed to forge a good relationship with Hristo Stoichkov, famously considered all but impossible to manage. 'He was a good coach, a real gentleman. I remember him very fondly,' Stoichkov says. 'Mind you, he had good players. He had players like me. That makes it easier.'

But for all that, Robson found Barcelona a stressful, claustrophobic environment. He had been given the impossible job, following Johan Cruyff, the man who had constructed the Dream Team. The club was still divided between those who accepted the Dutchman had gone and those who felt he should have been sacrosanct. So, too, was the fan base, and the city as a whole: as Robson wrote, Cruyff was 'the ghost in the machine'. 'The volatility was mind-blowing,' Robson remembered. 'Hysteria would sweep round the ground at the smallest invitation.' There was criticism of his tactics, of his team selections, of his over-reliance on Ronaldo and, from Cruyff, of his style. As Albert Turro, the journalist, wrote in *La Vanguardia* at the end of the 1996-97 season – one in which Robson was voted European Manager of the Year – 'no Barcelona coach has ever been the victim of such fierce, unjustified and indiscriminate criticism as Bobby Robson'.

Despite the storm whipping around him, Robson ended that season with three trophies. Barcelona won the Spanish Super Cup, the European Cup Winners' Cup and, sweetest of all, the Copa del Rey. The final was held at the Bernabeu. Victory is always even sweeter when it comes on enemy territory. Gaspart, mischievously, told the stadium's announcer to play the Barcelona anthem as they lifted the cup. Not once, not twice, but five times.

That moment – described by one former player, Sergi Barjuan, as the *rehostia*, the fucking bollocks – was not enough to save Robson. Barcelona had already offered Van Gaal a contract to start in 1997. Robson eventually decided discretion was the better part of valour and offered to take up another role, scouting, helping the development of the youth teams. He did it for a year and was ready to return to England when he was asked to help out, once again, at PSV Eindhoven. His adventure would end where it started. In 1999, he finally got home. Not to England, but to home: to Newcastle United, his boyhood club.

There is a curious footnote to the story of Robson's decade abroad, an anecdote that warrants further consideration. It may even be one of those sliding doors moments that litter football's history, where the game might have gone one way, only to end up travelling in precisely the opposite direction. It dates to his time at FC Porto. He had just won his first title there when he received word from England that Arsenal were looking for a new manager, and they rather wanted it to be him. He spoke to both David Dein, the club's chief executive, and Peter Hill-Wood, its patrician chairman. He agreed to take the job.

Pinto da Costa, the FC Porto chairman, saw things differently. He 'flew into a rage' when Robson told him he was intending to leave. He first begged him to stay and then warned him not to leave, threatening him with legal action and refusing to release him from his contract. Eventually, Robson was forced to call Dein to tell him that Porto were 'being thoroughly unpleasant' about the whole thing and, regretfully, to turn down his offer.

That Arsenal were paying attention to his exploits abroad suggested things had come full circle. English football, while he had been away, had ceased to look inwards, to be content unto itself, and had started to realise that there were not only lessons to be learned from the game abroad, but expertise to be imported. The sliding doors moment, though, is something else: Robson went on to win another title, to manage Barcelona, to have his romantic ending at Newcastle, to set Mourinho and Villas-Boas on their way, to influence Guardiola's thinking, to start his own dynasty.

Arsenal, unable to get their man, ended up extending their search further afield. They would go to Japan, to a Frenchman who had come highly recommended to Dein, and introduce Arsene Wenger to the English game. In other words, Pinto da Costa's obduracy defined the direction Arsenal would take over the next two decades. More than that, it would help break the seal on foreign coaches in the English game. By the time Wenger arrived, in 1996, foreign players were already a common sight:

a great welter had been brought in after the 1994 World Cup, stars like Philippe Albert and Marc Hottiger exciting fans up and down the land. In less than 20 years, England had ceased exporting talent and started importing it. Wenger would mark the start of yet another era, one in which more and more clubs look to foreign shores for their managers. Mourinho, of course, would benefit; so would dozens of others, from Chile and Argentina to Hungary and Norway. England had spent so long sending coaches out to help develop the game elsewhere. Now it found itself forced to bring in foreigners – the heirs, in fact, to many of the schools of thought those emissaries had founded – to help it catch up and compete. A couple of decades later, foreign coaches would be so popular in the multinational Premier League that the very idea that England might once have sent envoys out to teach the world to play would seem an unlikely relic of a dim and distant past.

11

Witch Doctors

Everything ended where it started, far from home. Alan Rogers called time on his career in the early 1980s. Football had taken him across the world, from the sweltering tropical heat of Manila to Iceland's bitter, Arctic cold. He had seen the brutal reality of dictatorship and the simmering chaos of revolutions. He had met empresses and gangsters. He had floated on yachts in the Caribbean and trekked on horseback through Africa. He had been away for two decades. In the early 1980s, he decided his time was up.

His last post was in Cyprus, but he could hear the clock ticking long before that. His previous job had been in Qatar, long before the tiny Gulf State harboured dreams of hosting World Cups. He had been there for two years and he had been quite happy, too, largely because of how handsomely he was remunerated. It all started to go wrong when the country's football authorities decided the fastest way to success was to hire a raft of Brazilian coaches. They assigned one to each club's youth teams, instructing them to nurture young players in the samba style.

As the sky turns pewter outside his Southport bedsit and evening draws in, his story starts to finish. 'I said to the sheikh who

owned the club that there are two philosophies,' he says. 'There is
my European style: four-three-three, pressing, hard tackling. And
then there is the Brazilian one, playing the ball around, rolling the
ball out from the back. These juniors had been taught in the Brazilian way by this coach. And then all of a sudden they are handed
over to me and I have to work with them in the European style. I
did two years and then said enough. No more.'

The English had never been the only teachers of football. They
had been rivalled, since the 1920s at the very least, by those other
nations who had forged a reputation in the game, most notably
those countries that had been influenced by Jimmy Hogan. Arpad
Weisz, a Hungarian player of some repute, was manager of Internazionale as early as 1926. In the 1940s, the *FA News* informed
readers that clubs in Iran were searching for Austrian players and
coaches to help develop their game, the legacy of the *Wunderteam*
that had so impressed in England the previous decade. As football's reach expanded, France, Germany and Holland in particular
would all start to send coaches further and further afield, just as
England and Scotland did. Some, like Rinus Michels, ended up in
high-profile jobs, consequences of the common market in Europe.
Others were sent to the backwaters, to educate and to inform.

What Rogers had noticed, though, was the first ripple of a more
significant tide. It was not just that some countries, some teams
preferred Brazilians to Europeans. It was not just that there was
now competition for those jobs – sometimes well paid, more often
not – in the game's most distant outposts, that England's status as the
homeland no longer carried such cachet. No, it suggested something
else, something more definitive. Ever since those first pioneers struck
out, England's voice had been heard loudest and clearest among its
peers and pupils. True, after a time others started to talk, too. Now,
though, they were drowning out the original calls. England's fall from
grace had been such that it was left to howl into the void. It was not

simply that it was felt they were not the only teachers out there. It was that the rest of the world did not want to hear what they had to say.

In football's developing world – across Asia, Africa and Central America – there is still a demand for foreign expertise. There is a desire to import coaches from the heartlands, from western Europe and South America, and a belief that doing so accelerates change. Even the most powerful nations on the game's new frontiers – Nigeria, Ivory Coast, Japan, South Korea, the United States – still turn to the old world for its guidance. There is always a Frenchman in a sodden white linen shirt sweating on the touchline at the Africa Cup of Nations, there is often a Brazilian legend looking after one of the rising powers of the East and there are even accounts of sun-bleached Germans with Californian accents taking charge of the USA. There are still countries out there who want to be taught how to play. All too few of them, though, look to England for inspiration. For all the popularity of the Premier League across the globe, there is a sense that English football itself is outdated, old-fashioned, unsophisticated. The Premier League appeals because it is international, not because it is English. The homeland is no longer seen as a source of knowledge; the fountainhead, it is felt, has dried up.

And yet a handful remain, heirs to a tradition that dates back a century and more, pioneers and mavericks and adventurers who have left home far behind to continue the spirit that first drove Fred Pentland and William Garbutt to set sail. Their work is in more exotic locations. Deprived of the benefit of hindsight, their impact is harder to measure. Their life, too, is harder. As one of their number, Scott Cooper, who has spent time working in Thailand, says, there is no 'respect for English coaches'. His arrival at his first club in Southeast Asia was accompanied by a chorus of cynicism and pessimism. One question kept surfacing, as he recalls. 'What have English managers ever done?'

*

The day Stephen Constantine's wife and baby daughter were due to join him in Nepal had been designated a *banda*, a general strike, by the country's Maoist rebels. For five days, Kathmandu had gone into lockdown. The streets stood empty, the shops closed, the police absent. The threat of violence against those who did venture out hung in the air. There was the very real chance that, when they landed on the Saturday, Constantine's family would be stranded at the airport, unable to leave until the strike was lifted on Monday. He was panicked. They would have access to a little food and water, and perhaps somewhere to change, but it was not the most auspicious way to start their new life. He contacted a member of the country's football association, who asked what time they were due to land, and instructed Constantine to stay in his hotel until he called. That afternoon, as Constantine waited, a police van drew up at the door. Eight gun-toting policemen, clad in full body armour, jumped out and rushed Constantine, a soft-spoken Londoner, inside. They raced to the airport. They did not go through security. They drove straight on to the tarmac, where the plane sat idling, its passengers waiting to disembark. The policemen leapt out and rushed up the stairs to the cockpit door. Constantine waited. Two minutes later, his wife, clutching their child, appeared at the top of the stairs. Her guard, holding their automatic rifles to their chests, marched her into the van and the arms of her husband. She looked at Constantine, bewildered, tired, a little frightened.

'What's going on?' she asked anxiously.

'I'm coach of a national team now,' he replied, deadpan. 'Don't worry about it.' It was only three months later that he finally worked up the courage to tell her the real reason for her unexpectedly dramatic arrival.

Constantine has spent the last two decades travelling the world as a football manager. He has worked on every continent, apart from Oceania and South America. He has taken charge of the national teams of Nepal, India, Malawi, Sudan, Rwanda and India again, as well as managing club sides in the United States and Cyprus and coaching them in Greece. He has braved civil wars and ethnic tensions – and Maoist rebels – and he has, by and large, had success wherever he has gone. In that, he is part of a tradition that dates back more than a hundred years, back through Terry Venables and Bobby Robson, Vic Buckingham and Roy Hodgson, George Raynor, Harry Game and Jimmy Hogan, all the way to Steve Bloomer, Fred Pentland, Jack Greenwell and William Garbutt. He is cast in their image. He is doing what they did, albeit in an age when contact with home involves a Skype call rather than a letter. He does not use the term – he is very much a coach – but he is the latest in the long line of *Misters*. He, like them, has spent his career and his life teaching the world to play.

The places where Constantine has worked may sound more far-flung than those countries where his predecessors spent their careers. We think of Spain and Germany and Italy, now, as being part of football's first world, at the centre of the sport's universe. But when Greenwell and Garbutt and the rest first set foot on their shores back in the dim and distant past, they were just as liminal to the game as India is now. They were places in need of guidance and knowledge, just as the countries that Constantine has called home are in the modern game. He is the heir to their throne.

His career follows much the same pattern as theirs did, though it comes with a thoroughly up-to-date twist. He grew up playing schools football in London, having trials at Chelsea and Millwall, before following his brother to the United States to study. At the age of 26, he tore his anterior cruciate ligament, all but ending his hopes of making a living as a player. Coaching, he thought, was 'the next best thing'. He did his initial licences in the States, finding work with a university team on Long Island, and then moved to Cyprus, where he had family connections. He landed a job working with the stiffs at Apollon Limassol. He was 29. Brief spells at Millwall and Bournemouth aside, he has never been back.

Nepal, in 1999, was his first national team job. The Football Association's Coaching Association had sent out a circular asking for coaches who would be prepared to work in Asia. It was part of an initiative from the game's governing body on the continent, the AFC, to attract foreign expertise. As many as 35 countries were looking for British, French, German managers. The deal was that the AFC would pay their salaries and the local associations would cough up for accommodation and travel. Constantine applied. His wife 'cried' when he was offered the position in Nepal, at the very top of the world. He stayed there for two years. The level of football he found was 'pretty basic', but he enjoyed the work. 'You find players who are prepared to jump off a bridge for you,' he says, 'but they have not received the same football education that players in Europe might. You are genuinely teaching them. They respect you because of your background and the knowledge that comes with it. It is a fantastic experience. The feeling of accomplishment is wonderful.'

Constantine was hooked. He recalls his three years in Malawi less fondly than the rest, but even there he found 'a group that wanted to learn'. He has grown used to being away from his family – there are three daughters now, one studying in Brighton, two living with their mother in Cyprus – passing his time playing on the Xbox, visiting them when his schedule permits. He is not put off by civil strife. He pays no heed to religion or to politics. 'I don't care where I am,' he says. 'I go for the football.'

His arrival in Sudan, for example, coincided with the United Nations issuing an arrest warrant for the country's president on charges of human rights abuses. The Darfur crisis was at its peak, Islamist militants wreaking havoc across a vast swathe of desert. 'All hell broke loose,' he says. He was summoned to see the chef de mission at the British embassy. He was told not to attend his first game, because they 'could not guarantee his security' in such a large crowd. 'There was no way I couldn't go,' he says. 'I had to. It was my job. Even if it was kind of scary.'

A couple of weeks later, he decided to go on a scouting trip to al-Hasahisa, four and a half hours south of Khartoum on a dirt road. He had seen a tall, elegant left back who he thought might fit nicely into his side. 'I was in the car with my driver and the president of the association calls,' he says. 'He asked me where I was. I said I was on the road south. He told me to put the driver on. He told him to turn round immediately. That area was dangerous for bandits, he said, it wasn't safe. There were militants linked to al-Qaeda who were operating there. We were only half an hour away from the ground. I told him to keep driving. The police met us outside the town and escorted us in. They said the only place they could make sure I was safe was if I sat next to the fourth official. It was 38 degrees, roasting. I stayed for 15 minutes. The atmosphere was not too good. But I had seen what I needed to. The guy was the first player from his village to play for Sudan.'

Rwanda – 'the cleanest place I have known in Africa; people go to jail for things like embezzlement' – was more peaceful; so, too, India, where he is when we speak. He keeps getting jobs because he is good at them. He took Nepal, who had spent five years before his arrival failing to win two games in a row, to a silver medal in a Southeast Asian regional championship. He led India to a continental trophy and Malawi into the final round of World Cup qualifying. He took Rwanda to their highest-ever Fifa ranking, guiding them to 68th in the world. He is good at them not just because of his coaching ability, but because of what he terms his 'chameleon' streak, his ability to adapt to whatever environment he is in, to absorb and understand whatever culture he finds himself in. His friends say he would 'change the colour of his skin' to blend in.

He keeps taking jobs not for the money or for the fame but because he enjoys the challenge and because, just like those early pioneers, there is no option to return. 'I love what I do,' he says, firmly. 'I would go anywhere in the world to coach, to build teams. I am very lucky to be able to do what I always wanted to do. I love every aspect of the game.

'Do I regret coming abroad? No. But it is very difficult. I'm a better coach now for all the experiences I have had, for sure, but with the lifestyle there are sacrifices, of course. My wife is the one to make the most. She is an absolute saint. It has been 25 years now that I have been away. Would I have liked the chance to coach in England, if a good job in the Championship or the Premier League was offered to me? Yes. But the clubs do not look at what you do abroad. I've been told it is a gamble to take me on by chairmen who see the safe option as being someone who has failed several times at three or four other clubs. And yet I am the gamble.'

Constantine admits the life he has chosen can be lonely, but he is not alone. It is hard to put an exact figure on the number of British coaches currently working abroad, but we know it is at least 145. That was the number, in August 2015, who had signed up to be part of the British Coaches Abroad Association, set up by Constantine and a journalist friend, Owen Amos, a couple of years previously. They keep in touch through an account on the social networking site LinkedIn, swapping stories and contact information, alerting each other to vacancies, problems or possible issues in whatever country or continent they happen to be working. 'There is nothing worse than going to a new place and not knowing the habits, the traditions, the customs,' he says. 'This way, if someone comes to India, say, if they need any help, I am there to provide it. The idea is to help those British coaches who have gone abroad to stay abroad.'

It is not an organisation designed for the likes of David Moyes, Steve McClaren or Gary Neville, the three most high-profile coaching expats of recent years. All three men left home at very different stages of their managerial careers, but their rationale for leaving was not dissimilar. Moyes and McClaren went to shake off the shadow of conspicuous failures, the former with Manchester United and the latter with England. They went to rebuild their careers. Neville, on the other hand, did not wish to take his first steps in management in the intense glare of the Premier League spotlight. He saw foreign shores as a productive place to start out.

All three, in their own way, were following the pattern set by Bobby Robson. To them as to him, Europe was a place to escape to. The presence of Moyes at Real Sociedad, McClaren at FC Twente and Wolfsburg was fuel to that age-old English conceit that you only travel abroad if you cannot make it at home. To Neville, Spain was his proving ground. In both interpretations, the English top flight is cast as the ultimate destination. The Premier League has inherited the Football League's old certainty that it stands at the very summit of the game. Moyes and McClaren were temporary refugees, hoping to pay their penance abroad before returning. Neville was almost on a coaching version of a gap year, taking the chance to discover himself in a less pressurised environment. McClaren had the most success, winning the Dutch title with Twente; Moyes did not last 18 months in San Sebastian, while Neville was offered only an eight-month contract. All three serve as proof that managing abroad might be seen as second best, but it is by no means a sinecure.

No matter how much help they might have needed, however, Constantine's organisation is targeted at those who do not have multi-million-pound pay-offs to cushion the blow when the axe finally falls, as it always does. The majority of the BCAA's members – like its founder – have spent most of their careers in foreign lands, forging their reputations in developing nations: men like Peter Butler, now coaching Botswana after years in Malaysia, or Simon McMenemy, who has become one of the most highly regarded managers in the Philippines. Neither has any particular pedigree at home.

Others, like Dave Booth, are a little different. An affable, down-to-earth Yorkshireman, Booth has had a quarter of a century abroad, after initially leaving England for what was supposed to be a six-week spell helping Sir Bobby Charlton with the Ghanaian club Ashanti Gold. 'I was supposed to stay out for a few weeks and then go home,' he says. 'I have been away ever since.' He has managed in India, Brunei, Cambodia, Myanmar, the Maldives and is, when we speak, in charge of the national team of Laos. It is a remarkable career path, made all the more unusual because there was a time when Booth – not entirely unlike Vic Buckingham – was well regarded within English football. In the mid-1980s, he was in charge of Grimsby Town as the club mounted a genuine challenge for promotion to the First Division of the Football League. There were spells with Darlington and Peterborough, too. Booth was on the treadmill. He had a foot in the door. He had, at that stage, 'no intention' of working anywhere other than England. He looks back on his adventure with great contentment – 'I could not have asked for a better one' – but you get the feeling it was, to some extent, accidental.

'It started in Ghana,' he explains. 'Bobby Charlton was acting as a consultant to Ashanti – this would be 1991 – and him and a guy called Ray Whelan, an English fixer in Africa, asked me to go out to help. They had eight games left. The idea was to keep them in the league. That eight weeks turned into three and a half years. I really enjoyed the work. You had such a dramatic impact on the players. You could see such drastic improvements after such a short space of time. But I can't really explain how it happened, how I ended up staying out for so long. It sort of snowballed.'

That is putting it mildly. His next job was in Brunei. 'I didn't even know they played football,' he says. He was summoned to the Dorchester hotel on Park Lane in London for an interview. 'I thought they were taking the mickey. I thought it was a wind-up.

The Dorchester! Then they offered me the job. They wanted me out there a week later.' His work there landed him the role of national team manager with Myanmar. He has spent most of the following 15 years in Southeast Asia. He is still not tired of what he describes as his 'fascinating adventure'.

In part, that is because of the pleasure he continues to derive from his work, even in his late sixties. He still relishes the chance to make a real difference to the players he encounters. 'I think I have done a decent job by the people I have worked with,' he says. 'I remember going back to Ghana and the players who I'd had coming up to me, desperate to show me the new car they had bought with their wages. It makes you feel humble. It makes you feel you have done a good job for them.'

He smiles to think of how much he has seen them – and the standard of the game – improve in his time abroad. He has endured his hardships, of course – 'leaping over a fence' after a snake was thrown under his bench in Ghana, dealing with pitches that had apparently been cursed by witch doctors – but he still looks back with pleasure on all that he has done, all the places he has been. 'The best quality of life was in Brunei,' he says. 'And the Maldives wasn't bad, I suppose. My best experience as a manager was at Mahindra United, in India. But all of the cultures I've seen, all of them, have been wonderful. There is terrible poverty in some of these countries, for the players, too, but the kindness of the people is incredible. There is nowhere that was a really bad experience.'

In part, though, he is driven by something more primal. He has a family in Thailand – three and a half hours' drive across the Mekong from Laos – and it is there that he will, most likely, settle when he does eventually lay down his clipboard. Not that he knows when that will be. Booth does not give the impression of wanting to give up any time soon, and he is well aware of the

reason why. 'Fear,' he says, without missing a beat. 'It is fear of
not being able to work. Not being able to get a club. I dread not
being wanted by football. If I leave, when I leave, I want it to be
on my own terms.'

As a Yorkshireman, he would, doubtless, regard such a theory
as psychobabble, but it is tempting to wonder whether this fear
of rejection stems from a sense that he has already been rejected.
In all his time thousands of miles from home, he has 'never really
tried' to get back to England, to find another job in the Football
League. He does admit, though, that if he had his time again, he
would change the way things have gone. He feels he could have
contributed something to English football beyond those seasons
at Grimsby. But as soon as he made the decision to go abroad,
any chance of that stopped. It is something Constantine said, too.
It is not bitterness, or resentment, but perhaps it is just a tinge of
regret. 'You are forgotten about straightaway,' says Booth. 'You
are off the radar. There is nobody watching.' It is an echo of the
past, reverberating over more than a century. English football continues to ignore its own emissaries.

Alan Rogers came from another age, another world. Like Vic
Buckingham, like George Raynor, he was a graduate of the coaching scheme first conceived by Stanley Rous and later put into
practice by Walter Winterbottom. The courses were designed, of
course, to help stimulate development within English football, but
both Rous and Winterbottom, whatever their flaws, understood
that England not only held a position but had a duty that compelled the country to help seed growth elsewhere.

What Constantine and Booth are experiencing is something older still, something more akin to the piecemeal process
that existed at the start of the last century. They are not fortunate enough to have the support network in place that Rogers,

Buckingham and Raynor enjoyed. They are not part of some grand centralised plan from within the Football Association. There is no sense that they are part of a mutually beneficial arrangement, aimed at helping to develop other nations at the same time as enabling coaches to garner more experience. Like Fred Pentland, William Garbutt and the rest, they are left to make their own way.

Indeed, listening to Constantine as he explains the reasoning behind setting up the British Coaches Abroad Association, it is hard not to be struck by quite how much English football's thinking has regressed. 'We could be doing much more,' he says. 'The Dutch, the Spanish, the German FAs are actively seeking positions for their coaches. They send out under-17 coaches and technical directors, whole staffs, to help a country grow. They ask how they can help other countries. We don't do any of that. The only people the FA have helped out with jobs are the likes of Bryan Robson and Peter Reid, when they went to Thailand. They paid part of their salaries. They were the two people who didn't need any help getting a job.'

The BCAA's members, by contrast, have had to rely on their own good reputations. Booth is a case in point. 'I don't want to sound big-headed,' he says, 'but in an area like this, where the teams play each other quite often, they get to know you. I have got a decent name as a coach. I tend to go into jobs from a position of strength. I have had some success at the level I have worked at. I have been to a few countries who couldn't win games – like Brunei – and managed to win a few.'

The rewards for their success are less tangible than money and glamour and fame. Constantine speaks for all of his peers when he says he loves 'every aspect' of his work, when he speaks of how 'privileged' he feels he is to do something that he cares about so much. But the life of the modern *Mister* is no less tough than that endured by their predecessors. 'You have to make sacrifices, just like any coach,' he says. The night before we speak, he has waved goodbye to his wife and daughters, visiting him in India for a whistle-stop three-day trip to the Taj Mahal. He dropped them off at the airport at 4am. He will not see them again for a few weeks. Then, too, it will be a few snatched days.

Thanks to his ingenuity, he and his peers have found a way to dull that sensation of isolation. The BCAA provides them with some form of community: informal, occasional, but community nonetheless. His frustration is that he feels there is much more that could be done to make all of the sacrifices worthwhile, if only the authorities at home would offer a hand. 'There is a great pedigree of coaching out there,' he says. 'They are honest people and hard-working people. They are trying to do something. It is not just the FA: the players' union and the League Managers' Association should get behind us more, too. We can use these guys who have learned so much abroad.'

That is a complaint that echoes through the ages. Again, Constantine is unaware of its historical familiarity, but there can be little question it is a sentiment that everyone from Pentland on would understand and appreciate. It conjures the voice of George Raynor: 'England misuses her assets.'

Its meaning, for the likes of Booth and Constantine, borders on the existential. Jobs that might go to one of them – or to other members of the BCAA – are far more likely to be given to Spanish or Dutch or German candidates. That is, in part, because of the phenomenon noted by Scott Cooper in Thailand: that while the Premier League is inordinately popular, while once again the world is looking to football played in England as the gold standard, it is scorning the very idea of English football.

For the game on these shores, the significance is more long-lasting. It is a century on and still the lesson has not been learned. English football has spent the first decade of this century in a period of intense soul-searching. There is never a year that goes by without the FA launching a root-and-branch review into some shortcoming, some failure. First, the concern was the absence of English players at the elite level of the game. Now, it is the shortage of English coaches. There has been much wailing and gnashing of teeth at the fact that the home of the game has just a fraction of the coaches available to Spain and Germany and the rest of the world's superpowers.

And yet, out in the world, there is a vast resource that has gone untapped and ignored. The FA's various projects to produce more coaches concentrate, as if in blinkers, solely on helping to develop English players, to help improve the England national team. That is the scale of the consequences of England's isolationism, of course: the motherland proved so deaf to the warnings she was given that now she finds herself desperately trying to claw back ground. But worse, almost, is that there is no thought of trying to stimulate the growth of the game elsewhere. There is no attempt to help those who are out there pursue their careers. It is not a situation that would surprise those who went out a century ago, but it would most certainly appal the likes of Rous and Winterbottom, unapologetic internationalists that they were.

A hundred years on, everything is ending where it started. England is looking only inwards. All that has changed is the nature of the navel-gazing. England failed once because it forgot to learn. It is failing again because it has forgotten how to teach. Out there, across the world, though, there are a few remnants left, a few standard-bearers for a tradition that dates back a century. They are doing it under their own steam, forging their own path, forgotten in their own country. There are still a handful of men ready to strike out from home, ready to teach the world to play.

Epilogue

Stories

On Wednesday, 4 September 2013, Greg Dyke gathered the great and good of English football together at Millbank Tower, in the heart of Westminster. He had been in position as chairman of the Football Association for a few months, but his reign had thus far been characterised by comparative silence. This would be his first major public intervention. He would use it to outline what he saw as the purpose of his role and to identify the priorities of his tenure. He took as his theme the very question that has occupied the game on these shores for almost half a century, ever since the afterglow of glory in 1966 finally dimmed. Why do England always lose?

Dyke highlighted a number of possible explanations. He considered whether the plethora of foreign players in the cosmopolitan, cash-soaked Premier League was holding back native talent. He vowed to look into what Roberto Martinez, among others, refers to as the '18 to 22 gap', the void into which so many youth-team prodigies fall before they can make an impact on their senior club side. He raised the spectre of strictly enforced quotas, limiting the number of imports permitted to take the field at any one time.

The Premier League, needless to say, was horrified at the very suggestion. The league's officials sought solace in European Union law, pointing out that the principle of freedom of movement precludes any such artificial restrictions. The clubs abhor the notion that they might not be able to recruit whoever they want, whenever they want. They have, after all, grown fat on the free market. Their television revenues continue to balloon because they can employ the best footballers the world has to offer. Limiting their ability to do so could only diminish their global appeal and with it their income.

Dyke anticipated that. He made sure to tackle, too, the unspoken prejudice that lies behind that fear. He addressed the issue that often dare not speak its name: whether, when all is said and done, English players are simply not good enough, whether they are somehow inherently, almost genetically predisposed to being less technically blessed than their foreign counterparts. '[Some say] that technically they do not learn enough when they are young, up to the age of 11,' he said. 'As a result, they cannot compete with Spanish, French, Dutch or German kids as they get older. This theory would also partially explain why we weren't winning European Championships or World Cups even when many more than 70 per cent of the old First Division players were English.'

He came prepared with a solution. If young English players are at a disadvantage because of a shortfall in their technical education, he vowed to make up the deficit. He pointed out that, according to Uefa, the number of qualified coaches in England pales in comparison to the numbers working in Spain, Germany and elsewhere. 'England has 1,161 coaches at Uefa "A" level, compared with 12,720 in Spain and 5,500 in Germany,' he said. 'At Pro Licence level, England has 203, Spain has 2,140 and Germany more than a thousand ... [the FA will appoint a] commission that will investigate all this, but on the face of it, the numbers are worrying.'

Dyke has been as good as his word. In the years since that speech, the Football Association's commitment to rearing more coaches has been steadfast. Ever since the new National Football Centre at St George's Park opened its doors in 2012, some 1,300 coaches have obtained their qualifications under the guidance of the FA. At whatever level they are working – in the mud and rain of the grass-roots game, in the sanitised world of professional academies, amid the Lamborghinis and Bentleys of the elite – they are taught to link their work to what the FA terms 'England DNA', a set of physical, technical and psychological attributes expected of all English players. The fruits of this labour will not be seen for many years. Dyke rather undermined his revolutionary, holistic approach by demanding that England win the World Cup in 2022, a ridiculous target given that such change will take a decade, perhaps more, to manifest. Nevertheless, his blueprint represents what is, unquestionably, a well-intentioned first step.

The men featured in the first half of this book, that first cadre of *Misters*, would have greeted Dyke's speech with rapturous, almost disbelieving applause. It is more than a century since William Garbutt struck out for Italy, Jimmy Hogan for Holland, Jack Greenwell for Spain and Steve Bloomer and Fred Pentland for their unhappy time in Germany. At last, England's football authorities have caught up with them. The suspicion of coaching that they saw to be so damaging, so stifling, has been obliterated.

It is now accepted throughout the game that young players – all players – must be properly taught and instructed in the finer aspects of technique and tactics. There is a willingness, at last, to look abroad and learn, to see how other countries do things and ask if perhaps their methods might work here. Their warnings might have gone unheeded in their own lifetimes; they might have been condemned to toil in the darkness because of England's insularity, but, long after their deaths, their homeland has finally seen their light. Dyke's speech was their vindication.

Indeed, the change has been more complete than they could ever have envisaged. They worked in a world that believed unquestioningly in the unimpeachable superiority of English players, the conceit that only in the country that invented the game was there such a thing as a race of 'natural footballers'. Now, the opposite is true: it would have been unthinkable to them that the most powerful man at the FA might ever stand up and wonder if English footballers had a genetic disadvantage compared with the French or the Italians.

Within that total volte-face, only one thing has remained constant: the abiding sense that talent is innate. It is not. How important those early pioneers were in the development of the game can be gauged from the scale of England's self-doubt: Hogan, Pentland, Greenwell and the rest laid the foundations so well that the rest of the world caught and overtook the game's homeland, turning it into an importer of talent – in the form of both players and managers – and leaving it so far behind that it must institute radical policies to try to arrest the slide. That does not prove that Spaniards, say, are more naturally gifted than the English. That is no more true than the old idea that the English did not need to be coached as much as foreigners because they were naturally superior. What it proves is that ability is something that can be nurtured, developed and, yes, taught. It demonstrates the importance of coaching. The most important thing that England can learn from the game abroad – the game that was given to them by those early pioneers – is the importance of learning.

This book started as a collection of stories. Initially, there were a dozen or so. There are some, like George Raynor and Jimmy

Hogan, who played such a significant role in the spreading of football's vine across the world that their inclusion was obvious, almost compulsory. There are others, like Fred Pentland and William Garbutt, who rank among the most important figures in the growth of the game in specific countries. There are more, still, who warranted inclusion because they have been so unjustly forgotten, almost written out of history, men like Jack Greenwell and Randolph Galloway.

For each one, though, there are many more stories that have had to go untold. For every maverick, every missionary whose contribution is described here, there are dozens of others who could have taken their place. The impact Pentland had on Spanish football, for example, is no more or less than that which William Townley – one of the defining figures in the history of Bayern Munich – had on the German game; Jack Reynolds could legitimately be held to be as significant to the development of Total Football as Vic Buckingham. Some, like Patrick O'Connell and John Madden, slipped through the gaps by mere accident of birth: a story about how English football contributed to the world could only have been muddied by the inclusion of an Irishman and a Scot. It should be noted, however, that both of those nations – especially the Scots – had a significance which is too often overlooked.

History is a compendium, a collective conflation of individual stories. The stories included here were not chosen scientifically; they were, if anything, selected journalistically. They are, on their own, good stories: stories of adventure and courage and sorrow and regret. Together, they are something else. They offer an insight into a greater truth. They each contribute a little to another narrative, a larger picture. Together, they become a little piece of history.

Amid all of those personal stories, those lives lived, there are, though, essentially just two. One is a story of arrogance and ignorance. It is a story of how England taught the world and forgot to learn, of how the game's homeland gave the planet the goods and promptly lost the knack of making them. It is a story of short-sightedness and, to some extent, naked, craven stupidity. It is a story of how a country was entirely complicit in its own demise, of how it failed to heed warnings and read signs, of how it remained so content unto itself that it lost its primacy and its place in the world. It is a story that, in many ways, reflects England's changing status throughout the 20th century, its shift from imperial power to cultural dynamo to sick man of Europe to standard-bearer of the free market. It is a story of where England was and what it became.

The other story is quite different. It is one of intense generosity and lasting effect. It is the story of how England – first through the enthusiasm of its mavericks and then, later, through its own sense of missionary purpose – disseminated its gift to all four corners of the globe. It is the story not of the men who gave the world the game they knew but who taught it the one we have now. England now looks abroad for inspiration. It looks to Spain and to Germany and to South America and asks why they can do things we cannot. It sees in Ajax and Barcelona, among others, something intrinsically foreign, something that it envies and does not quite understand. This is the other story: the story of how all that seems so exotic has its roots in something familiar, of how the work of Jose Mourinho and Pep Guardiola – the modern game's two defining, opposing forces – can be traced back to Bobby Robson and Vic Buckingham and beyond, all the way into the game's distant past, to Jimmy Hogan and Fred Pentland.

There is a theory, in anthropology, that the entire human race can trace its lineage back to just six women in Africa, that the seven billion people now on the planet all came from the same place and the same people. Perhaps, in its own small way, the same can be said of football. Perhaps all of the many and various ideas we see now, all of the different tactical variations, the local flavours that make the game so enticing, so popular, all have one common root, one shared beginning. This is the second story that emerges from all of those personal stories. It is the story of the *Misters*, the men who taught all of the world to play.

Select Bibliography

As far as possible, I have tried to attribute the work of other authors in the text. The list that follows contains those books and sources which proved particularly helpful in compiling the stories contained here.

A number of newspaper archives – some digital, some held both at the British Library and in the James Catton archive at Arsenal – proved crucial. In England, *The Times* and *Sunday Times*, *Guardian*, *Athletic News*, *FA News*, *In Ruhleben Camp* magazine, *Navy and Army Illustrated* and *All Sports Weekly* provided a huge amount of original material. Abroad, I became worryingly familiar with the digital editions of *ABC*, *El Mundo Deportivo*, *Gijon Hemeroteca*, *La Vanguardia*, *La Stampa* and *El Observador*.

Other first-hand accounts came from:

Bob Ferrier, *Soccer Partnership* (Sportsmans Book Club, 1961)

Brian Glanville, *Soccer Nemesis* (Secker & Warburg, 1955)

Brian Glanville, *Football Memories: 50 Years of the Beautiful Game* (Robson Books, 2004)

Howard Kendall, *Love Affairs and Marriage: My Life in Football* (De Coubertin Books, 2013)

George Raynor, *Football Ambassador at Large* (Stanley Paul, 1960)

Bobby Robson, *Farewell but not Goodbye: My Autobiography* (Hodder & Stoughton, 2006)

Stanley Rous, *Football Worlds: A Lifetime in Sport* (Faber & Faber, 1978)

Ivan Sharpe, *40 Years in Football* (Sportsmans Book Club, 1954)

Peter Swan, *Setting the Record Straight* (The History Press, 2007)

Terry Venables, *Born to Manage: The Autobiography* (Simon & Schuster, 2014)

I have also drawn from (among others):

Phil Ball, *Morbo: The Story of Spanish Football* (WSC Books, 2011)

Dominic Bliss, *Erbstein: The Triumph and Tragedy of Football's Forgotten Pioneer* (Blizzard Media Ltd, 2014)

Jimmy Burns, *Barça: A People's Passion* (Bloomsbury Publishing, 1999)

Jimmy Burns, *La Roja: A Journey through Spanish Football* (Simon & Schuster, 2012)

Paul Edgerton, *William Garbutt: The Father of Italian Football* (Sportsbooks, 2009)

John Foot, *Calcio: A History of Italian Football* (Harper Perennial, 2007)

Norman Fox, *Prophet or Traitor?: The Jimmy Hogan Story* (Parrs Wood Press, 2003)

David Goldblatt, *The Game of Our Lives: The Meaning and Making of English Football* (Viking, 2014)

Geoffrey Green, *Soccer: The World Game* (Sportsmans Book Club, 1954)

Ashley Hyne, *George Raynor: The Greatest Coach England*

Never Had (The History Press, 2014)

Pierre Lanfranchi, '"Mister" Garbutt: The First European Manager' (*The Sports Historian*, 22, 2002)

Sid Lowe, *Fear and Loathing in La Liga: Barcelona vs Real Madrid* (Yellow Jersey Press, 2013)

Simon Martin, *Football and Fascism: The National Game under Mussolini* (Bloomsbury Publishing, 2004)

Graham Morse, *Sir Walter Winterbottom: The Father of Modern English Football* (John Blake Publishing, 2013)

Peter Seddon, *Destroying Angel: Steve Bloomer – England's First Football Hero* (Breedon Books, 1999)

James Walvin, *The People's Game: The History of Football Revisited* (Mainstream Publishing, 2000)

David Winner, *Brilliant Orange: The Neurotic Genius of Dutch Football* (Bloomsbury Publishing, 2000)

Acknowledgements

This book started with a snatched conversation in the foyer of the Epstein Theatre in Liverpool. It was there that Jamie Bowman first mentioned the name Alan Rogers to me. It meant nothing then; over the last three years, it has come to mean an awful lot.

From there, it was simply a matter of persuading my agent, David Luxton, that pursuing the story of Alan and those like him would not be a complete waste of time. I owe a huge debt of gratitude to David for listening to my rambling explanation of the story I had mapped out in my head and realising it was not, necessarily, complete gibberish. Thankfully, he described it to Ian Marshall, at Simon & Schuster, rather better than I ever could. Ian's help, guidance and patience served to make the process as painless as possible.

It would require hours to go through all of the people who have unwittingly 'volunteered' their time to help me get my thoughts straight, but prime among them are Ian Herbert, Jack Pitt-Brooke, Tony Barrett, Jonathan Wilson, Barney Ronay, James Montague, Ian Hawkey and Sid Lowe. Their support, wisdom and advice kept me on the straight and narrow. Sid, in particular, read far more rough copy than anyone should have to.

There are more, countless more, people who lent me their

time. Michael and Barbara at Crook Town helped piece together the early years of Jack Greenwell, and Carl Worswick in Colombia did the same for his final few months.

Mark Whittle, Emanuele Gamba, Gary Lineker, Paddy Barclay, Brian Glanville, Martin Swain, Geoff Snape, Graham Williams, Alec Jackson, Brian Whitehouse, Chemi Torres, Hristo Stoichkov, Anthony Hindmarch, Gabriele Marcotti, Jan Ferguson, Richard McColl, Goncalo Lopes, Julien Laurens, Fernando Arrechea, Professor David Wood, Naomi Westland, Dominic Bliss, Andy Mitten, Oier Fano, Joaquin Aperribay, Ernesto Moreno and Pichi Alonso all listened to my questions, in a variety of languages. Kate Laurens and Tony Sandell at Arsenal deserve a special mention for helping me go through the Catton archive, and Asier Arrate's work in preserving collective memory of Athletic Bilbao allowed me to gather information on Fred Pentland. It was a pleasure talking to Scott Cooper, Stephen Constantine and Dave Booth, men who are still out there, teaching the world to play.

Thanks to all of those at *The Times* for pretending not to notice that I wasn't being especially constructive on the day job: to Tim Hallissey, Richard Whitehead, Oli Kay, George Caulkin, Tony Evans and Clive Petty, in particular. And thanks to the staff at Grounded, and especially Amanda and Sara, for allowing me to use their rather lovely cafe as my office.

Alex Jackson, at the National Football Museum, went way above and beyond what might have been expected, and even managed to give the impression he was not bored by the endless requests for help.

My family – my mum Alison, Robert and Rachel, Ken and Ann – did well not to refuse to speak to me for 18 months. I promise not to mention it again. My wife, Kate, has suffered more than most, but never faltered in her support. She now knows more about Spanish football in the 1920s than she may have wanted.

My dad, Rod, pored over pretty much every chapter, offering hints here and tips there and scouring the text for a single missing apostrophe. I'm sorry you didn't find it, but we'll always have 'neutering'. Thank you for your time and your ideas.

The biggest thanks of all, though, have to go to the likes of Doris Hahn, Jack Greenwell's granddaughter, who guided me through his adventures. I hope I have been able to add to it. To Carole and family, too, for inviting me into your home to meet your father, Harry. And, finally, to Harry and Alan Rogers, for allowing me to listen to your stories. I hope this book is suitable testament to all your yesterdays.

Index